2.50

COACHING DAYS
&
COACHING WAYS
BY W. OUTRAM TRISTRAM

The Postboys.

WITH ILLUSTRATIONS BY

HERBERT RAILTON AND HUGH THOMSON

BRACKEN BOOKS
LONDON

Previously Published by Macmillan & Co
London in 1888

This edition published 1985 by Bracken Books,
a division of Bestseller Publications Ltd,
Brent House, 24 Friern Park, North Finchley, London

ISBN 0 946495 96 3

Printed and bound in the German Democratic Republic

CONTENTS.

LIST OF ILLUSTRATIONS.

b 2

Coaching Days
and
Coaching Ways

Setting Out.

COACHING DAYS AND COACHING WAYS.

I.—THE BATH ROAD.

In setting out on the Great Roads of England—whether in the lumbering six-inside vehicles of the seventeenth century, or in the light four-inside Fast Coaches which in about 1823 marked the meridian of road travelling—I propose to take an inconstant course of my own. And by inconstant I mean that I shall bind myself neither to time, place, nor consistency of attitude to my subject. I shall now look at it, for instance, in the company of Mr. Stanley Harris, Lord William Lennox, Captain Malet, Mr. James Hissey, and other Knights of the Ribbons (whose experienced enthusiasm shine so pleasantly in such works as *The Coaching Age; Coaching and Anecdotes of the Road; A*

Drive through England, &c., &c.), purely from the coachman's point of view; and then I shall look at it from the point of view of Miss Burney and Mr. Samuel Pepys. With kindred assistance I shall try to get some glimpses of the social life which passed to and fro between London and the provinces from the time when men began to travel, up to the time when they began to arrive at places, but to travel no more. I shall show our ancestors of all ages in all kinds of costumes—trunk hose, doublet and ruffles, sacks and sarcinets, periwigs and full-bottomed coats, beavers and top-boots, busy at those nothings which make travelled life—eating, drinking, flirting, quarrelling, delivering up their purses, grumbling over their bills—a motley crowd of kings, queens, statesmen, highwaymen, generals, poets, wits, fine ladies, conspirators, and coachmen. With the assistance of my able illustrators, I shall picture these worthies in all sorts of positions—on the road and off it, snowed up, in peril from the great waters, waiting for the stage coaches, &c., alighting at the inns—those inns for which England was once famous, with their broad corridors, their snug bars, their four-posted beds hung with silk, their sheets smelling of lavender, their choice cookery, their claret equal to the best that could be drunk in London. Here too I shall hope now and again to make the violet of a legend blow among the chops and steaks; and besides mere chance travellers, to call upon some ghostly and romantic figures who lived near the

The Lower Ship Inn at Reading.

road when in the flesh, whose residence by it seems to make them of it, and must have caused them many a time to post up and down

Waiting for the Stage Coach.

it on business or pleasure bent, before grim Fate sent them posting to Hades.

Any time between the years 1667 and 1670 the issue of some such announcement as the following made Londoners stare:—

"FLYING MACHINE.

"All those desirous to pass from London to Bath, or any other Place on their Road, let them repair to the Belle Savage on Ludgate Hill in London and the White Lion at Bath, at both which places they may be received in a Stage Coach every Monday, Wednesday, and Friday, which performs the whole journey in Three Days (if God permits), and sets forth at five in the Morning.

"Passengers to pay One Pound five Shillings each, who are allowed to carry fourteen Pounds Weight—for all above to pay three halfpence per Pound."

Bill posting was in its infancy in the days of the Restoration, but the above effort drew a crowd to the Belle Savage even at five o'clock in the morning. This crowd eyed the Flying Machine, drawn up in the inn yard ready for its flight with a wild surmise. With a kindred expression they also eyed the six intrepid passengers who had been received into it, and their fourteen pounds of luggage to each man piled on the roof—that roof on which no passenger dared venture himself for fear of his neck. And the six inside intrepid passengers turned upon the onlookers twelve eyes estranged and sad. They were practised travellers all of them, but even for practised travelling this was a new departure. They had booked for Bath; with a proper regard for the proviso in the advertisement, they had committed themselves to Providence; but they did not very well know whither they were going. They knew however that they were going five-and-thirty miles a day instead of twenty, over roads called so out of courtesy, and the thought, now that they were seated, gave them melancholy pause. They felt probably as the passengers by the first railway train felt a century and a half later. They cursed the curiosity which pines for a new experience, and wished themselves on the fixed earth again. And as they did so the huzzas of the crowd and a supernatural jolting told them they were off it.

The streets of that London in which woodcocks were killed in Regent Street, in which bears danced and bulls were baited in Lincoln's Inn Fields, in which the dead cats and dogs of Westminster were shot into St. James's Square, were not mediums for making coach-riding a bed of roses—in point of fact they were in as dangerous a condition as they could well be. Long before the Flying Machine had cleared the metropolis—the metropolis which knew Chelsea as a quiet country village with a thousand inhabitants, Marylebone as a space where cattle fed and sportsmen wandered—the six inside passengers had been twice nearly upset and shaken out of their seven senses; and it had scarcely begun its creeping passage over Hounslow Heath when it was stopped abruptly, and the six inside passengers had their six purses taken away. When their eyesight, temporarily obscured by agitation, returned to them, they recognized the French page of the Duke of Richmond as the author of this graceful feat, and having spoken strange words to the guard for having neglected the fleeting opportunity presented to him for the discharge of his blunderbuss (which was rather wild of them, the said blunderbuss being a mere vehicle for the release of coach guards who were weary of their lives, and perfectly well known as such), they jolted forwards on their way to Bath pale and purseless.

The Bear at Reading: its days are gone!

The French page of the Duke of Richmond will recompense us for their departure. Claude Duval was about this time in the zenith of his fame; indeed in 1670 his brilliant career was cut short with the suddenness in character with such shooting stars, and at the usual time and place. To speak plainly, having sacrificed unduly to the Rosy God of

Mr. Swiveller at "The Hole in the Wall," in Chandos Street, the gallant Claude was surprised in that elegiac retreat, arrested without expense of blood or treasure—"and well it was for the bailiff and his men that he was drunk"—committed to Newgate, arraigned, convicted, and condemned, and on Friday, January 21, executed at Tyburn in the 27th year of his age. "A sad instance of the irresistible influence of the stars and the fatality of the climacterical years; for Venus and Mars were in conjunction at the hero's birth, certain presages of good fortune, but of short continuance."

He was I think the greatest of the highwaymen; and lately I have read the records of most of them; have admired the reckless buoyancy of their enterprising lives; have thought how colourless the history of the roads would be without their brilliant presences. I have become acquainted, amongst others, with the dashing Augustin King, educated at Cambridge, hanged at Colchester; with the great William Nevison, whose name still haunts the hamlets of the northern moors, hanged at York; with the magnanimous Bliss, hanged at Salisbury; with the Brothers Weston, the Peaces of the last century, who frequented the best society at Winchelsea, and robbed in the surrounding country, hanged at Tyburn—a cultured pair, whose lives were pleasant, and in death they were not divided; but I declare that none of them—no, not Turpin himself, the Turpin whose ride to York has been labelled by Macaulay a myth—seem to me to attain to that high standard of elegant rascality displayed by this importation from France. For Claude, alas! was not a native product. No, to our sorrow we say it, he was born at Domfront, in Normandy, a place very famous for the excellency of the air and the production of mercurial wits. His father moreover was a miller, and his mother a tailor's daughter. Early in life the boy was troubled with the stirrings of young ambition. He was wanted by the local police, but was out when they called. He had gone to Paris, where he did odd jobs for Englishmen and got his hand in, and in this improving exercise he continued till the Restoration brought him over to England to be a spectator of the Jubilee. He now entered the service of the Duke of Richmond, gamed, made love, drank (a vice for which his indulgent biographer cannot pardon him, though for our part we admire this graceful participation in a national pastime), soon fell into want of money, took to padding to pay his debts, quickly became so accomplished in his business that in a proclamation for the taking several notorious highwaymen he had the honour to be named first. How brilliant a rise to eminence! What a record for a short public life!

That so gifted and elegant a ruffian as this should in an age of gaiety and fine manners, when morality was never considered, have met his fate by having a cart pulled away from under him, is, to my thinking, a melancholy reflection on the ingratitude of mankind. Why, this was a man after Charles II.'s own heart, and not unlike him, except that he was better looking! To do the King justice however I think he would have spared the highwayman if he had had his way. It was the judge who presided at the trial who hanged the accomplished Claude; as it was the judge who with so flagrant a disregard for right feeling interrupted the solemn *post-mortem* celebrations, when the defunct hero lay in state in the "Tangiers Tavern," St. Giles, in a room covered with black cloth, his hearse blazing with escutcheons, eight wax tapers burning, and as many tall gentlemen with black cloaks in attendance. "Mum was the word, as if for fear of disturbing the sleeping lion; and the night was stormy and rainy, as if the heavens sympathized with the ladies, echoed over their sighs, wept over again their tears."

I read that as they were undressing him "in order to his lying in state," one of his friends—one of the tall gentlemen in black cloaks, that is to say—in an abstraction natural no doubt to so solemn an occasion, and with a gesture full of melancholy meaning, put his hand in the defunct hero's pocket and—produced not his purse but his Dying Confession. I much regret that I cannot reproduce this elegant effort here. It is written in a blithe spirit of Christian resignation, not unmixed with a Stoic's contempt for the pleasures of the life he was leaving. It contains a surprising summary of Duval's good fortunes. But the concluding lines in which he so to speak rounds his philosophy are so truly conceived in the spirit of the Restoration, so faithfully reflect the polished manners of the times, that they are quite unfit for publication.

Duval was buried in the middle aisle of Covent Garden Church. The fair sex formed the larger part of the crowd which attended. Flambeaux blazed, and the hero was laid under a plain white marble stone, "whereon were curiously engraved the Du Vall arms," and under them written in black this epitaph :—

"DU VALL'S EPITAPH.

"Here lies Du Vall: Reader if Male thou art
Look to thy Purse: if Female to thy Heart.
Much Havoc has he made of both; for all
Men he made stand and Women he made fall.
The second Conqu'ror of the Norman Race
Knights to his arms did yield and Ladies to his Face.
Old Tyburn's glory, England's illustrious Thief,
Du Vall the Ladies' joy: Du Vall the Ladies' Grief."

What is an inscription in Westminster Abbey to this surprising offering at the tomb of genius? "The Second Conqu'ror of the Norman Race." Can anything be more magnificent? "Du Vall the Ladies' Grief." This sorrow is heavenly. Let us take our leave of this great man and follow the Flying Machine that he has lightened. We shall not have to go far to catch it up in spite of our digression. It has been off the Road as well as we have, has got into one of those ruts or rather trenches, which filled foreigners with strange oaths—and there it sticks fast—the six horses with flanks distended, the coachman scarlet in the face with thonging them, the guard armed with a stick in aid of his amiable exertions; all powerless to move it. The state of the roads at this time in early spring and winter must have been something awful. So late as 1797, Middleton, in his *Survey of Middlesex*, speaking of the Oxford road at Uxbridge, observes that during the whole of the winter there was but one passable track on it, and that was less than six feet wide and was eight inches deep in fluid sludge. To be in character, on a sliding scale, all the rest of the road was from a foot to eighteen inches deep in adhesive mud, which was better. Earlier roads, more

A Breakdown: Taking on the Mails.

adhesive mud. And when snow was on the ground, more adhesive snow; causing coaches to stand on their heads in snow drifts; and guards with blue noses to mount the unharnessed leaders and "take on the mails." Small wonder then that in 1668 the Bath Flying Machine sticks fast and needs four cart horses, pressed into the service, after much bawling, to pull it on to firm land again. Meanwhile it has blocked the road for an hour to all but the fortunate people who can afford to ride post. Amongst these envied ones of the earth is his Grace the Duke of Buckingham, who rides furiously by scattering the mud far and wide on each side of him—his rich dress disordered and travel-stained, his horse covered with foam—his attendants spurring to keep up with his headlong pace and cursing the Bath Coach as they ride by it. His Grace is making for Cliefden,

"The bower of wanton Shrewsbury and of Love,"

which lady's husband he has just run through the right breast and shoulder at Barne Elms; her ladyship, who now rides by the Duke's side in a page's dress, having shed the light of her graceful presence on the amiable formality; in her office of page holding her lover's horse as he exchanged thrusts with her better half. Delightful society! So picturesquely free from care and scruple!—who would not have lived in those days? The travellers in the Flying Machines of Charles the Second's day must have seen much of that brilliant, sparkling, outrageous society fly by them. That seems to me to have been the chief advantage of the Flying Machines. Everybody flew by them—at least everybody who was worth seeing.

This Hounslow Heath, which the Flying Machine has now left behind it—the creaky, mud-covered old caravan is drawn up now outside the Inn, at Cranford, the horses are in the stable feeding, the coachman with a pot of beer in his hand lying about his heroic resistance to six highwaymen—it seems to have been the province of coachmen at all periods to lie—("*compare*, Tom," said I, "I think you can whistle louder, hit a horse harder, and tell a bigger lie than any one I ever knew;"—words spoken to a great coachman on the Northern Road, Tom Hennessey by name, to which, with Spartan frankness, he replied, "You're right, sir,")—but this is a digression—the Hounslow Heath, I say, which the Flying Machine has left behind it, holds a prominent

True—every word of it.

C 2

place at all periods in the *Annals of the Roads.* To us it is chiefly remarkable for its Powder Mills, which explode once or twice a year; but besides highwaymen in Charles the Second's time (in the spontaneous production of which it, in all ages, held a high place in national esteem), it had in James the Second's time a camp of thirteen thousand men placed there to overawe the London which was ripe for the rebellion, and which had an exactly opposite effect—a visit to Hounslow Camp becoming a favourite holiday amusement for Londoners; and later on in the great Era of Coaching, when it was the first stage out of London for all coaches going westward, there used to be kept here for the purposes of posting and coaching two thousand five hundred horses, which perhaps gives as good an idea of the scale of an undertaking as anything can.

It has its lists of accidents too. It was not a good place even in the best days of the road to cross in a fog. The celebrated Charles Ward was an eye-witness of a calamity which happened in 1840 when some thick weather prevailed. He was bound for Bagshot and had to be escorted out of London by torches. "seven or eight Mails following one after the other, the guard of the foremost lighting the one following and so on till the last." He took three hours to do the nine miles, and on his way back to London, the same weather prevailing, he found the old Exeter Mail in a ditch. The leaders had come in contact with a haycart, which not unnaturally caused them to turn suddenly round. They foolishly did not stop here or all would have been well. No! They broke the pole, blundered down a steep embankment, and brought up in the bottom of a deep ditch filled with mud and water. The wheelers were drowned and the Mail Coach pitched on the stump of a willow tree that hung gracefully over the scene. Meanwhile where were the outside passengers? They were thrown into the meadow beyond in company with the coachman. The two inside passengers however remained where they were, wherever that was, and were extricated with some difficulty. Fortunately no one was injured, which, considering the somewhat mixed condition of men, beasts, and things, was fortunate, and lends some colour to the fine distinction drawn between railway and coaching accidents by a devotee of the roads :—" You got upset in a coach or chaise," he cries, " and there you were. You get upset in a railway and where are you ? "

The same authority discourses more of fogs on Hounslow Heath as follows :—

" There were eight Mails," he writes (they ought to be sung, these old coaching yarns, gray legends of a life that has faded, and out of which much meaning has gone, turned into Border Poetry by some horsey Scott, so that they should possess some form at least to future generations who may be grappling in the central blue), " there were eight Mails," he writes, " that passed through Hounslow. The Bristol, Bath, Gloucester, and Stroud took the right hand road from Hounslow ; the Exeter, Yeovil, Poole, and 'Quicksilver,' Devonport (which was the one I was driving), went the straight road towards Staines. We always saluted each other when passing with 'Good-night, Bill,' 'Dick,' or 'Harry,' as the case might be. I was once passing a Mail, mine being the fastest, and gave the wonted salute. A coachman named Downs was driving the Stroud Mail. He instantly recognized my voice, and said, 'Charley, what are you doing on my road ? ' It was he however who had made the mistake ; he had taken the Staines instead of the Slough Road out of Hounslow. We both pulled up immediately. He had to turn round and go back, which was a feat attended with much difficulty in such a fog. Had it not been for our usual salute he would not have discovered his mistake before reaching Staines."

After leaving Cranford Bridge—where I shall leave the Flying Machine and its passengers, it is much too slow for me, considering the ground I have to get over, and with the help of the York House fast day coach, or the Bristol Mail, or the Beaufort Hunt, I shall be at Bath before they "inn" for the night at Reading. After leaving Cranford Bridge with its White Hart Inn, the memory of which

St. Mary's Butts, Reading.

is in the nostrils of old stage coachmen as a sweet-smelling savour, the Bath Road runs through flat pastoral country (indeed, this side of Reading there is hardly a rise), past Sipson Green, where at the

Magpies post horses could be procured, past Longford where they couldn't, till it enters Buckinghamshire just before reaching Colnbrook.

And in entering Buckinghamshire we are on classic ground. Every yard of the way burns with memories—not of broken poles, of runaway teams, of chains snapped and coaches running on wheelers, and like data of purely horsey history; the Bath Road is not rich in this kind of recollection, being a flat, comfortable road almost as far as Newbury, and as a consequence not as remarkable as many others for great catastrophes, and cunning coachmen; but the memories which haunt it about Colnbrook no less belong, it seems to me, to its history; memories of great names famous in art, fashion, poetry, scandal, politics, which have posted down it, coached down it, sauntered by its side, lived within touch almost of its ceaseless, hurried pulse.

For on the right of Colnbrook is Ritchings—where Lord Bathurst, the pleasant kindly Mæcenas of the last century, loved to entertain the literary celebrities of his time. Round his table Addison, Steele, Pope, Prior, and Swift constantly gathered. An old bench in the grounds used to be covered with the autographs of these immortals—post-prandia mementoes of a pleasant jaunt from town. Here the great Congreve, fresh from some recent stage triumph, wrote his great name in juxta-position, of course, to the equally great name of some fine lady. It is pleasant to think of these symposiums of wit, poetry, and politics; of the wine taken on the site of the chapel to St. Lawrence, the tutelary saint of Windsor forest; of the drive back to London in the cool of the evening; of the laughter which echoed to some forgotten good thing, which made the sixteen miles back to London seem six, and this part of the Bath Road classic.

My Lord Bathurst, after having enjoyed the society of Addison, Steele, Swift, Pope, and Prior, came at the end of his long and cultured life to know Sterne, and in doing so touched hands with the wits of two generations. The most original of English authors however and the most misunderstood did not grace Ritchings with his quaint presence, at least not as Lord Bathurst's guest, the place having passed from his lordship's hands in 1739 into those of the Earl of Hertford. This nobleman's wife continued the literary traditions of the place. She was the Eusebia of Dr. Watts and the Cleora of Mrs. Rowe. Minor poets piped about her feet and listened, with the enthusiasm which authors in company of their kind can feign so well, to her poems. For Eusebia not only wrote poetry, but recited it too; and this is the deuce, as every one knows, and as Thomson found it. The author of the *Seasons*, dedicated his poem of "Spring" to her; and, no doubt, according to his delightful custom, wandered round her garden in his dressing-gown, and bit off the sunny side of her peaches; but when Eusebia cried, "Lend me your ears," and produced a manuscript, the sleepy poet plied his pinions and betook himself to a less intellectual feast; in point of fact, he went off and caroused with Eusebia's husband; and of course Eusebia was annoyed.

This dual tenancy of Ritchings has connected the Bath Road with some famous literary characters already—with, indeed, the lions of two periods and their jackals; but its passage through Colnbrook connects it with a greater memory still. It was here—or, to speak more accurately, in the neighbouring village of Horton—that young Milton lived, from the time he was twenty-four to the time he was thirty. It was here, in the quiet Buckinghamshire hamlet, and before the shadow of political convulsion informed his genius with a sterner bent, that he gave to the world those rich fancies of a yet courtly Muse, which some hold still to be her most precious bequest. At Horton he wrote "Lycidas," the "Comus," the "Sonnet to the Nightingale," and probably the "Allegro" and "Penseroso." Hence it was that he wrote to his friend Diodati, "You ask me of what I am thinking. As God shall help me, of immortality; but how shall I attain it? My wings are fledging, and I meditate a flight." I like to think that the travellers on the Bath Road between 1634 and 1637 may have often passed

D

and noticed the romantic figure of the young poet, his fine face aflame with genius, his comely head bent to catch the music of the spheres. The ladies in the Bath Machine or the Post-Chaise of Charles the First's time would, I am sure, have noticed him; would have awakened their sleeping husbands,

A Winter Day's Amusement.

heavy with the dinner at Cranford, and pointed him out to them; would have looked back at him, admired him, wondered who he was.

But let us get back to our horses and coachmen; for the history of the Bath Road is not all a literary history, though, of all the great roads of England, I have found it the most literary road. At one end of it must be remembered was Bath, and to "The Bath"—as it was till quite lately called—jaded authors and other literary wild fowl rushed to rouse sedentary livers. The Bath Road, as I say however, has its coachmen as well as its poets, and they must be chronicled in their courses. Down this part of the road, then, where we are resting, the following great men, who are now, let us hope, driving in august procession by the Styx, exercised their superlative craft—Isaac Walton—not he of fishing fame, but the Mæcenas of whips, the Braham of the Bath Road—who could pick a fly off his leader's right eyelid with all the friendly dexterity discovered by Mr. Vincent Crummles; Jack Adams, the civil and obliging pastor, who taught the young Etonians how to drive—(how schoolboys must have enjoyed coaches, by the way; how the slow rate of travelling must have drawn out the delicious luxury of departure from the seat of learning; how postponed the horrid moment of arrival; with what pride the first driving lesson must have been taken on so conspicuous a box; with what unerring aim peas must have been launched at equestrians on restive horses, from how great a point of vantage!)—then, to proceed with the catalogue of the coachmen, there was the gallant Jack Everett, who upset his coach near Marlborough, broke one of his own legs, and one also belonging to a female passenger, but who, disdaining an ignominious flight, allowed himself to be conveyed to the nearest surgeon in the same barrow with his victim, who was neither fair, fat, nor under fifty; who, moreover, after uttering the ever-memorable exclamation, "I have often kissed a young woman, and why shouldn't I kiss an old one?" suited the tender action to the candid word; neither did shrieks issue from the barrow. Lastly, of those whom I have space left me to mention, Jack Stacey must not be forgotten; one of four brothers who worked on the Western roads—known, all of them, for equal skill, courage, punctuality, and hats with brims destitute of all curl; but Jack notorious above them all for having, for the first time on record, driven a Mail out of Piccadilly with more than four passengers inside. The deed, hateful alike to men and Mail inspectors, is thus pleasantly told by Mr. Stanley Harris, in his erudite and amusing work, *The Coaching Age*:

"One night the Bath Mail was full inside all the way down, when a gentleman who was a regular customer wanted to return home to Marlborough, and there was no means of his getting there. Stacey held a council with the book-keeper, observing that it wouldn't do to leave the gentleman behind as he was a regular customer, but how they were

Newbury Bridge.

to get out of the dilemma neither of them was able to explain. Ultimately it was, I believe, solved by the gentleman himself getting in just as the mail was starting. A squeeze it must have been if they were small men; but on this point I have no information. Arrived at the Bear, at Maidenhead, where they changed, Stacey went to the coach door and said, 'There's time for you to get a cup of coffee here, gentlemen, if you just like to get out.' No one moved, fearful that if once out he might not be able to get in again. In this way they travelled down to Newbury, fifty-six miles from London, and the end of Stacey's journey. They had then however seventeen miles to go on to Marlborough, the extra passenger's destination, and he got out without any expression of regret either on the part of himself or his fellow passengers at the parting."

Here is a picture of a fearful possibility in a coach. Degenerate travellers of to-day, we know what glances of flame are exchanged, even in an hour's journey, between the ten occupants of a first-class special and the accursed eleventh who projects himself into their midst at the very moment when the train is moving from the platform. But here was an agony prolonged for seventy-four miles, and suffered in a sinister silence. Why that silence when experience would lead one to expect curses? I should much like to know the secret history of that ride. How did the fifth passenger so impress his presence on his victims that they said no word when the coachman asked them whether they would like some coffee? Did he administer some narcotic on entering the coach, or—those were fighting days—was it by knocking them "out of time" that he "sent them to sleep?"

The issue is lapped in mystery; but much of the Bath Road lies beyond Colnbrook, where I have been pausing, and it is time to get along it. The fast coaches out of London soon covered the twenty-two miles to Reading, and there is no need for me to dawdle by the way. The purely coaching record is a blank. There was however a fine inn at Slough, where there is now a draughty railway station; and at Salt Hill, six furlongs on, the Windmill was noted for its dinners. Here was also one of those unlimited establishments for the supply of posting horses, to be found years ago on all the great thoroughfares out of London. After crossing over Maidenhead Bridge the road enters Berkshire, and immediately afterwards the town of Maidenhead itself. An industrious curate, once resident in the town.

has filled a large volume with its history; but there is nothing in it; and were it not that Royalty here first sets its foot on the road, we might hurry on to Maidenhead thicket, where we should have our purses taken. Such a lot, at least, would in all likelihood have been ours, had we travelled in the good old days, and properly provided. The place had such a bad reputation so far back as Elizabeth's time that the Vicar of Hurley, who did duty at Maidenhead, drew an extra salary as amends for having to pass it.

In July, 1647, Charles the First was allowed, after several years separation, to see his children, and children and father met at Maidenhead, at the Greyhound Inn. The meeting must have been a pathetic one, but the town was strewn with flowers and decked with green boughs. The united family, so soon to be so terribly divided, dined together, we read, and afterwards drove to Caversham. It must have been a pleasant journey that down the Reading Road, and would make, I think, a pretty picture; the king, with a sad smile on his fine face, pale from imprisonment, the children laughing and talking gaily, innocent of what the Fates were preparing unseen, the stern guard of Ironsides, not unmoved at the sight, riding grimly behind. I wonder what Charles and his children talked about on that historic journey. Not of past troubles, I suspect. Care had been too constant a companion ot late years to be chosen as a topic. I dare say that the king, who knew his folk-lore and his Berkshire too—and who was a capital story-teller, if we are to believe Mr. Wills—simply discussed the places of interest on the road, and acted as *cicerone* to his children. It would be a natural event at so critical a meeting, just as it was natural that Heine, after careful consideration of what he should say to Goethe when he met him, found when the crisis came that he could only talk about plums; and Charles if he did discuss scenery had a subject. Half a mile south of Maidenhead, he might have pointed out the spire of Bray Church, and told his children the story of the immortal Vicar. Perhaps at his children's request, he sang them a song, or perchance a ballad, according to prescription, though I am not quite sure whether one was extant at the time—probably it wasn't. At any rate, the Vicar alone would make a subject for an afternoon drive. There are few characters in English history that I admire more than the soft-hearted Simon Aleyn. This genial churchman had seen some martyrs burnt; he thought the game was not worth the candle, and at the same time discovered in himself no particular *penchant* for martyrdom. The result was that he was a papist in Henry the Eighth's time, a Protestant in Edward the Sixth's time, a papist in Mary's, and in Elizabeth's a Protestant again. I cannot sufficiently admire the genial adroitness of this bending to circumstance, or weary of considering what seas of precious blood might have been saved to England if Simon Aleyn's contemporaries could have added a leaven of his circumspection to the fury of their faith. But I do not think that his contemporaries thought very highly of poor Simon—though from all I can read, he made as good a vicar as many of them, and a better one than most. No! they "lay low" for him in the cruellest manner, and asked him at the end of his life, whether, if he was not a turncoat, he was not an inconstant changeling? But Simon, though he must have been about a hundred, was ready for

The Jack of Newbury.

Sign of the Angel, Woolhampton.

them. "Not so," said he, "for I have always kept my principle." Upon this the wicked desired him to "go to," when he "went to" in the following fashion. "My principle," he said, "is this: to live and die the Vicar of Bray." Then his questioners "went too," and the good Simon died according to his principles in 1588.

His genial presence must have passed up and down the London Road many times during his life, for the purpose of taking fresh oaths under varying conditions, signing recantations and executing more important commissions, and his jolly ghost should haunt it still if ghosts were not like stage coaches—so hideously out of fashion; and Simon would be in good company too if he would walk, for the Bath Road *is* haunted, and by two of his contemporaries.

I shall have occasion later on to remark on the curious way in which Henry the Eighth's name has attached itself to certain counties, with which, if we are to credit historians, for want of other pastime, he had no earthly connection in life. It is not surprising however that between Windsor and Reading, the much married and much whitewashed king should be the hero of every tale. And it is of a ghost story of which he is particularly the moving spirit—a story which I shall tell here because it connects another royalty with the Bath Road.

In the days, then, when people used to sit round ingle benches and frighten each other with horrid tales to make an excuse for taking strong waters, travellers by night on the Bath Road used often to have a fright on this side of Reading. They met, or rather were confronted with—confronted is the proper word—two figures with their faces set towards London. The usual preliminaries in the way of hair standing on end, eyes shooting out of sockets, horses trembling violently and then running away, having been adjusted, the traveller looked at the apparitions and found one was a fat king in Lincoln green and the other a pale abbot extremely emaciated, having his hand pressed meaningly on the place where his supper ought to have been and clearly was not—

under which presentment the two figures passed on towards London, the king beckoning the churchman. So far so good. But what occurred when the apparitions in a marvellously short space of time were seen returning Reading-wards? Why, a change had come over the spirit of the dream and the order of the procession. The churchman rode first, and his complexion, so far as a ghost's can, had recovered all its roses—his face moreover had filled out and his priestly hands folded before him embraced a portly person. Behind him rode the fat king tossing a purse

Henry the Eighth and the Abbot of Reading.

"I would give £100 could I feed so lustily on beef as you do.

of gold and shaking his royal sides with paroxysms of ghostly inaudible laughter! The whole thing was a mystery.

Its key can be found in Fuller. It seems that Henry the Eighth one day lost his way out hunting, and as he had started the chase at Windsor, and found himself outside the Abbot of Reading's house at dinner-time, he must be allowed to have got some distance from his bearings. Clearly however the next thing was to dine, and this he did at the Abbot's table, the bat-eyed churchman having taken him for one of the Royal Guard. A sirloin was produced and the king "laid on," much marked of the Abbot, who had as much appetite as a peahen. When the roast had almost disappeared before the royal onslaught, the churchman could contain himself no longer.

"Well fare thy heart," he exclaimed to the supposed man-at-arms, "for here in a cup of sack I remember thy master. I would give a hundred pounds on condition that I could feed as lustily on beef as you do. Alas! my weak and squeezie stomach will hardly digest the wing of a small rabbit or chicken." How cruel a case of dyspepsia in the Middle Ages! I recommend it to the notice of the faculty, as a proof that there is nothing new under the sun, not even in this "new disease that is stealing upon us all." Meanwhile the king pledged his host and departed. Some weeks after, the Abbot was committed to the Tower and fed for a short space on bread and water—a novel treatment for loss of appetite which threw the pious patient into the most horrid dejection, "yet not so empty was his body of food as his mind was filled with fears as to how he had incurred the king's displeasure." At the very climax of this emptiness a sirloin of beef was set before him, when the good Abbot verified the proverb that two hungry meals make a glutton. He in point of fact rivalled the king's performance at Reading, and just as he was wiping his mouth, out jumped the king from a closet. "My Lord," quoth the king, "deposit presently your hundred pounds of gold, or else no going hence all the days of your life. I have been your physician to cure you of your 'squeezie stomach,' and here as I deserve I demand my fee for the same." Too replete for repartee the Abbot "down with his dust," and presently returned to Reading as somewhat lighter in purse so much more merry in heart than when he came thence. I hope that when Henry the Eighth suppressed the monasteries he remembered that the good Abbot had got a renewed digestion and left him something to buy beef with—but it is probable that he didn't.

This I believe to be the right interpretation of the vision of the two horsemen on the Reading Road; which I hope will not be considered a digression from my subject, because the travellers are somewhat pale and insubstantial, and ride by us on ghostly old horses instead of in a spick and span fast day coach. Everything is a subject in my eyes provided that it has travelled on the road, and if Henry the Eighth and his patient travelled on it some time since, they have at all events brought me to Reading, which is thirty-eight miles seven furlongs from Hyde Park Corner, and a third of the way to Bath.

Reading has a history like many other provincial towns which nobody has read of. That is to say the usual number of Parliaments have been held there at which no particular measures were passed. Queen Elizabeth visited it six times, but seems to have omitted to shoot a stag during her stays; there was a siege or two undertaken in the Civil Wars; and a Benedictine Abbey turned into a palace—the Abbey of the unfortunate Abbot. What is more to the purpose however is that here the Flying Machines of the early days of coaching inned, as they called it, after the first of their three days' journey to Bath, and the coaches of the palmy days changed horses. The Great Western Hotel now reigns of course instead of the Bear, the Crown, and the George; but it was at the latter signs that the passengers in the Flying Machines rested their jolted limbs on the sheets smelling of lavender that we have read of, and their more hurried descendants had just time to drink the great drink of a tumbler of fresh milk, one fair lump of sugar, two tablespoonfuls of rum, and just a thought of nutmeg grating on the top of all, a trifle that could be tossed off in a minute and so far as I can read was perpetually so being tossed off, before the guard applied "the yard of tin" to his lips and the four fresh horses whirled them off to Newbury.

I have said that the Bath Road has appealed to me as being more particularly the literary road than any of the other five great thoroughfares out of London. The next thirteen miles out of Reading go to bear out this view. They teem with literary and romantic recollections. Two miles out of Reading and on the right of the road is Calcott House, once the seat of the Berkshire Lady. In the pleasant park which lies in front of the square, formal-looking old house, the beautiful Miss Kendrick, the rich, the whimsical, confronted Benjamin Child, Esq., Barrister-at-law—masked, rapier in hand, and under the pale moonlight. The lady had refused numberless offers of marriage made in due form. Due forms however were her aversion, and so seem men to have been, till one fine day, when

> "Being at a noble wedding
> In the famous town of Reading,
> A young gentleman she saw
> Who belonged to the law."

In fact Benjamin Child, Esq. To him the lady sends a challenge unbeknownst, as Mrs. Gamp would say, to fight a mortal duel in Calcott Park. Nor did she trouble to assign any cause why Child—if such lot were to be his—should be skewered like a chicken. This sounds like Dumas, but the barrister thought it meant business, and repaired to the place named sword in hand. He found the fair Miss Kendrick, masked, and still "unbeknownst," awaiting him,

> "'So now take your chance,' says she,
> 'Either fight or marry me.'
> Said he, 'Madam, pray what mean ye?
> In my life I ne'er have seen ye.'"

In fact he proposed point-blank that she should unmask, not perhaps caring to take a pig in a poke. The lady however remained firm and *incognito*, when the intrepid Child, fortified perhaps by a view of Calcott House, which formed a grateful background to the scene, told the lady that he preferred to wed her than to try her skill. Upon which in the twinkling of an eye he found himself

> "Clothed in rich attire
> Not inferior to a squire"—

Doctor Swift and Bolingbroke.

in fact master of Calcott. Fortunate man; romantic times, say I. They were only so far back as 1712.

Two miles beyond Calcott the Bath Road runs through Theale, where on the Old Angel inn the traveller's eyes at least may be feasted. And in this neighbourhood, the memory of Pope once more adds lustre to the way. For at Ufton Nervet lived Arabella Fermor, the Belinda of *The Rape of the Lock.* Arabella must have passed down the road many a time on her way from Ufton to Hampton Court.

> "Where mighty Anna, whom three realms obey,
> Doth sometimes counsel take and sometimes tea,"

perhaps in the society of her celebrator; for Pope himself was frequently a visitor at Ufton. Many of his most delightful letters are dated from there—letters in which he gives charming sketches of English country life in the last century, and paints the old house for us, with its haunted staircase, secret chambers, formal gardens, and the raised terrace behind it where Arabella must often have walked. Bucklebury, in the immediate neighbourhood, is associated with even greater names. This was the country seat of Bolingbroke the magnificent. Here the great statesman who was half Horace and half the elder Pitt, forgot the distractions of political intrigue in the smiles of Burgundy and the calm pleasures of country life. Bucklebury was his Sabine farm. Here he played the fancy farmer and gathered round him the finest intellects of the day. Swift was a constant visitor, and in a very delightful letter to Stella, he has drawn Mr. Secretary for us as the perfect country

The Old Angel at Theale.

gentleman, smoking his tobacco with one or two neighbours, inquiring after the wheat in such a field, visiting his hounds and calling them all by their names, he and his wife showing Swift up to his bedroom just in the country fashion. "His house," writes the author of Gulliver, "is just in the midst of 3,000*l.* a year he had by his lady, who is descended from Jack of Newbury, of whom books and ballads are written; and there is an old picture of him in the room."

Courtyard of Angel, Woolhampton.

At Woolhampton, a little over ten miles from Reading, still stands all that is left of the Angel, a celebrated old posting inn, with a most curious sign, and three miles five furlongs further on is Thatcham. Here the passengers by the "New Company's elegant light four inside post coaches," which in the palmy days of coaching did the hundred and five miles from Bath to London in twelve hours and a half, used to dine at the King's Head. Here prodigies in the way of taking in provisions were performed in half an hour. The attack on the table must have been tremendous, and the tables were well fortified for the attack. These were the days, be it remembered, when English cookery was English cookery, unpolluted as yet with

"Art, with poisonous honey stolen from France."

The distinguished author of *Tancred* and the Treaty of Berlin has described the half hour for dinner at such an inn as the King's Head with much spirit.

"The coach stops here half an hour, gentlemen: dinner quite ready."

"'Tis a delightful sound. And what a dinner! What a profusion of substantial delicacies! What mighty and iris-tinted rounds of beef! What vast and marble-veined ribs! What gelatinous veal pies! What

The King's Head, Thatcham.

colossal hams! Those are evidently prize cheeses! And how invigorating is the perfume of those various and variegated pickles! Then the bustle emulating the plenty; the ringing of bells, the clash of thoroughfare, the summoning of ubiquitous waiters, and the all-pervading feeling of omnipotence from the guests, who order what they please to the landlord, who can produce and execute everything they can desire. 'Tis a wondrous sight!"

F

Three miles farther on and we are at Newbury, or rather at Speenhamland, a kind of suburb of inns and posting houses which connected it with the Bath Road; and at Newbury, and indeed right on to Hungerford, we are on historic ground. It is out of my province to describe in detail the rise and fall of the fortunes of the fight during those two tremendous days, September 16th, 1643, and October 27th, 1644, when the best blood of England was poured out like water on Speen Hill, and the cause of Charles the First was upheld by an uncertain triumph; nor have I space to do more than make passing mention of the famous personages in the world of history, romance and letters, whose memories throng the road as far as Hungerford, and indeed beyond it, "thick as leaves in Vallombrosa." I see Charles the First dressing in the bow window of the drawing-room of Shaw House on the morning of the battle, and the divinity that hedges a king turning aside the rebel bullet; and the gallant Carnarvon measuring the gateway with his sword to see how Essex horns could pass through when they should lead him in as prisoner (Carnarvon's dead body came into Newbury the same evening stretched across a horse); and Sunderland dying sword in hand at twenty-three; and Falkland the blameless, who foresaw much misery to his country, riding into the battle in the belief that he would be out of that misery before night; I see the travellers on the Bath Road smacking their lips over the Pelican dinners, and losing their colour over the Pelican bill, each equally notorious at that great house.

> "The famous inn in Speenhamland
> That stands below the hill,
> May well be called the Pelican
> From its enormous bill,"

as Quin sang of it. On the 16th of June, 1668, Mr. Samuel Pepys came to "Newberry," as he spells it, and there dined "and musick: a song of the old courtier of Queene Elizabeth's, and how he was changed upon the coming in of the King did please me mightily, and I did cause W. Hewer to write it out. Then comes the reckoning (forced to change gold), 8*s.* 7*d.* servants, and poor 1*s.* 6*d.* So out and lost our way; but

Shaw House,
Newbury.

come into it again." I do not see Chaucer writing the *Canterbury Tales* under the oak named after him in Donnington Park, because, in spite of the tradition that says he did so, the Park did not come into the family's possession till eighteen years after the poet's death, but I can see Burke, and Johnson, and Goldsmith, and Reynolds posting along the road towards Sandford, where they are going to stay with Mrs. Montagu, and I can see Evelyn eating "troutes" at Hungerford, and William of Orange receiving the commissioners of King James. This important episode in the Rebellion is graphically described by Macaulay:

"On the morning of Saturday, 8th of December, 1688, the King's commissioners reached Hungerford. The Prince's bodyguard was drawn up to receive them with military respect. Bentinck welcomed them and proposed to conduct them immediately to his master. They expressed a hope that the Prince would favour them with a private audience; but they were informed that he had resolved to hear them and answer them in public. They were ushered into his bed-chamber where they found him surrounded by a crowd of noblemen and gentlemen. Halifax, whose rank, age, and abilities entitled him to precedence, was spokesman. Halifax having explained the basis on which he and his colleagues were prepared to treat, put into William's hand a letter from the King and retired. William opened the letter and seemed unusually moved. It was the first letter which he had received from his father-in-law since they had become avowed enemies. He requested the Lords and Gentlemen whom he had convoked on this occasion to consult together unrestrained by his presence as to the answer which ought to be returned. To himself however he reserved the power of

The White Harte, Thatcham.

Littlecote.

deciding in the last resort after hearing their opinion. He then left them and retired to Littlecote Hall, a manor house, situated about two miles off, and renowned down to our own times not more on account of its venerable architecture and furniture than on account of a horrible and mysterious crime which was perpetrated there in the days of the Tudors."

I do not think that the travellers on the Bath Road, whether posting or coaching, knew much about "this horrible and mysterious

Great Chatfield Manor, near Bath.

crime" which has made Littlecote Hall and Wild Darrell notorious, till Scott told the story to the general world in a fine foot-note to *Rokeby;* for Evelyn—to take one example—on his journey to Wiltshire, in 1654, passes the place with the remark that it "is a noble seat, park, and river," which is perfectly true, but not much to the point; and Pepys—to take another—on Tuesday, June 16th, 1668, after paying the reckoning at the Hart at Marlborough—"14*s.* 6*d.;* and servants, 2*s.;* poor 1*s.;* set out, and passing through a good part of this county of Wiltshire saw a good house of Alexander Popham's," and with that passes on to Newbury, where he dined, and heard that song of the old courtier of Queene Elizabeth, and how "he was changed at the coming in of the king," which pleased him so mightily, and to which I have already referred. Now we expect nothing but pragmatical practicalness from the delightful Samuel, but to call Wild Darrell's haunted home "a good house of Alexander Popham's," is really to touch bottom in an outrage on the eternal fitness of things. Worse however remains behind. One might at least be led to expect mention of a romantic legend from a literary lady; but Miss Burney, on her journey to Bath in 1780 with Mrs. Thrale, viewed Littlecote's storied towers unmoved, that is to say if she saw them at all, and was not looking out of the other window of the post-chaise; at all events she makes no mention of there being such a place in Europe, or her *Diary*, though she tells us that she slept at Maidenhead the first night, Speen Hill the second, the third at Devizes, and dwells on the Bear Inn there at great length—where we will join her in a quarter of an hour.

Meanwhile it is not for me to pass with such travelled indifference the scene of that wild story of Elizabethan crime and mystery, which reads even in these practical times like some page of horror torn out of Sheridan Le Fanu, and to which the great magician of the world fantastical could alone have given fit form and colour. Summoned by his eerie genius, with what terrible vividness would each incident, each actor in the buried infamy, rise from the dead! The whole story would pass before us under a ghostly, shimmering, ghoul-like glamour: the midwife at Shefford, a village seven miles off, waked in the dead of night, with a promise of high pay for her office on condition that she should be blindfolded! the headlong ride through the wild weather behind the silent serving man! the arrival at a large house which was strange to her! the mounting of the long stairs, which the woman, shadowed already with some grim foreboding, counted carefully as she

Littlecote Hall.

passed up them! the delivery in a gloomy, richly furnished room of a masked lady! the entrance of a tall man "of ferocious aspect", who seized the newborn child, thrust it into the fire that was blazing on the hearth, ground it under his heavy boot till it was cinders! then the trembling departure of the pale spectator of the hideous scene, blindfolded as she had come, aghast, speechless, carrying a heavy bribe with her as the price of guilty silence, but carrying also a piece of the curtain which she had cut out of the bed—all this scene of horror how the author of *The Dragon Volant* would have described it for us! And all this horror is history!

The original deposition made on her death-bed by the midwife, whose name was Mrs. Barnes, and committed to writing by Mr. Bridges, magistrate of Great Shefford is in existence to this day, and is proof beyond cavil. It is from this point that rumour begins. That rumour, backed in my opinion by damning circumstance, has for two hundred years connected the tragedy with Littlecote House and William Darrell, commonly called Wild Darrell, then its proprietor. It is alleged that the midwife's depositions set justice on the murderer's track, and that the fitting of the piece of curtain which Mrs. Barnes had taken away with her into a rent found in the curtain of the Haunted Room at Littlecote, marked the scene of the murder. Wild Darrell was tried for his life, it is said, but escaped by bribing the officers of the law with the reversion of his large estates. But—so runs the rumour—the memory of his crime pursued him. He was haunted by ghastly spectres which he tried to forget in wild excesses, but which no seas of claret would lay. Finally as he was riding recklessly down the steep downs, with the scene of his atrocity in sight, at headlong speed, the reins loose, his body swaying in the saddle, pale, wild-eyed, unkempt, the very picture of debauched and guilty recklessness, tearing from the Furies of the past, that past confronted him. The apparition of a babe burning in a flame barred his path. The horse reared violently at the supernatural sight. Darrell was as violently thrown, and the wicked neck, which had escaped the halter by a bribe, was broken at last as it deserved to be. The stile is still shown by the country people where the wretched, haunted man, met his fate; the spectres of the pale huntsman and his hounds often cross their simple paths in the gloaming of summer evenings when the downs loom gray and ghostly—or did cross them, rather, before School Boards, the franchise, the abolition of the smock frock, and the general improvement of everything on and off the earth, banished such inspiriting sights for

Haunted Room, Littlecote.

ever. Wild Darrell is remembered but as a name now, and as a name for all that is wicked.

And yet not quite so if we are to judge from a recent publication ; in point of fact "not at all so by any means no more," as the South Sea Islanders say when they have eaten a Wesleyan missionary. For we live in an age of the rehabilitation of condemned reputations, and a generation which has learnt from a German professor that Tiberius was an amiable potentate, and not a fourteen-bottle man, and from an English historian that Henry the Eighth was a confirmed theological student for whom women's society offered no charm, will not raise their eyebrows even when Mr. Hubert Hall tells them in his delightful *Society in the Elizabethan Age* (Sonnenschein & Co.), that Wild Darrell, far from being the monster that rumour and I have made out, was in point of fact a plain, courteous, much abused lord of wide acres, which rapacious neighbours passed their lives in trying to take from him, and who was compelled as a painful consequence to ruin himself in Chancery law-suits. The William Darrell that Mr. Hall draws for us is indeed almost too good to be true. He bears an ominous resemblance to the "good young man who died," and far from roasting live children at midnight and breaking his neck by furious riding, spends his whole days in totting up his accounts, drawing up amateur legal documents to the utter confusion of his legal advisers, giving away estates in order that these documents may be heard in court, reading philosophy, cultivating strawberries and trout with the aid of a Dutch gardener (the strawberries not the trout), smoking tobacco, and finally dying in his bed, comfortable and orthodox. Mr. Hall does indeed take pity on his hero and permits him, with many graceful excuses, the sentimental license of running away with his neighbour's wife (the injured husband, as is customary, coming in for no consideration whatever); but at best his hero is but a dowdy sort of Elizabethan Edgar Ravenswood, attired in a gray jerkin, with an elderly Lady Hungerford for a Lucy Ashton.

Now all this is very sad, and bad, and mad—at least it will make most people feel so if their cherished illusions are thus ruthlessly shattered In the present instance however it does not seem to me that the romance of private history has been deprived of a lawful possession, or that the wicked Wild Darrell of our youth, "the tall man of ferocious aspect", has been turned for good and all into an agricultural goody-goody. Nevertheless in an age when documentary evidence is considered everything, and all other kind of evidence as nothing at all, Mr. Hall's defence of Darrell must command respect, for it is a defence based entirely on a series of Darrell papers lying in the Record Office, which have been carefully edited, and give us as interesting a glimpse into Elizabethan country society as can have been got for some time. The cry of documentary evidence is not however one at which I stand instantly

Wild Darrell.

abashed, because I know that not only have documents relating to issues wherein the honour of families has been at stake been frequently tampered with in public collections, but have been found, on search being made, to have vanished off the face of the earth. Who supposes for instance that in our Record Office is to be found anything approaching even to a complete account of an event so important as the Gunpowder Treason? Who wrote the letter to Monteagle? and at whose instigation? Was the Government cognizant before that letter was written of the exact nature of the conspiracy? Where are the documents which should point most clearly to the complicity of the Provincial of the English Jesuits? Echo answers "Where?" and will continue to answer so to the end of the chapter.

It is from this point of view, though not from this point of view only, that Mr. Hall's defence of Darrell seems to me inconclusive. The Darrell papers, or rather such as are now in the Record Office, are all that he relies upon; and the Darrell papers really have little to do with anything but farm accounts. Mr. Hall, in truth, has only got hold of one end of the stick. There is a lack of cause for effect, as a consequence, at the very basis of his argument. And the same flaw, if I may say so, runs through it. We are shown at the outset, a man at feud with all his neighbours, accused of one murder, suspected of another, his name a by-word for profligacy and something worse, and we are told that the only reason for this notorious reputation was that he was a wealthy landowner, and that his neighbours wanted to grab his farms! As if the whole energies of an Elizabethan country gentleman—the contemporary of Raleigh, Sidney, Essex, be it remembered—were devoted to this pastoral pursuit! Mr. Hall indeed would have us believe that they were; as he would have us believe, as an excuse for Darrell's *amour* with Lady Hungerford, "that it was as common for men of his class to debauch their neighbours' wives, as for two yeomen to draw on each other at a country fair;" but surely Mr. Hall is thinking of times when carving-knives were made of flint-stones and authors lived in caves and ate each other. And the arguments that he adduces to prove that his hero was not the ruffian that contemporary opinion made out, are really not conclusive at all. If Darrell, for instance, is accused of being a wine-bibber, we are confronted with a most interesting collection of *menus* during his last stay in London, from April 16th to July 14th, 1589, in which we find constant entry of a "pynt of clarett" in connection with "a legg of mutton," and so forth. But waiving the fact that the wicked squire was at this time playing the courtier, with a suspected reputation to keep up, does this formal entry for the benefit of the steward preclude the possibility of private drinking? I think that many a confirmed drunkard's house books would show as temperate a return. It is that private store of Rhenish which does the business, which remains unentered in ledgers, or if entered, appears as "dressinge for ye chickens." Then again, and this touches the root of the whole matter, Mr. Hall expressly declares that Darrell did not "keep a brace of painted madams at his own command." But has he heard of a certain letter dated 2 January, 1579, from Sir H. Knyvett of Charlton, to Sir John Thynne of Longleat, which was discovered by the Reverend Canon Jackson of Leigh Delamere, in which the writer asks Sir John Thynne to tell a Mr. Bonham, who was in his employ, "to inquire of his sister touching her usage at Will Darrell's; the birth of her children; how many there were and what became of them; for that the report of the murder of one of them was increasing foully and would touch Will Darrell to the quick"? This surely seems rather grave! and does not look like "the best years of a life devoted to a Platonic intercourse with a highly cultivated woman." Nor is Mr. Hall more satisfactory with regard to the alleged bribe to Sir John Popham of the reversion of Littlecote, to which rumour assigns the salvation of Darrell's neck. He looks upon it indeed, so far as I can judge, as a sort of Elizabethan refreshing fee to counsel. Will Mr. Hall tell us next that it was the custom of an afternoon for Elizabethan squires to convey away estates "of thousands of broad acres upon the famous downland of three counties", simply to hurry on a chancery lawsuit? I think that even his able and earnest advocacy will fail to arouse such a belief. The truth is that the weakest point of the latest defence of Darrell is the graceful negligence with which his advocate avoids the main, the one, issue. We have pages of farm accounts and household expenses, all very interesting and creditable, but only a contemptuous allusion here and there to the alleged horrible and mysterious crime.

Mr. Hall, to be plain, treats the whole accusation of murder brought against Darrell as so much vindictive cackle. On what grounds it is difficult to conjecture, unless indeed it be that Darrell, when accused of murder before the magistrates, "replied to the wild charge with a mournful dignity"—but so did the late Mr. William Palmer of Rugeley notoriety

The Black Bear, Hungerford.

under similarly embarrassing circumstances; and he could keep accounts as well as Darrell could, ay, and make a book too. I trust, I am sure, that the author of *Society in the Elizabethan Age* will give us many more charming works of the same kind, but he must really not try to destroy all romantic faith that is in us with such doubtful arguments as these. Meanwhile I wonder whether he has seen all those papers that Popham's agent seized almost before Darrell's breath was out of his body, and despatched in chests to London, there to await the arbitration

The Young 'Un.

promised between the respective claims of the Attorney-General and the Secretary of State, who also had a finger in this mysterious pie. Why this almost indecent despatch on the part of Popham ("faithful to the last, though wise only for himself") I should much like to know. I wonder!

In the *interim* I must hurry after Miss Burney and Mrs. Thrale, who are waiting for me all this while at the Bear Inn at Devizes, three and twenty miles or so down the road. I cannot find much to record in the way of history, coaching or otherwise, between Hungerford and Marlborough. The road between Newbury and Bath was called the "lower ground", and being remarkable chiefly for its hills, necessitated much skidding and unskidding. Nor even in the palmy days was it unrenowned for accidents. On the contrary, the Beaufort Hunt fast day coach from London to Bath, run by the celebrated Sherman, he of the moustachios (a prodigy, a blasphemy I had almost said, in those days; of the three old ladies also, wived in succession; distinguished, moreover, for the colour of his coaches, which was yellow; and for their strange shape, which was heavy, peculiar, and old-fashioned as Noah's Ark)—the Beaufort Hunt, I say, was upset in this part of the world three times in less than three weeks, an event, or rather a trilogy, which made passengers nervous, affected the receipts, and led to the removal from the box-seat, whence he had directed these acrobatic manœuvres, of a so-called Captain Jones, whoever he may have been. From which I infer that there were coach-driving captains even in those days, though I have never read of one before. However, the captain retired into private life, and a young man who was a very good coachman, but whose name is unknown to me, though it was very well known on the road, reigned in his stead. This change of cast brought up the receipts of the Beaufort Hunt with a run; places were booked three or four weeks in advance by passengers who wished to travel eleven miles an hour without breaking their necks. The coach became

H

quite the fashion, crowds of people standing about the White Lion in the Market-place at Bath to see it start.

This coach used to change horses at Froxfield, three miles out of Hungerford, and the next stage was Marlborough, seven miles on; the last two miles of the road skirting Savernake Forest, which is a horrible place to hunt in, is sixteen miles in circumference, and the only forest in the country in the possession of a subject, which seems very strange and wild.

One begins to be ashamed of saying of English country towns that they stood a siege in the great Civil Wars, yet this must be said of Marlborough, which was, as a matter of fact, a most important place, considered from a strategical point of view, and a thorn for a long time in the side of the royal cause; for it was not only the most notoriously disaffected town in all Wiltshire, remarkable for the obstinacy and malice of its inhabitants (why, I wonder, this strange malignancy on the part of the good burghers of Marlborough?) But, standing as it does on the Western Road, it seriously menaced Charles's communications with the loyal West. It accordingly underwent the proverbial harmless, necessary siege, and was stormed by Wilmot in December, 1642. In April and November of the following year, Charles himself was at Marlborough, as Henry the First was here five hundred and thirty-three years before, keeping Easter; but with the royal junketings of the scholar king we have nothing to do, though he went to Bath himself two years later, curiously enough, as we are going now.

In the days of the great Roads Marlborough possessed in the Castle (where we will in a minute or two rest a while) one of the finest inns in the three kingdoms. As to the town itself, Evelyn, who dined there on the 9th of June, 1652, found it fresh built from a fire (it has had about four in its history), but he found nothing else in it, except "My Lord Seymour's house," which was afterwards this very same famous Castle

Inn, and the Mount, which he climbed dejectedly for want of something better to do; "ascending by windings for neere halfe a mile," and

Old Marlborough.

remarking that it seemed to have been cast up by hand—which indeed it was by some one or other—weird and legendary, the betting at the present moment being in favour of Merlin, for lack of anybody better known; while Pepys, on the 15th of June, 1668, after lying at the Hart, which he describes as a good house, walked out and found Marlborough "a pretty fair town only for a street or two." After which, having sagely observed that what was most singular was, that the houses on one side had their pent houses supported by pillars, which made a good

The Castle Inn,
Marlborough.

walk, and also, what is more to our purpose, that all the five coaches that came that day from Bath were out of the town before six, went to bed, and the following morning, according to the immortal prescription, "after paying the reckoning, etc., etc., set out."

But the Castle Inn at Marlborough is the question after all, or rather was, for the celebrated caravansery is now part of the College, and ingenuous youths acquire the Greek accidence where their ancestors drank port and recalled their casualties; a striking example of what strange uses an inn may return to as well as a human being. The Castle however has had a three-fold destiny, for not only has it changed from a caravansery into a college, but it was a nobleman's palace before it was a caravansery. Here lived, amongst others, a noble lady whose acquaintance we have made further up the road, to wit, Frances, Countess of Hertford, afterwards Duchess of Somerset, she who at Ritchings entertained Thomson till she found that he preferred to entertain himself; though some say that it was in this very castle that the august patroness to whom "Spring" was dedicated, discovered the horrid truth that her poet was, alas! little better than a drunkard. And it was in her noble lord's society that Eusebia discovered her bard carousing—that was the pity of it—no doubt in one of Eusebia's grottos, which, in company with cascades, artificially formed, it pleased her to scatter about the castle grounds with a lavish and pastoral hand. With what divine anger must she have confronted the guilty pair—both their wigs off by reason of the heat—drinking punch in her pet cave! That divine anger proved at all events too enduring for Thomson's powers of pacification. It was in vain that he piped off—

> "Hertford, fitted or to shine in courts
> With unaffected grace, or walk the plain
> With Innocence and Meditation joined
> In soft assemblage."

In vain! In vain! The lady declined to listen to his song, "which her own season painted" (the season was spring by the by, but surely under the circumstance it ought to have been winter), and the unfortunate bard had to pack his portmanteau and leave the castle for ever, with a flea in his ear. So much for poets who prefer iced punch to the streams of Helicon, and so much also for the great Frances's connection with the castle. The family seat of the Seymours became an inn soon after this, being leased by the Northumberlands (who also found Marlborough slow, and preferred Alnwick) to Mr. Cotterell, and an inn the old place remained, with the reputation for being the best in England almost to the time when it closed its doors in 1843 and was turned into a public school.

And it was an inn in the best sense of the word, an inn such as Macaulay describes, whose equal was not to be found on the Continent, whose "innkeeper, too, was not like other innkeepers." It was of this sort of place that Johnson was thinking when he declared that a chair in it was the throne of human felicity, though it was not at the Castle, Marlborough, that he spoke his great speech on taverns, but at the celebrated Chapel House, Cold Norton, in Oxfordshire, on the North-Western Road. But the Castle, Marlborough, might quite as justly have earned the advertisement. Not that it wanted it, for it had the advertisement of all the nobility, wealth, fashion of a century, that thronged, as all history in those days thronged, to that centre of the valetudinarian and the voluptuary, Bath.

I should like to have the visitors' list of the Castle, during the days of its prime. It would be a Homeric catalogue of guests, compared with which the ship business would be commonplace. Consider that everybody of note in England for over a century entered those doors, ate, drank, slept, gamed there, grumbled over their bills, paid their reckoning, thronged to their post-chaises or coaches, and posted off Bath-wards or to London. Why, the mere writing of the names would make a history, and a more suggestive one than many chronicles of the kings. Chesterfield and Lady Mary Wortley Montagu making for scandal and the waters; Walpole reclining in his chariot, meditating his ailments and the ancient legend of Bath; hypochondriasis and antiquities usurping equal halves of that delicate, indolent brain, his nostril curled at the horsey atmosphere of the old inn yard, his white hand raised in deprecating horror at mine host proffering refreshment on a salver as big as a coach wheel; Selwyn, most good-natured of voluptuaries, who however liked to see a man hanged, taking his ease before dinner in the inn's best room, while his delightful chaplain, Dr. Warner, who had Rabelais and Horace at his finger ends, is busy below with the cellarman, assuring himself of the quality of his patron's claret; Sheridan

Eloped!

running away with his beautiful wife; Garrick posting to Bath in search of new talent and to depreciate Barry; Byron, (already on his biscuit and soda-water *régime*), eying the bill of fare misanthropically; and Brummell incubating a new cravat; and Gentleman Jackson surrounded by his backers on his way to a prize fight. But why proceed with the list? The names of the visitors at this celebrated inn are written in the letters and diaries of three generations.

Of all the great people who put up at the Castle in the days of its prime, perhaps the greatest of them, as is meet and right, has left the most lasting impression behind him. But he did so by rather out-of-the-way means, and advertized himself as a great statesman, not indeed at all more than is customary at the present day, but with a naïve absence of affectation that raises a smile. There were no paragraphists in the land in those times, be it remembered, to announce to an expectant world that a prime minister had cut a tree down, or read the first lesson in church; so Lord Chatham having been attacked by gout on his way from Bath to London, in 1762, took a more picturesque way of acquainting his countrymen with his whereabouts. He made it an insistive condition to his staying at the Castle that every servant in the place from the waiter to the stable boy should wear his livery. Now I do not know what the livery of the noble Lord was, but it was very well known to the England of his day, and as gout kept him in his room at the Castle for several weeks, and as the establishment of that inn, (temporarily clothed as his servants) was the largest in England, the good town of Marlborough simply exhaled its distinguished visitor. People ran against his attendants at every turn. The streets swarmed with them. The inn was alive. The name of Chatham was on every lip, and the great tide of travel which ebbed and flowed night and day along the Bath road, carried the strange news to the uttermost parts of the kingdom.

So political celebrities advertized themselves before the *Daily Telegraph* was, or editors of fashionable papers wanted copy—but I must get on to Devizes.

The fourteen miles odd between this town and Marlborough is sacred to the antiquary, who delights to dig up mounds on plains, and discover two human skeletons or more in a sitting posture, and two laid horizontally as the case may be, which is what was done at West Kennett, four and a quarter miles down the road. At this West

Kennett, to complete the celebrity of the spot, is made and stored the celebrated West Kennett Ale, and that it is also drunk here in large quantities, is not beyond the pale of reasonable human hope. The travellers on the once thronged Bath Road, now as deserted, alas! as the old Roman highway which here coincides with it, took a good deal

A Quaint Corner in Marlborough.

of this ale, I suspect (if it was brewed in those days, of which fact I am not certain), to fortify themselves against down air; and at the same time no doubt some antiquary, perched on the box seat with pince-nez pinched firmly on red nose, observed Silbury Hill immediately on the left of the road, which some sages suppose to be posterior to the Roman invasion, and some anterior to it, but which is the biggest artificial hill in Europe, and is indeed "very fine and large."

Now Beckhampton Inn looms in sight. Here the Beaufort Hunt, and all the principal coaches changed horses, passengers refreshed the inner man, and the different roads to Bath diverged. The Beaufort Hunt and other fast coaches going by Cherhill, Calne and Chippenham, making the whole distance from town 105 miles 6 furlongs; other coaches less known taking the next shortest cut by Sandy Lane and Bowdon Hill to Lacock. Here there is an Abbey with a romance attached to it, which tells how a young lady, discoursing one night to her lover from the battlements of the Abbey church, though strictly forbidden to do so by her papa, remarked "I will leap down to you" (which was surely very unwise), and leapt. The wind came to the rescue and "got under her coates," (the ulster I presume of the 16th century) and thus assisted, the young lady, whose name was Sherington, flopped into the arms of the young man, whose name was Talbot, and killed him to all appearances fatally dead on the spot, at which she sat down and wept. Upon this the defunct Talbot, who had been only temporarily deprived of breath, came to life again, and at the same moment the lady's father, with a fine instinct for a melodramatic situation, jumped out of a bush and observed, that "as his daughter had made such a leap to him she should e'en marry him," meaning Talbot, which was rather obscure, but exactly what the young lady wanted, and married she was to Talbot, whose Christian name was John, brought him the Abbey as a dowry, and lived happily ever after. Leaving Lacock behind, the coaches which took this second route from Beckhampton passed through Corsham, Peckwick Box, and Batheaston, where they entered Somersetshire, and so into Bath, making the whole distance from London 106½ miles.

The third route however is the one which I shall follow more closely, not because it is a mile longer than the last (on the map it looks five miles longer at the very least, but this is a geographical optical delusion), but because it was the route of the Bath mail particularly as distinguished from the Bristol, and because it passes through Devizes,

A Change of Horses.

where there is or was, a celebrated inn at which two distinguished travellers, in the persons of Miss Burney and Mrs. Thrale, have all this long while been waiting for me. But I have not got there yet. After leaving Beckhampton, and not going to Avebury on the right of the road, which is a remarkable temple after the manner of Stonehenge,

The Old Market House, Marlborough.

which some suppose to have been built in the time of Abraham, whenever that may have been, and some modestly proclaim a Serpent's Temple.

"Now o'er true Roman way our horses sound,"

as Gay sings; and three miles and a half or so from Beckhampton the road runs through Wandsditch (perhaps Wans Dyke will be preferred by etymologists), which magnificent earthwork was, according to Dr. Guest, the last frontier of the Belgic province, and can be traced through Wiltshire for nineteen miles. All about here the Bath Road is as exposed as an ancient Briton or Belge could wish it to be; but for warmer and more modern fancies it is not a good place for a kilt. To tell the truth it blows on these downs confoundedly, and here all coaches which were about in the great snow-storm of 1836 wished they were out of it. Nor does the present appearance of Shepherd's Shore, a lone house standing by the roadside, look as if it could have proffered much in the way of shelter; yet this is the last stage of all, of an inn, which, like Winterslow Hut on the Exeter Road, has had its day, and which, when that day was in the ascendant, gave shelter and refreshment to any number who wanted it.

Hungerford Chapel, Devizes.

It is in standing by such a deserted relic of bygone days as this, in looking up and down the silent coach road—that great artery which once gave Shepherd's Shore life, and which is now as empty as the heart which it fed—that we get some sense of the poetry of the old coaching days, some perception of the gulf which separates our manners and our methods from theirs; the difference, indeed, which lies between travelling to a place with such due pauses for romance and adventure as were provided in the old days of posting and flying machines, and arriving at a place with no pauses at all save for collecting tickets—which are not always to be found—as are provided for by our limited mails and flying Dutchmen. For it was this very deliberation of our ancestors which has given to such inns as this Shepherd's Shore on the great roads, much of their historic charm—a deliberation which permitted these old houses to catch, if I may say so, something of the personality of the great people, whether kings, queens, highwaymen, conspirators, or coachmen, who halted at their hospitable doors, dined at their liberal tables, or passed by them at that decorous speed of from five to nine miles an hour, which, even without a stoppage, permitted however faintly some sort of individual impression. And what sort of individual impression, may I ask, can a distinguished traveller to Bath in these days—whether statesman, on his way to the waters, or modern highwayman, armed with the three-card-trick (we live in degenerate days!), or conspirator, fresh from Parliament—make, let us say on Reading, whose platform he can only just see as he whizzes by it; or on Swindon, in whose refreshment-room he has five minutes in which to bolt hot soup? Why, he makes no impression at all, and his characterless transit from one spot to the other (to call it a journey might raise the indignant ghost of some great departed coachman) will remain ignored and unrecorded for ever.

Yes! Railway days and Railway ways, or rather the romance of them will not be written even when posterity has taken to balloons, for the hurry of the concern is not only fatal to romance, but is fatal to any collection of it, if any romance at any period existed; and some sort of prophetic insight into this truth, a sort of sad perception of what posterity, by its rejection of stage coaches, would be eternally bereft, breathes through the following threnody of a great coachman, whose poetic heart could not remain silent under the introduction of the new gods, but whose name, as Keats supposed his to be, is writ in water, or perhaps in rum and water, which would in this case be a fitter emblem of effacement.

St. John's Church, Devizes.

"Them," he cries, with a fine directness of pathos, "them as 'ave seen coaches afore rails came into fashion 'ave seen something worth remembering! Them was 'appy days for old England, afore reform and rails turned everything upside down, and men rode, as nature intended they should, on pikes, with coaches and smart active cattle, and not by machinery like bags of cotton and hardware. But coaches is done for ever, and a heavy blow it is! They was the pride of the country; there wasn't anything like them, as I've 'eerd gemmen say from forrin parts, to be found nowhere, nor never will again."

To descend from these high regions of prophecy and metaphor to firm earth again, the Bath Road, after leaving Shepherd's Shore, runs through a district whose inhabitants must have been regarded by the drivers of Mr. Thomas Cooper's coaches between London and Bath with appreciative eyes; for the Wiltshire men resident between Shepherd's Shore and Devizes have been notorious through all ages for being "very fine and large," as were Mr. Thomas Cooper's coachmen. The inhabitants, indeed, of Bishop's Canning, a village about three miles from Devizes, might, in the seventeenth century, according to Aubrey, have challenged all England to the exquisitely diversive exercises of music and football. In James the First's time the village boasted a peculiarly musical vicar, one George Ferraby, who I trust played football as well as he played the lute, armed with which instrument and attired in the costume of a druid bard (lent by the local costumier of the day), he, at the head of his parishioners, disguised for their part as shepherds, assaulted the ears of Queen Anne of Denmark at the Wansdyke, in April, 1613, with a four-part song of his own composing. Let me hope that it was not as windy an April day on those downs as I have known it, or our reverend druid must have cursed his ancestors' airy taste in costume; and our royal Solomon himself, who on this occasion accompanied his queen, would have found a pipe of that tobacco, which he had lately counter-blasted, greatly beneficial to his health. I make no doubt that Queen Anne herself caught a cold in the head, but she was gracious enough notwithstanding to express her great liking and content to the Reverend George Ferraby, and her ladies joined their congratulations to hers, though they had no doubt caught colds too.

The practised enthusiasm of these Wiltshire musicians found fresh vent in 1702, when, on the occasion of the second Queen Anne's return from the Bath, they indulged themselves and their august audience with another musical junketing, this time however according to the pamphlet in the British Museum, accompanied with a less scrupulous regard to archæological correctness in costume. The Reverend George Ferraby, being dead many years, no longer stage-managed the ceremonial, nor did he, unless as a spirit, indulge in choryambic exercises at the head of his parishioners, lightly attired as a druid. A more simply pastoral atmosphere consequently prevailed. The pamphlet I have referred, to thus describes the scene :—

Wraxhall Manor.

"Her Majesty and her Royal attendants passed over the downs in Wiltshire, where they were met by a great number of Shepherds from all parts of the country, all dressed in their long, coarse white cloaks with their crooks, shepherd scrips, and Tarboxes, playing all the way they marched upon their pipes of Reeds, humbly presenting themselves to her Majesty; who was pleased to hear their country Songs and Musick with a great deal of Satisfaction, and as a Demonstration of Her Royal Acceptance of their Duty, was pleased as a mark of her condescending Goodness and Bounty to give 20 or 30 guineas among 'em, which they received with repeated acknowledgments of loud and repeated prayers and acclamations for Her Majesty's Long Life and Prosperity: after which a great number of Spinners with their Spinning Wheels presented themselves before her Majesty, and were favourably received, and tasted very liberally of Her Majesty's bounty."

"And so on to Bath," as Pepys would have said, and as I must be going,

I have first however to pause a while at Devizes, 88¾ miles from Hyde Park Corner, a town famous in coaching days, and whose name has long been the subject of discussion among the learned. What however is in a name, when one thinks that no less persons than Miss Burney and Mrs. Thrale have been waiting for me at the famous Bear Inn ever since the beginning of the chapter. Coachmen remember this famous house principally for its fine stables. Memoir hunters know it best probably from the diary of the lady who has so long been waiting for us, and from her meeting there with a young gentleman, son of the landlord, destined afterwards to be as great a celebrity as her own fair self.

To be plain, at this Bear Inn at Devizes in April, 1780, Miss Burney met the future Sir Thomas Lawrence—the portrait-painter of a whole generation of court beauties—clothed in knickerbockers, and with a precocity for catching likenesses, not often found in an inn. Miss Burney and her friend, in their journey from London, posting—which was after all the equivalent to first-class travelling in those days, coaching being the second-class compartment of the then travelling scheme, and riding in damp straw at the bottom of stage waggons drawn by six horses, the third—Miss Burney and her friend, I say, posting from London, stopped for the first night at Maidenhead, the second at Spleen Hill, and for the third put up at the same Bear Inn at Devizes. Here a strange series of accidents befell them, which the fair diarist elaborately describes. Having observed that the inn was full of books as well as paintings, drawings, and music, and that their hostess, Mrs. Lawrence seemed something above her station in her inn, the two visitors, according to habitual contemporary prescription, and before supper, sat

The Bear at Devizes.

down to cards. I wonder, after reading our ancestors' feats in this line, that aces are not found stamped on the persons of all the present generation. But this is a psychological digression. It is now that

Miss Burney's adventures at the inn began. Scarcely had she and Mrs. Thrale warmed to their work when their artistic abstraction was surprised by the sound of a pianoforte. This, at first, in the way of an interruption at an inn, may strike my readers in the words of the Laureate as

> "New old, and shadowing sense at war with soul."

Miss Burney however, who had not had the advantage of reading Tennyson, jumped up and ran to listen whence the sound proceeded. She found it came from the next room, where the overture to the *Buono Figliuola* was being performed—a piece not often heard, so far as I can learn, at the Promenade Concerts, Covent Garden. Mrs. Thrale however though hardly for this reason, determined to know from whom it came, and tapped at the door. And who confronted her when it was opened? A young highwayman of the Paul Clifford type, with pale face, eyes full of music, and pockets full of pistols? Not at all. But a very handsome girl with fine dark hair upon a finely-formed forehead; and at the same moment another girl advanced, and obligingly and gracefully invited the intruders in and gave them chairs. And who were these houris? Miss Burney soon discovered that they were the daughters of the hostess and born and bred at Devizes. "Oh, what a surprise!"

"But though these pretty girls struck us much," she writes, "the wonder of the family was yet to be produced. This was their brother, a most lovely boy of ten years of age, who seems to be not merely the wonder of their family, but of the times, for his astonishing skill at drawing. They protest he has never had any instruction, yet showed us some of his productions, that were really beautiful."

The future Sir Thomas had ample opportunities at the Bear for keeping his hand in. His father used to use him now as a stimulant to his guests, now as a sedative. Instead of offering lame excuses when the roast had gone wrong, or saying that a bad bottle of claret was simply "sick from a journey," this original in the way of a host, used simply to introduce his son to the malcontents, and in a moment where there had been disgust there was wonder. At the simple talisman, "Gentlemen, here's my son; will you have him recite from the poets or take your portraits?" the most confirmed bald-headed grumbler

Old Street in Potterne.

ceased his monotonous drone, and the storm in the coffee-room fell before the smile of the young genius.

I shall go on with Miss Burney and Mrs. Thrale to Bath in their post-chaise instead of waiting sixty years later for the Monarch, or one of Thomas Cooper, Esquire's fast day coaches, not only because the ladies went by the old Bath Road, on which I propose to travel, but for the further reason that they met during their stay at Bath some unhackneyed society to which I should like to make my readers known.

Asking the Way.

Miss Burney however, I observe in her memoirs, declares her intention of "skipping to our arrival at this beautiful city," meaning Bath, and I am not certain that there is much reason for not following in her diary-writing wake, for there is not much in Trowbridge or Bradford to chronicle, though Seend, about three miles before the first-mentioned place, or rather Poulshot, which lies on the left before reaching Seend, is connected with an atmospheric catastrophe and a celebrated character. In the vicarage at Poulshot lived the son of the great Izaak Walton, he whom Byron (who was no angler) would fain have seen impaled upon a hook in the manner prescribed by the great fisherman for spring frogs; and to the same vicarage, as guest of the great fisherman's son, came the good Bishop Ken, his uncle, "with all his coach-horses, and as many of his saddle-horses as he could bring," to prevent their being seized by the invading force of William of Orange.

Poulshot vicarage gave the good bishop shelter from other troubles than that revolution, for, in 1703, while Ken was sleeping under his nephew's roof, the "Great Storm," sung by Addison, broke over the country and buried Bishop Kidder and his wife, (who had usurped Ken's place at Wells) even in the episcopal palace. The deposed bishop lay awake in Poulshot vicarage meanwhile escaping all harm, though the beam which supported the roof over his head, was shaken out to that degree, that at the conclusion of the hurricane it had but an inch to hold.

My readers will not probably be unprepared to learn that the name of the town of Trowbridge, 96 miles from Hyde Park Corner, has much perplexed etymologists, but they will remember that the poet Crabbe (who ought to have been a three volume novelist) was vicar of the place; with which mention I may leave the plain-looking town behind, and, passing through Bradford with all convenient speed, and still in the company of Miss Burney and Mrs. Thrale, go, by Walcot into Bath, which is 107¼ miles from Hyde Park Corner, and according to Walter Savage Landor, the next most beautiful city in the world to Florence.

In 1780 Miss Burney was much of the same opinion, though Florence she had not seen; but the houses of Bath she found elegant, the streets beautiful, the prospects enchanting, and she alighted from

High Street, Bath.

her post-chaise at the York House. To her and Mrs. Thrale, as they were in the act of alighting, entered instantly Sir Philip Jenning Clerke "with his usual alacrity to oblige," and told them of lodgings on the South Parade. Mrs. Thrale immediately hired a house at the left corner. "It was deliciously situated," Miss Burney tells us. "We have meadows, hills, Prior Park, the soft-flowing Avon, whatever Nature has to offer, I think, always in our view."

So ends pleasantly what seems to have been a pleasant journey down the Bath Road in 1780, and it is outside the scope of my scheme to describe the terminus, or to follow our travellers further through their three months' stay. They met however some characteristic figures, travellers like themselves on the Bath Road, some known to fame, others not. Amongst them a Mr. W., a young clergyman, who had a house on the Crescent. He was immensely tall, thin, and handsome, but affected, delicate, and sentimentally pathetic, and his conversation about his "own feelings", about amiable motives, and about the wind which, at the Crescent, he said in a tone of dying horror, "blew in a manner really frightful," made Miss Burney open her diary; then there was Mrs. Byron, grandmother of the poet, who was very far from well, but whose charming spirits never failed her; and Mrs. Siddons, playing in Belvidera, who did not move Miss Burney greatly; and Mr. Lee, playing Pierre, who did; and Mr. Anstey, author of the *Bath Guide*, who on the first occasion on which Miss Burney met him, had no opportunity of shining, and appeared not unnaturally "as like another man as could be imagined"; and Mrs. Ord, constant to the Pump-room; and Georgiana, Duchess of Devonshire, of whose style of beauty "vanity was such a characteristic that it required it indispensably", and who put her face to the glass of her chair as she passed Miss Burney and remarked, "How d'ye do?'"

Mass House on Bridge, Bradford.

These travellers on the Bath Road came personally under the

author of *Evelina's* piercing ken, and are accordingly types for ever. The *Bath Miscellany* of 1740 enlarges the list with some unfamiliar names—to wit, a Miss Jeffery, junior, who danced well and had "a poem wrote her in the rooms"; a nameless gentleman, likewise celebrated by

Courtyard of
The Castle and Balls.

the local bard, "who was observed never to go to church till Miss Potter came to Bath, when he went twice a day as constant as she;" a parson, also nameless, who played *Pharaoh* (note the spelling), and who suffered for his imprudence by an impromptu delivered to him on a card; and a hundred other figures—old, young, beautiful, decrepit, bent on health, pleasure, scandal, wine, or the waters, but travellers on the Bath Road, all of them, and any of whom, when the inevitable time for separation and departure had come, might have been seen standing in groups about the White Lion Inn in 1780, much as their ancestors stood about the Belle Sauvage a hundred and thirty years before, but with less surprise on their faces, eying some such announcements as these, and prepared for the worst:

"MACHINE IN TWO DAYS.

"From Bath for London, Mondays, Wednesdays, and Fridays; arrive at London from Bath, Tuesdays, Thursdays, and Saturdays. The machines from the White Lion Inn at the Bell Savage, on Ludgate Hill; those from the White Hart Inn, at the White Swan, Holborn Bridge, and the Three Cups in Bread Street; and those from the Bear Inn at the Swan with Two Necks in Ladlane.

"Passengers to pay One Pound five Shillings each, who are allowed to carry fourteen Pounds Weight—for all above to pay three halfpence per Pound."

I do not think that I can close my review of the old Bath Road, a review which pretends only to deal with its more salient features, with an excerpt more suggestive than this. What perils does it not breathe of by flood and field—perils due to increased confidence and a reckless acceleration of pace. And acceleration of pace was not the only sign on the time-bill of increased recklessness. The lapse of a century had marked a departure in advertisement. The coach proprietors in Charles the Second's time did, it will be remembered, in assuring the public that their flying machines would reach Bath from London in *three* days, add a proviso which committed the safety of their passengers to Providence. The coach proprietors of George the Third's time however, in assuring the public that their machines would reach London from Bath in *two* days only, appear to have forgotten this formality.

The George, and High Street, Salisbury.

II.—THE EXETER ROAD.

WHEN the elegant and accomplished Barry Lyndon, about the 17th of May, 1773, and shortly after his marriage with the widow of the late Right Honourable Sir Charles Lyndon, K.B., set out to visit his estates in the West of England, where he had never yet set foot, he and his Honoria and suite left London in three chariots, each with four horses; an outrider in livery went before and bespoke lodgings from town to town; the party lay in state at Andover, Ilminster and Exeter; and the fourth evening arrived in time for supper, "before that antique baronial mansion of which the gate was in an odious Gothic taste that would have set Mr. Walpole wild with pleasure."

Now this was good travelling in the days when full-bottomed wigs were in wear, and the roads of England in the state that I have described them. It was natural however that the fine gentleman whose pocket permitted him to fly "Flying Machines" as a slow form of lingering death, should have made better time with the aid of outriders, constant changes, and the finest cattle that could be procured, than the sad citizen whose wish was to pass from London to Exeter in the shortest time possible, and whose purse only permitted him to pass there behind six cart horses harnessed to a diving bell.

For such I take it was very much the sort of appearance that the Exeter Fly presented in 1773, as it set out for its weekly flight from the Bull and Gate in Aldersgate, at five o'clock on some wintry morning, with the snow already falling thickly. Nor did the passengers seated in it, or rather clinging to its inside, aspire to Barry Lyndon's good fortune. They did not look forward to lying in state at Andover the first night, at Ilminster the second, at Exeter the third. Far other were their dreams. The young lady of the party (Belinda, Leanthe, Lucinda—what you will) drew her furs round her, and nestled closer to her mother, who took snuff at short intervals, and returned with interest the opposing captain's impudent gaze. The captain had been at Dettingen, as he somewhat raucously informed the company on entering the coach, a fact of which they appeared doubtful, though they agreed *nem. con.* that he had since been in liquor. Him (whenever, that is to say, he dared to look at the young lady of the party) the young man of the party—(Ranger, Mirabel—what you will) eyed furiously as if he would eat him, sword, Dettingen and all; while the lawyer, who sat between these two men of mettle, tried his best to preserve peace, and wished himself on the other side of the coach. All this party were bound to Exeter; but none of them, I say, hoped to reach it in three days. The lawyer indeed, who was a great traveller, having made the journey three times in his life, blew his frozen nose and publicly revelled in a more moderate ideal. "If," he said, "in spite of highwaymen, snowdrifts, ruts a yard deep, and Bagshot Heath, we compass the 172 miles in six days, we may think ourselves lucky, and may thank our stars, when we are safe at The Swan at Exeter, that we are not wandering among the bustards on Salisbury Plain."

And so they rumbled and jolted along what is now Piccadilly, till they got to what is now Apsley House; there the coachman alighted for a drink at the Hercules' Pillars, the Hatchett's of the period, which stood where Apsley House now stands. Readers of *Tom Jones* will remember this Hercules' Pillars well, will fancy that they have stayed in the place, as they can fancy that they have stayed in every inn which Fielding has described. Was it not here that Squire Western alighted on his arrival in London in pursuit of the fair Sophia? Certainly it was; and it was here that he cursed the chairmen, who, true progenitors of our cabmen of to-day, asked him for another shilling. "D—— me," in point of fact, the immortal old gentleman exclaimed, "D—— me, if I don't walk in the rain rather than get into one of their hand-barrows again. They have jolted me more in a mile than Brown Bess would in a fox chase." The travellers in the Exeter Fly of 1773 did not regard The Hercules' Pillars from the Squire Western point of view, it is more than likely; but they were thankful for its light in the gray winter's morning; and as they saw the guard in the inn doorway somewhat ostentatiously getting his blunderbuss under control, recollected that they were near Knightsbridge, and experienced a qualm.

Considering that Knightsbridge is only two furlongs from Hyde Park Corner—measured to what was once the cloth manufactory—this early perturbation of our ancestors may seem strange; but the truth is, that a little more than a century ago those who, on nearing Knightsbridge, sported prayer books, felt for pistols, and generally put themselves into a posture of defence, did the right thing in the right place. The Arcadian tract indeed, which we now associate with guardsmen and nurserymaids, was known to travellers in the Exeter Fly as a place of bogs and highwaymen. For here the Great Western road crossed the stream—Where is the stream now?—and the stream's bed was composed, "especially during the winter months," as the advertisement has it, of impassable mud.

In the rebellion of 1554 Wyatt's men discovered this fact to their cost. After having marched all the way round by Kingston to cross the Thames, the stream at Knightsbridge proved a harder nut to crack, and utterly annihilated their reputation on entering town. Instead of being welcomed as Defenders of the Protestant Faith, the crowd saluted them as "Draggletails," and how, after such a reception, could they look for anything but defeat?

And, though this sort of thing may appear in keeping in the sixteenth century, Knightsbridge was no better place for travellers in 1736. "The road between this place and London," writes Lord Hervey, dating his letter from Kensington, "is grown so infamously bad that we live in the same solicitude as we should do if cast on a rock in the middle of the ocean; and all the Londoners tell us there is between them and us a great impassable gulf of mud."

Into this great impassable gulf of mud the Exeter Fly presently descended, and after desperate flounderings which only made matters worse, stuck fast. To it, when thus safely anchored, entered a gentleman in a vizor and riding a dark chestnut mare, who good naturedly recommended the coachman to alight, and offered to relieve the passengers of their purses. The first to take advantage of this amiability and give up his purse was the warrior from Dettingen, who had been loud in his contempt for highwaymen ever since the Fly left the city, and had sketched, with an elaborate garnishing of oaths, the horrid fate to which any marauder would be subject who ventured to bar the way. He spoke no more now of Dettingen, and of the standard he had taken from the musketeer of the French guard. Far from it. He gave his little all to the gentleman who asked for it, counselled submission to his

An Alarm by the Guard.

companions, and disappeared to eat straw in the bottom of the coach. The highwayman now asked the ladies to oblige, parenthetically observing that time pressed. The words were hardly out of his mouth when Mirabel, who had been biding his time, obliged him with a sudden blow on that jaw which he had somewhat ostentatiously intruded upon the company, and at the same moment jumped from the coach and seized the bridle of the chestnut mare. The highwayman now said "Zounds!" and discharged his pistol; but as the chestnut mare reared and fell back with him just as he was firing it, the aim was not so true as the intention; in point of fact, instead of shooting Mirabel through the head, he shot the guard through the hat, who announced in stentorian tones that he was a dead man, and let off his blunderbuss at the morning star. Meanwhile the highwayman and Mirabel had closed and were wrestling in the mud, the ladies viewing the progress of the strife in a state of pleasing suppressed excitement, and the coachman flogging his horses with a view of driving off and leaving Mirabel and his antagonist to decide their interesting difference in solitude and peace. This genial intention was frustrated by the mud which held the coach fast, and by the guard, who, mounting one of the leaders succeeded in waking some watchmen, who, by way of performing their patrol between Kensington and Knightsbridge, were lying in graceful sleep at The Half-way Public House. They came upon the scene just as Mirabel was binding the highwayman's hands behind his back, the man having yielded himself for worse when he felt eleven stone and a half kneeling on his chest and saw that the chestnut mare had run away. The watch now with great intrepidity took charge of the bound prisoner, helped the Exeter Fly out of the ditch, and Mirabel into the coach, who joined his companions in a somewhat mud-stained, flushed, and exhausted state, but not inwardly unpleased at what he had done.

Those of my readers who may be surprised at such an affair having taken place a little more than a century ago in the immediate neighbourhood of the present barracks of life-guards, may be glad to learn that such adventures were, at the time I speak of, of almost daily occurrence. In April, 1740, the Bristol Mail was robbed a little beyond this spot by a man on foot, who took the Bath and Bristol bags, and mounting the post-boy's horse, rode off towards London. On the 1st of July, 1774, William Hawke was executed for a highway robbery here, and two men were executed on the 30th of the ensuing November for a similar offence. In the same year, December 27th, Mr. Jackson, of the Court of Requests at Westminster, was attacked at Kensington Gore by four footpads, and even so late as 1799 it was necessary to order a party of light horse to patrol every night from Hyde Park Corner to Kensington, all of which strange facts will be found chronicled in Mr. John Timbs's pleasant work on the *Romance of London*, who at the same time tells a good story of a footpad's capture at this very place.

It seems that during the year 1752, the chaise to Devizes had been robbed two or three times, and at last, the thing becoming no doubt monotonous, a gentleman of the name of Norton, not unknown to the authorities, was asked to try his hand at abating the nuisance, With this end in view he entered the post-chaise on the 3rd of June, and had got just as far as Knightsbridge on the way to Devizes, at half-past one o'clock in the morning, when a man came up on foot and said, "Driver, stop." The driver, who was a post-boy, did as he was bid in the twinkling of an eye; and the man held a pistol tinder-box to the chaise and said, "Your money directly; you must not stay—this minute your money." Mr. Norton now commenced business. He took a pistol from his coat pocket, and from his breeches pocket a five shilling piece and a dollar, holding, it is unnecessary to say, the pistol concealed in one hand and the money in the other. He held the money pretty hard. This puzzled the footpad, who said, "Put it in my hat," a very gentlemanly request surely. Mr. Norton however preferred to let him take the five-shilling piece out of his hand; but directly he had done so, was rude enough to snap a pistol in his face. The highwayman naturally incensed at this surprise, staggered back, held up his hands and remarked, "Lord! Lord!" He then incontinently ran away, hotly pursued by the indefatigable Norton, who took him about 600 yards off. But how did he take him? It pains me to say that he hit him a blow in the back. To take his neckcloth off after this, and tie his hands with it, was a mere matter of adding insult to injury, but Norton did not disdain the deed. He then took his captive back to the chaise and told the gentlemen "that was the errand he had come

The Three Swans, Salisbury.

upon" (which was surely an unnecessary confidence), and then he wished them a good journey, and brought his captive back to London.

The customary preliminaries at the trial which ensued having been adjusted, the prisoner was asked whether he had anything to urge against his being taken to Tyburn in an open cart. Said he, pointing to the indefatigable Norton, "Ask him how he lives!" To which question, meant to be insulting, the indefatigable Norton replied in these meaning words—"I live in Wych Street, and sometimes I take a thief."

But where is the Exeter Fly *viâ* Salisbury all this time? Why, the coachman has recovered his reins and his senses, and the Fly has resumed

The Catherine Wheel, Salisbury.

its flight, and while its passengers are busily discussing footpads from a personal experience, it passes, about a furlong further down the road, a noted house of entertainment at which footpads used to congregate.

This was the celebrated Half-way House, an inn midway between Knightsbridge and Kensington, which stood on the present site of the Prince of Wales' Gate, Hyde Park, and which was pulled down in the autumn of 1846. Every highwayman of the period had drunk within its doors, a recollection of which fact did not incline the driver of the Exeter Fly to try the quality of its beer. Meanwhile all the way through Kensington (just outside which charming village the Fly passes two blue nosed sportsmen, out snipe shooting) the passengers with much excitement and heat review the recent adventure. A scene from Smollett slips in so well here that I cannot refrain, a scene which I grieve to have to tone for ears polite.

"When," writes Roderick Random (after a similar adventure), "when I had taken my seat, Miss Snapper, who from the coach had seen everything that had happened, made me a compliment on my behaviour; and said she was glad to see me returned without having received any injury; her mother, too, owned herself obliged to my resolution; and the lawyer told me I was entitled by Act of Parliament to a reward of forty pounds for having apprehended a highwayman. The soldier observed with a countenance in which impudence and shame struggling produced some disorder, that if I had not been in such a —— hurry to get out of the coach, he would have secured the rogue effectually without all this bustle and loss of time, by a scheme which my heat and precipitation ruined. 'For my own part,' continued he, 'I am always extremely cool on these occasions.'

"'So it appeared by your trembling,' said the young lady.

"'Death and the deuce!' cried he. 'Your sex protects you, madam; if any man on earth durst tell me so much I'd send him to —— in an instant.'

"So saying he fixed his eyes upon me, and asked if I had seen him tremble. I answered without hesitation 'Yes.'

"'D—e sir,' said he, 'd'ye doubt my courage?' I replied, 'Very much.'

This declaration quite disconcerted him ; he looked blank, and pronounced with a faltering voice, ' Oh, 'tis very well! I shall find a time.'

" I signified my contempt of him by thrusting my tongue into my cheek, which humbled him so much that he scarce swore another oath aloud during the whole journey"—or perhaps till he got as far as Brentford, let us say, where our travellers in the Exeter Fly breakfasted at The Pigeons.

Brentford is seven miles from Hyde Park Corner, and is a noted town in the opinion of some experts, though others, I observe, prefer to describe it as a filthy place. The Pigeons was, at any rate in the old coaching days, a noted inn for post-horses, two of whom, tired of life and the vile paving stones which adorned the streets, tried early in the century to drown themselves in the Grand Canal, in the decorous company of a clergyman from Buckinghamshire, who was seated in the chaise with twelve volumes of Tillotson's sermons, two maiden daughters, and their aunt. On being recovered from the waters, the Buckinghamshire clergyman sought his sermons, or rather Tillotson's, wildly, and when he found they had gone to improve the fishes, he lifted up his voice and said the strangest things. He told one of his daughters that he could better have spared her aunt, and spoke in monosyllables to the post-boy, who was duly discovered to be drunk.

This, however, has nothing to do with the Exeter Fly, which is standing before The Pigeons, refreshed as to men and horses, and ready to start. The snow is still falling, the coachman's nose beams a benignant purple, and the ostler recommends another glass as an antidote to the weather, of which he presages the worst. Recovered by the aid of Nantes brandy from his previous dejection, the captain hears these words of ill omen as he issues from the inn, and meditates falling back on the bar for further support. The guard however tells him that it is time to get forward, and the man of war somewhat sadly joins his company and the coach. The talk now among the passengers is of Hounslow Heath ; and the ladies fearing as to

In a Snow-Drift.

what may happen there, in the way of highwaymen, the captain, full of a temporary valour, lets fall something about the cold which will make a little martial exercise enjoyable. He is instantly however reduced to abject silence by a glance from the hero of the recent episode, who at the same time eloquently squeezes the younger lady's hand. A delicious glance is exchanged. At the same time the coach begins to jolt unspeakably, and enters the town of Hounslow. Here they are advised by the landlord of The George not to go forward, as the Bath Flying Machine up to town has been snowed up beyond Colnbrook, and six beds at The George are aired and empty. As sole answer to this appeal, the coachman, full of valour, calls for more brandy, and two more horses, to take them comfortably over the heath, and the captain adjourns for a little something in the bar which may serve the same purpose. Inspired by a like exercise, the coachman now imagines himself to be Jehu, the son of Nimshi, and the Fly leaves Hounslow behind it at six round miles an hour. The first thing to be seen on the notorious heath is the Salisbury Fly in a terrific snow drift, or rather the coachman's hat, two horses' heads, the roof of the coach, and two passengers standing on their luggage bawling "Help." The driver of the Exeter Fly observes this catastrophe, but he does not regard it, or regards it purely as a landmark, and majestically avoids the pit into which his less fortunate brother has fallen. Surely in vain is the snare laid in sight of any coachman. But to see at all has become difficult by this time. The snow drives; the wind blows it full in their faces; the horses begin to show signs of suddenly capitulating. The coachman now has recourse to all the dark arts of persuasion and the whip; "fanning" them, which in the tongue of coachmen is whipping them, "towelling them," which is flogging them, "chopping them," which is hitting the horse with the whip on the thigh (a barbarous practice very common among the coachmen of the Iceni, who however preferred a spear head for the purpose), in vain!—absolutely in vain! The six horses fall into a walk, and can only be kept to that by incredible exertions and oaths. The passengers now give themselves for gone, in the expressive language of the day; but presently, when things are at the worst, their clouds break a bit, and the snow ceases driving. The coachman does the opposite with redoubled vigour, and presently draws up before The Bush, at Staines. The Exeter Fly has taken nearly three hours to come the seven miles from Hounslow. The landlord of The Bush, Staines, hearing this, follows the lead of the landlord of The George, and counsels rest and dinner; and the passengers, who to

St. Anne's Gate, Salisbury.

speak truly, have never before in their lives come so near to the experience of riding in the air in a hollowed-out iceberg, incline their ears to the advice. Success, stimulant, and the lull in the snow storm have, however, made the coachman daring. He observes thickly that *he* is an Englishman, and declares his intention of inning at Bagshot for the night, whether the passengers leave the coach or stick to it. Upon this the young captor of the highwayman says, blushing with ingenuous shame, that he is willing to go on; upon which the young lady, blushing also, says that she is willing too. This necessitates the mother also putting her neck in jeopardy, and she, too, re-enters the coach. The lawyer, seeing himself in danger of being divided from the proprietress of a snug estate in Devonshire, free from encumbrances, and perhaps divided from her for ever, takes his heart out of his boots, recites a by-law to the coachman on the subject of catastrophes, and drivers committed for manslaughter, and sits by the widow's side; the captain, for his very uniform's sake, feels bound to follow the lawyer's suit; and amidst faint hurrahs from half-frozen pot-boys, the Exeter Fly starts gallantly on its last flight. At Egham, one mile three furlongs on, it begins to snow again, and as the coachman pulls up at the Catherine Wheel, the lawyer desires the captain not to stare at the widow; the captain threatens to send the lawyer to a place where legal documents are not of the faintest use; the lawyer threatens the captain meanwhile, if he moves a finger, with an immediate action for assault. Upon this the captain, not being a man of immediate action, subsides, and the Exeter Fly enters upon the most perilous part of its journey. Now the snow falls as it should at Christmas time, when men are seated round blazing fires in snug inn parlours, and not braving the blasts in antediluvian flying machines. The coachman foreseeing the worst, and that every moment the snowfall is heavier, tries to churn his horses into a canter as the gloom of a winter's afternoon begins to fall upon Bagshot Heath. The guard now fingers his blunderbuss delicately, and sees a highwayman behind every bush; but highwaymen are not such fools as to be out in such weather, and the driver, who can see nothing at all, drives into a rut a yard deep.

> "Now shriek'd the timid and stood still the brave—"

among whom the captain may not be numbered. He bellows indeed like a bull, and jumping out of the coach, seeks refuge in a snow-drift, leaving his head exposed above it, to show how the land lies. The coachman sees, and double thongs his wheelers, who drag the coach out of the rut to the side of the captain, and upset it in a gravel pit. The captor of the highwayman now tells Belinda not to be alarmed, and seats her with her mother by her side on the side of the overturned Fly, from which point of vantage they scream in concert, and look upon as dismal a scene as two upset women ever saw. A moan is heard from the lawyer, bound on most important law business to Salisbury, but now studying the laws of nature, &c. &c. after the manner of the inhabitants

Courtyard, King's Arms, Salisbury.

of the island of Formosa, with his feet out of the window and his head under the seat; the coachman and guard are enjoying the experience of the Laplanders, who never think so deeply as when they are lying on their back in the snow; and the captain all the while is being rapidly converted into New Zealand mutton.

Having collected his scattered companions one by one, and propped them in various attitudes of frozen dejection against the side of the overturned coach, the young gallant of the party proposes that some one shall go on to The King's Arms at Bagshot and procure help—with which end in view he cuts the traces and leads up one of the wheelers for a charger. The only answer to his appeal comes from the guard, who raises his blunderbuss gravely and mistaking a too curious shepherd who approaches from behind a bush for a footpad, shoots him, before he has time for effectual flight, in the hinder parts. The shepherd has now to be dealt with. He is given brandy and placed on his chest beside the coachman who, still believing himself to be on the box, mechanically drives air-drawn horses. Despairing of the others, the young man now commits Belinda and her mother to the care of the lawyer, who has lost all feeling in hands, feet, and arms, but declares he will look after the mother, mounts the patient wheeler and rides off for help to Bagshot. In under an hour the landlord of The King's Arms is seen approaching, with anticipation of a week's good company beaming in his eye, and surrounded by a goodly array of stable boys bearing torches, and ostlers armed with staves. There is also brandy for the frost-bitten, and a post-chaise for the wounded. The timely succour is greeted by the castaways with a faint cheer. Truth to say it has not come before it was wanted, or before the guard, still on highwaymen intent, has fired off his empty blunderbuss at the party of rescue. All the way to The King's Arms he babbles of the hundred pounds due to him for ridding the heath of a footpad; the shepherd consults the lawyer meanwhile as to damages and as to how an action would lie; the captain swears that his recent experience was nothing to what he has known in the Low Countries; Mirabel presses Belinda's hand, and the pressure is ever so faintly returned; the snow falls and falls as if it never intended to stop, and the party arrive finally at The King's Arms, Bagshot, where a wonderful display of good cheer oppresses a groaning table—"Iris-tinted rounds of beef, marble-veined ribs, gelatinous veal pies, colossal hams, gallons of old ale, bins full of old port and burgundy."

And here, in the midst of old English plenty, my travellers are snowed up for nearly a week. And Mirabel proposes to Belinda, and is accepted; and the man of law drinks a congratulatory bottle of port with the fortunate wooer; and proposes himself to the widow next day, and is refused; and Mirabel drinks a bottle of port with him—a consolatory one this time; and the guard is forgiven by the shepherd; and the captain is rude to Betty the chambermaid, and gets his face slapped for his pains in a long oak corridor; and so in the old coaching days, when Exeter was five days' journey from London, and ladies wore hoops and farthingales, and gentlemen bag wigs and three-cornered hats, the old coaching world went round.

It went round at a very different pace though in another fifty years, when the dashing young Mirabel of 1771 was a septuagenarian with the gout and grandchildren, and the guard of the crazy old Exeter Fly was practising on a ghostly horn by the banks of the Styx, and the coachman cracking empty jokes with pale, insubstantial highwaymen destined never to cry "Stand and deliver" any more. Let us skip fifty years, I say, and imagine our Mirabel an old man of seventy, a stranger to reforms in coaching, and in 1823 making the same journey to Exeter again! The great and ingenious Nimrod has described such a scene with such extreme facetiousness and point, that I may well take a leaf from his book, *The Chase, the Turf, and the Road* (Murray, 1852), with many acknowledgments and thanks.

Full of scepticism, then, but guided by a friend, our Mirabel of the Exeter Fly takes his stand outside The Gloucester Coffee-house, now the St. James's Hotel, on a winter's morning near Christmas 1823. His life since he married Belinda has been passed out of England in the great new world beyond the sea, and he has come back to see his grandchildren and the old home in the west country before the allotted time arrives for him to leave off travelling for ever. Behold him then with much of 1773 about him in dress, deportment, and speech, set

The Meet at an Inn.

down suddenly in Piccadilly. The street is crowded. Bucks about to travel are hurrying into The White Horse Cellar for a last rum and milk, or lolling outside the doors attired somewhat after the manner of our more modern masher, but having broader shoulders, curlier hats, longer hair dressed *à la* George the Fourth, parted behind, and distilling the subtle odours of Macassar the Incomparable to the morning air. They stare at the old-fashioned cut of the once fashionable Mirabel's clothes with fatuous incredulity, over cravats *à la* Brummel half-a-yard high. The newest things in the way of exclamations are abroad; "zounds" have had their day. The talk is of the six bottles drunk overnight, of the recent battle on Crawley Down, and Lord Byron's expedition to Missolonghi. Mirabel listens with ears intent, and is at the instant accosted by a ruffianly-looking fellow, made after the manner of the desperadoes who pursue our cabs for miles when we return with our families from the sea-side, and insist upon tendering assistance with the luggage. Their progenitor of 1823 snatches Mirabel's portmanteau out of his trembling hands, breathes upon him brandy, and says, "What coach, your honour?" betraying, I fear, a Celtic origin.

"I wish to go home to Exeter," says Mirabel mildly. Upon which the desperado tells him he is just in time, and that in point of fact, "Here she comes! Them gray horses!"

Pleased at having timed the thing so well, Mirabel looks in the direction thus grammatically indicated. He expects to see the Exeter Fly—a trifle improved upon possibly—but still the Exeter Fly. And what does he see in its stead rapidly approaching? Why, a turn-out drawn by four spanking grays, which he takes to be a gentleman's carriage, and which would do credit to a crowned head. He communicates this impression to the desperado, who remarks "Bah!" or "Yah!" (a more common use). "It's the Comet, and you must be as quick as lightning!" with which words he projects his victim into the coach, the victim's luggage into the boot, pockets his fee without a thanksgiving, and remorselessly attaches himself to another innocent.

Before he got into the coach Mirabel has stared at the coachman, and as soon as he is seated, asks what gentleman is going to drive. "He is no gentleman, sir," says a person who sits opposite to him, and who happens to be the proprietor of the coach; "he is no gentleman! He has been on the Comet ever since she was started, and is a very steady young man." "Pardon my ignorance," Mirabel replies. "From the cleanliness of his person, the neatness of his apparel, and the language he made use of, I mistook him for some enthusiastic Bachelor of Arts, wishing to become a charioteer, after the manner of the illustrious ancients." At which piece of simplicity the coach proprietor suspects Mirabel of *delirium tremens*, but says, "You must have been in foreign parts," and at the instant the wheels begin to go round. In five minutes they are at Hyde Park Corner; but where is The Hercules Pillars? Never to be seen by Mirabel again, who remarks somewhat pointlessly, "What, off the stones already?" He is informed that they have never been on the stones, and that there are no stones in London now. [This seems strange to me—I seem to have met some in my wanderings in hansom cabs!] Wrong however as regards stones and coachmen, the next thing Mirabel remarks is that they seem to be going very fast; but here also he is hopelessly out of his bearings. "Fast!" says the proprietor. "We never go fast over this stage. We have time allowed in consequence of being subject to interruptions, and we make it up over the low ground. Notwithstanding which apology for lack of speed, in five and thirty minutes, the Comet careers into Brentford.

At the jolting of the coach on the old familiar paving stones Mirabel becomes young again. The past reappears. He is in the Exeter Fly once more, with the blooming Belinda—whose bright eyes are dimmed now; with her mother, who has long since vanished off the

Giving them a Start.

face of the earth; with the lawyer of Salisbury who, whilst she was upon it, had aspired to keep her company; with the blue-faced warrior from Dettingen, intoxicated and timorous to the last.

> "Wounds bleed anew; the Plaint pursues with tears
> The wanderer through life's labyrinthine waste;
> And names the Good already past away,
> Cheated alas! of half life's little day,"

as Goethe sings of a similar condition of affairs. To be brief, the old man feels sad, and looks it; but when his companions ask him what the matter is, and whether they may prescribe, he observes, "Hah! . . . . . What! . . . No improvement in this filthy place? Is Old Brentford still here? A national disgrace." In answer to which somewhat splenetic attack on a perfectly respectable town, he is informed that Old Brentford *is* here; and a second after it could only have been described as *there*, for the Comet leaves it at ten round miles an hour, and fifty-five minutes precisely from leaving Hyde Park Corner draws up at Hounslow.

Mirabel is delighted, for he wants some breakfast. "Thank Heaven," he says, "we are arrived at a good-looking house," with which words he stands up for the purpose of alighting at it; but he is violently and with horrid suddenness reseated, and the waiter, the inn, and indeed Hounslow itself, disappear in the twinkling of an eye. By and by, when he has recovered from the painful shock of nearly swallowing his teeth, he eyes the proprietor sternly, and says, "Sir, you told me we were to change horses at Hounslow," searching meanwhile for the address of the Society for the Prevention of Cruelty to Animals—or its equivalent in those days. The proprietor, smiling superior, blandly tells him that they have changed horses while he was putting on his spectacles. "Only one minute allowed for it at Hounslow, sir, and it is often done in fifty seconds by those nimble-fingered horse-keepers." The coach at this moment begins to rock violently, bounding about the road like a pea on a drum, and showing other outward signs of being

Crane Bridge, Salisbury.

attached to runaway horses, which phenomena, having been remarked upon by Mirabel (who clings to his seat as tenaciously as ever he did fifty years before to the seat of the Exeter Fly), are thus explained by the omniscient proprietor, in words full of darkness and doubt.

"Oh, sir, we always 'spring them' over these six miles. It is what we call the 'hospital ground';" which fateful phrase being interpreted

Putting-to the Team.

turns out to mean that it is ground particularly adapted to horses suffering from the varying peculiarities of (1) having backs which are getting down instead of up in their work; (2) of not being able to hold an ounce down hill, or draw an ounce up; (3) of kicking over the pole one day, and over the bars the next; all of which gifts qualify them to work these six miles, because here they have nothing to do but to gallop. This they proceed to do in the fullest acceptation of the term. Some expletives in vogue when George the Third was king are now heard inside the coach, and seem to come from the old gentleman's corner. He looks out and sees death and destruction before his eyes, the horses going at the rate of a mile in three minutes, and the coachman in the act of taking a pinch of snuff. The last of these three sights tends to reassure him, and he remarks to the coach proprietor that fortunately for their necks the road seems excellent. "They are perfection, sir," says the proprietor. "No horse walks a yard in this coach between London and Exeter, all trotting ground now." "But who has effected this improvement in your paving?" says Mirabel. "A party of the name of M'Adam," is the reply, "but coachmen call him the Colossus of roads. Great things likewise have been done in cutting through hills and altering the course of roads; and it is no uncommon thing nowadays to see four horses trotting away merrily down-hill on that very ground where they were formerly seen walking up-hill."

When the Comet arrives at Staines, Mirabel, reassured by this soothing syrup, alights to see the horses changed. On seeing a fine thoroughbred led towards the coach, with a twitch on his nose, he experiences a slight feeling of nausea; but recollects his inside friend's assurance that the next stage requires cattle strong and staid, and takes his seat again just as the artist on the box says, "Let 'em go, and take care of yourselves." All goes well for a while till they reach what is termed on the road a long fall of ground, when the coach presses upon the horses. The thoroughbred at once breaks into a canter, and by doing so disqualifies himself from being of any service as a wheeler, and this done there is nothing for it but to gallop. The coach rocks awfully, nevertheless she is not in danger; the master hand of the artist keeps her in a direct line, and meeting the opposing ground, she steadies and is all right.

Not so old Mirabel, who feels extremely sick and shaken, and leaves the Comet at Bagshot for good and all, congratulating himself on the safety of his limbs. He once more after a lapse of fifty years enters

Courtyard of Church House, Salisbury.

The King's Arms, recalls the journey to Salisbury in 1773, finds the place much changed, rings the bell for the waiter, and mistakes the well-dressed person who answers it for the landlord. "Pray, sir," said he, "have you any slow coach down the road to-day?"

"Why yes, sir," replies John; "we shall have the Regulator down in an hour."

Upon which Mirabel remarks that the Regulator will do, as it will enable him to breakfast, which he has not done that day. Upon which John breaks into lamentations, which must often have been heard in those days when fast coaches had come into fashion and were killing old inns.

"These here fast drags," he cries, "be the ruin of us. 'Tis all hurry, scurry, and no gentleman has time to have nothing on the road." Here he breaks off. "What will you take, sir? Mutton chops, veal cutlets, beef-steaks, or a fowl?" (to kill.)

Having duly breakfasted off tough beef-steak and memories of the past, old Mirabel sees the Regulator draw up at the door. He sees also that it is a strong, well-built drag, painted chocolate, bedaubed all over with gilt letters, a bull's head on the doors, a Saracen's head on the hind boot, and drawn by four strapping horses. Amongst other sights which inspire him with confidence the coachman must be numbered, who has neither the neatness nor the agility of the artist of the Comet, but is nearly double his size. Mirabel now asks what room there is in the coach. "Full inside, sir, and in front," is the answer, "but you can have the gammon board all to yourself." "Ah!" says Mirabel, "something new again, I suppose;" and mounts up the ladder to inspect it. He finds himself on a seat which enables him to sit back or front to the horses as he may like best, thinks himself lucky, and at the same moment the Regulator leaves the village of Bagshot at a steady pace, to the tune of "Scots wha hae wi' Wallace bled," and continues at that steady pace for the first five miles. Mirabel now congratulates himself; but his song of gladness is soon, unlucky man, to be turned into a dirge. For the Regulator, though a slow coach, is timed at eight miles an hour through a great extent of country, and has therefore—to borrow an illustration from poetry—to make play when she can. This occurs after she has left The Golden Farmer and The White Hart at Blackwater behind her, and entered upon a very dreary and dismal tract of country known as Hartford Bridge Flats. To the lover of scenery this place affords few attractions, but it is as a sweet-smelling savour in the nostrils of old coachmen, being known indeed as the best five miles for a coach in all England.

The ground being firm, the surface undulating, and the Regulator

The White Hart at Blackwater.

being timed twenty-three minutes over the five miles, the coachman proceeds to "spring his cattle." The coach being heavily laden forward, rolls in a manner which it is quite impossible to find a simile for, and Mirabel utterly gives himself up for gone. In the midst of one of its best gallops the Regulator meets the coachman of the Comet driving his up coach. He has a full view of his quondam passenger, and thus described his situation :

"He was seated with his back to the horses, his arms extended to each extremity of the guard irons, his teeth set grim as death, his eyes cast down towards the ground, thinking the less he saw of his danger the better;" and in this state he arrived at Hartford Bridge. Here he dismounted from the Regulator with the alacrity of lightning. "I will walk into Devonshire," he cries. Then he thinks better of this, and says he will

The Lion, at Blackwater.

At Whitchurch.

post; then he is told that posting will cost him twenty pounds; then he says this will never do, and asks whether the landlord of The White Lion can suggest no coach to his notice that does not carry luggage on the top.

Here he lays himself open to the unkindest cut of all, which the landlord hastens to avail himself of with all the unbending remorselessness of his kind.

"Oh yes," he says, "we shall have one here to-night that is not allowed to carry a band-box on the roof; the Quicksilver mail, sir, one of the best out of London. Jack White and Tom Brown—picked coachmen over this ground; Jack White down to-night."

The Poultry Cross, Salisbury.

"Guarded and lighted?"

"Both, sir; blunderbuss and pistols in the sword-case, a lamp each side of the coach and one under the footboard—see to pick up a pin the darkest night of the year."

"Very fast?"

"Oh no, sir! Just keeps time, and that's all!"

"That's the coach for me!" says the credulous Mirabel; "and I'm sure I shall feel at my ease in it. I suppose it is what used to be called the Old Mercury?"

Alas! not at all. The Devonport, commonly called the Quicksilver, mail, is half an hour faster than most in England, and is indeed the miracle of the road. She has no luggage on the top, it is true, but she is a mile in

The White Hart at Hook.

the hour quicker than the Comet; at least three miles in the hour quicker than the Regulator; and she performs more than half her journey by lamplight. Imagine Mirabel's condition when he discovers into what sort of coach he has been beguiled! Past Hartley Row he flies, past Hook, where in The White Hart there was and is a splendid old inn; but it is the dead of night now, and the inn is shut up if the Quicksilver stopped at it, which it didn't. The climax comes when old Mirabel awakens from the sleep of exhaustion on a stage which is called the fastest of the journey—it is four miles of ground, and twelve minutes is the time. Mirabel now loses his head, and in spite of the assurances of the passengers that all is right, thrusts it out of the window to see where the deuce they are going to, sees nothing but dust and whirling wheels, and loses his wig. The unfeeling passengers remark, "I told you so," according to invariable recipe.

Courtyard, White Hart, Hook.

Mirabel cries, "Stop, coachman!" The coachman hears him not. In another second the broad wheels of a road waggon have done the accursed thing; and a short time after the Quicksilver mail thunders through Basingstoke, which is forty-five miles one furlong from Hyde Park Corner, and as uninteresting a town as can be seen in a day's march.

And at Basingstoke I shall leave Mirabel and the Exeter mail, and go down the rest of the road in slower and more historic company.

Amongst the most distinguished of these must be mentioned Cromwell, who was extremely busy on this part of the Exeter road in 1645, taking Basing House (which had defied the Parliamentarians for four years), stripping lead off the roof of the Abbey for casting bullets for the purposes of the siege, and generally impressing his iron personality on everything about. Little remains, thanks to him and time, I regret to say, of Basing House, except a ruined gateway and the indelible memories of its gallant defence for the king; but a great deal remains of the town of Basingstoke, which is a modern growth from old Basing, and which, though I understand it had once a large share of the silk and woollen trade, is chiefly remarkable, from my point of view, as being the place where many of the West of England coaches stopped for their passengers to dine.

The road between here and Andover, about eighteen miles, runs through a desolate country, which already begins to anticipate in its lonely monotony some of the more engaging peculiarities of Salisbury Plain. Through this tract (it being give-and-take sort of land) the fast coaches made fast time; past Worting, once famous for its White Hart; past Overton, six miles and a half further on, famous for its trout stream and foxhounds—the celebrated Vyne; and so on to Whitchurch, which is fifty-six miles six furlongs from Hyde Park Corner, and is not the bustling place now that it was when the coaches from London to Salisbury, and from Oxford to Winchester, crossed each other here, as they used to. It may be perhaps unnecessary for me to say that the inn at Whitchurch is The White Hart, but what adds interest to the fact is that it was here, while waiting for the down mail to Falmouth, that Newman began the *Lyra Apostolica*, with the lines, "Are these the tracks of some unearthly friend?"

Seven miles further and we are in Andover, which though a small place, has a railway junction and a history. Here Henry VII. rested from his labours after suppressing the insurrection of Perkin Warbeck; but whether the miserly Tudor put up at the Star and Garter, or the everlasting White Hart, or their mediæval equivalents, if there were any, is more than

I can say. It was upon Andover, to link another royalty with the place, that James II. fell back, after the breaking-up of the camp at Salisbury. Here it was that he was deserted by Prince George, remarkable for his impenetrable stupidity and his universal panacea for all contingencies in a catch-word. Whatever happened, "Est-il possible?" was his exclaim. He supped with the king, who was at the moment overwhelmed naturally

The White Hart, Whitchurch.

Corridor in White Hart.

enough with his misfortunes, said nothing during a dull meal, but directly it was over slipped out to the stable in the company of the Duke of Ormond, mounted, and rode off. James did not exhibit much surprise on learning the adventure, being used to desertion by this time. He merely remarked, "What, is 'Est-il possible?' gone too! A good trooper would have been a greater loss;" and left for London—I was going to say by the next coach.

At the Lion inn, readers of Thackeray will remember, the ingenious Barry Lyndon lay on the first night of his journey to Hackton Castle, county Devon; here he called up the landlord to crack a bottle with him in the evening; here Lady Lyndon took umbrage at the proceeding; and here

Barry Lyndon Cracks a Bottle.

the great Barry "who hated pride," "overcame," as he delicately puts it, this vice in his haughty spouse.

To become geographical for a moment, it is at Andover, or to be quite accurate, half a mile out of the town, that the two great coaching roads to the West of England diverge—one going by Little Ann, Little Wallop, Lobton Corner, and Winterslow Hut (celebrated as the residence of Hazlitt, and as the scene, on the evening of October 20, 1816, of an attack by an escaped lioness on the Exeter Mail) to Salisbury; the other route being by Weyhill, Mullens Pond, Park House, Amesbury, and thence to

A Christmas Visitor.

Exeter by Mere, Wincanton, and Ilminster. Of this road, which was the one taken by the Telegraph, more anon. The Quicksilver, the other crack coach on the Great Western road, which was timed eighteen hours for the 175 miles, changed horses at Salisbury, which is one of the most picturesque towns in the south of England, and will make a convenient halting-place for me, it being situate almost exactly half way between Exeter and London.

The town of Salisbury, which is eighty miles seven furlongs from Hyde Park Corner, is chiefly remarkable for its cathedral; and it owes this agreeable notoriety to the north wind. This may sound strange in the ears of those who have not, attired as shepherds, highwaymen or huntsmen, braved the elements in the surrounding plain. Those however who have enjoyed this fortune, will not be surprised to learn, that when the winds raged in the good old days of 1220 round the original church of Old Sarum, which was quite unprotected and perched upon a hill, the congregation were utterly unable to hear the priests say mass; and no doubt they were unable to hear the sermon too. This fact much exercised the good Biship Poore; and so, a less windy site having opportunely been revealed to him in a dream by the Virgin—he got a license from Pope Honorius for removal. Which done—with a mediæval disregard for the safety of the local cowherd or government inspector—he aimlessly shot an arrow into the air from the ramparts of Old Sarum, and (unlike Mr. Longfellow's hero), having marked where it fell, there laid the foundations of the existing beautiful church.

To pass from ecclesiastical matters, with which we have really little to do, Salisbury, from the fact of its position on the great thoroughfare to the west of England, has always played a prominent part in the history of the road—in times of civil commotion indeed, a part perhaps second to no other provincial town of its size and commercial insignificance. And so, long before coaches were built or flying machines dreamed of, this part of the Exeter road was trod by kings and queens, and courtiers and statesmen, who made at different times in their august and calculating lives, the town of Salisbury their headquarters, cracked their mediæval old pleasantries in the quaint old streets, caracoled along them, not in coaches and four, but on such gallant steeds and so

Quadrangle of House, Exeter.

caparisoned, as our eyes are feasted with on Lord Mayor's Day, gorgeous without and within, resplendent with velvet, and cloth of gold, and ermine, and stiff embroidery.

First perhaps among the royal visitors to Salisbury was Richard the Second, who was here immediately before his expedition to Ireland, where he should clearly never have gone. But this visit does not seem to have been a success. There was, I fear, not enough largesse about during the last of the Plantagenets' stay, not enough tournaments and junketings, and conduits running rhenish, and cakes and ale; for the good inhabitants seem to have been impressed so little with what was to be got out ot Richard, that they a short time after expressed their thanks for his visit, by, with almost indecent alacrity, espousing the cause of Henry. Perhaps though it was the other way, and the disappointment of the good men of Salisbury at Richard's visit was caused by contemplation —not of how little they got out of Richard, but of how much Richard got out of them. For the kind king had an amiable inclination towards charging his subjects with his outings; and as his household consisted of ten thousand persons, three hundred of whom were cooks, and as this enormous train had tables supplied them at the king's expense; some good quarters of an hour were spent by the purveyors, whose action was one of the chief reasons of public discontent, and who, no doubt, gave Salisbury good reason for recollecting their activity.

The next arrival of importance at Salisbury was one of the four quarters of Jack Cade, a fifteenth century politician, of Irish origin, who held views on deep questions of rent and labour extremely in vogue at the present day but which in 1450 were, unfortunately for Cade, premature. Yes, like all really great men, Cade was considered to be before his time! And so instead of being returned to Parliament as a Home Ruler, a price was set on his head, and he was killed by a Liberal Unionist of the period, one Iden, a gentleman of Sussex. Not however before Cade had had a good time of it with the fifteenth century unemployed, who saying (and quite correctly) in their hearts, "There are no police," demonstrated in London for some time, unopposed

The Elephant Inn, Exeter.

by law and the authorities, till a rich house or two were broken into, and plundered, when the Londoners felt that the time was come for action, and took the law into their own hands.

Thirty-four years after Cade had suffered for advanced political principles by having one of his legs exposed in a cathedral town, the hunchbacked Richard honoured Salisbury with his presence ; but he was not I expect in the best of tempers, for here to him was brought the Buckingham we have all read of in the play, who had just seized the fleeting opportunity to head an insurrection against the king, in an unprecedentedly wet season in Wales. The result was that he was unable to cross the Severn, and this misfortune brought him too to Salisbury, where Richard was waiting to superintend his execution at what is now the Saracen's Head.

In the courtyard of this inn, which was then called the Blue Boar, and not "in an open space," as Shakespeare has described it (as if he were speaking of Salisbury Plain), Buckingham had his head cut oft according to contemporary prescription. We have none of us seen the episode presented on the stage, but we have read the carpenters' scene, which Shakespeare wrote in, to give the gentleman who originally played Buckingham a chance, and allow a few moments more preparation for Bosworth Field. And we may recollect that it consists principally in Buckingham asking whether King Richard will not let him speak to him, and on being told not at all, informing the general company, at some length, that it is All-Souls' Day, and that as soon as he has been beheaded, he intends to commence "walking".

After Richard and Buckingham, there came to Salisbury in the way of kings, Henry VII. in 1491. Henry VIII. in 1535 with Ann Boleyn, already in all probability engaged in those sprightly matrimonial differences as to men and things which culminated the year following on Tower Green. Next in order, came to Salisbury, Elizabeth, bound for Bristol, bent, as on all her royal progresses, on keeping her nobility's incomes within bounds, and shooting tame stags that were induced to meander before her bedroom windows. After the virgin queen came James I., who liked the solitudes which surrounded the Salisbury of those days, for the two-fold reason, firstly, because they saved him in a large measure from the invasion of importunate suitors (who were afraid of having their purses taken on Salisbury Plain before they could

R 2

proffer their supplications), and, secondly, because they were well stocked with all sorts of game on which he could wreak his royal and insatiable appetite for hunting. The "open" nature of the country might perhaps be added as another reason for the sporting king's liking for the place: for James was no horseman, and as he was in no danger of

Christmas Eve.

meeting a hedge in an area of thirty miles, the going must have suited him down to the ground. Indeed I do not doubt, but that in ghostly form he still follows the celebrated Tedworth on their down days, riding on an invisible horse, propped on a well-pillowed and invisible saddle, and having an invisible bottle of Greek wine dangling on either side. His royal preference for Salisbury however drew a greater presence to the place, and associated the old cathedral town with a genius whose head James cut off, but in whose presence he was not worthy to stand. For here came Raleigh on his last journey to London, broken down by the shameless ingratitude of princes, pining with the sickness of hope deferred. Here he sought a last interview and explanation with James, who sent word that he was sorry, but was hunting; here he tried to gain time for his suit (foreseeing the Tower at the end of his journey to London) by feigning sickness by the aid of a French quack; failing of course to move his drunken and hunting master's compassion in the least; here he wrote his apology for the voyage to Guinea; and hence he started on his last journey from Salisbury to London, the last of many journeys up the Exeter Road, from that west country which saw his birth—as it saw the birth of the best and greatest of English manhood—which fed his stirring genius with many a wild tale of sea romance and adventure, and whose pleasant green hollows "crowned with summer sea," still hold the decapitated head, in which that wonderful, wild, restless brain throbbed, and schemed, and laboured.

It is a long way from Raleigh to Charles II., though not so far from Raleigh to Cromwell, who was at Salisbury and on the Exeter Road on October 17, 1646, after the taking of Basing House, as I have already remarked. The merry monarch was here twice, but on neither occasion, I suspect, was he peculiarly merry; for after the battle of Worcester, when he lay concealed near the town for a few days, and his companions used to meet at the King's Arms in John Street, to plan his flight, the Ironsides were much too close on his track to allow opportunity for jesting; and when he came here as king in 1665, all but the most forced mirth was banished from a court which dreaded every day to be stricken by the plague.

I have already recalled the fact that it was from Salisbury that James II. fell back upon Andover, when the army which he had con centrated there to bar the way of William of Orange, departed on the more pastoral errand of conducting him in triumph to London; and this episode in the Revolution closes, I think, Salisbury's historical account,

St. Mary's Steps.

which I am rather glad of, as I am tired of kings, and pine for the more congenial society of horses, hosts, footpads, of guards blowing horns, and coachmen staring at broken traces.

The Broken Trace.

And Salisbury was, of course, a big coaching centre. Apart from the Quicksilver Mail, the wonder of foreigners, the envy of rival coach proprietors, which did the 175 miles in eighteen hours, and caused rustics to stand in turnip fields motionless, gaping, paralytic with surprise, for minutes after it had passed—when they set with trembling hands the correct London time on Brobdingnagian watches; apart from the Devonport Mail, I say, a large number of coaches halted at and passed through Salisbury, some bound for Exeter, others bound no further, others bound for places like Weymouth, on the south-western coast. I have a list before me of some of these crack turn-outs, which constantly used to enliven the streets of the now sleepy old town with the clanging of horses' hoofs on macadamised roads, the sounding of horns, the objurgations of passengers irritable after a long journey, and in a hurry to start on another, with the friendly greetings of rivals of the whip as they passed each other on their journeys up and down the great Exeter road.

In 1821, then, there set out for Salisbury, from the Angel, St. Clement's, what was known as the Post Coach, which started at 7 in the morning daily, and arrived at the White Hart, Salisbury, at 7.30 in the evening; from the Bell and Crown, Holborn, the new and elegant Post Coach, which left London every evening at 6.15, and arrived at the Black Horse, Salisbury, at 6.15 next morning; from the same inn in Holborn also departed at 3.30 daily, Saturdays excepted, what was known as the Old Coach, which arrived at 7 the next morning at the same Black Horse. Besides these, all more or less known to fame, there passed through Salisbury the Royal Auxiliary Mail, which started every afternoon at 6.15 from the Bell and Crown, Holborn, and arrived at the New London Inn at Exeter at 7 next night; the Eclipse, which left the Golden Cross, Charing Cross, daily at 7.30 a.m. for Exeter, going by Salisbury, Blandford, Dorchester, and Bridport; also the Royal Mail to Exeter, which left the Swan with Two Necks, Lad Lane, every

College Hall, Exeter.

evening at 7.30, and going by the same route as the last coach, arrived at the New London Inn at Exeter at 9.30 next morning; also the Regulator, whose acquaintance we have made already, which reached Exeter from London in twenty-six hours, starting daily at 3 o'clock in the afternoon from the same celebrated London house. Nor was the

Weymouth Union, which left the Saracen's Head, Snow Hill, every afternoon at 4, less known in the streets of Salisbury than any of these former; and with it the Accommodation post coach from the Swan with Two Necks entered into brilliant rivalry, and leaving London an hour earlier in the afternoon, arrived at 9 o'clock next morning at the same seaside resort.

The names of many celebrated coaches will be found missing from this list, some of which were not running at the time it was made, others of which were; but it is not in my design to compile coaching statistics, for statistics I abhor; and those on coaches, as on all other subjects, whether in the heavens above or on the earth beneath, may be sought by students in the British Museum, where, if due pertinacity be theirs, they will, after many months, be voluminously found. No! statistics are neither my object nor my *forte*. I wish only as I hurry along them (and this reminds me that Exeter is still ninety-one miles seven furlongs off) to give faint glimpses of the old life on the old roads, looking upon that life from all possible different points of view, and trying more to render its sentiment perhaps than to write its history.

My readers, then, who have been loitering with me all this while at Salisbury, may remember that had they been travelling to Exeter in the finest age of coaching by the Telegraph, the fastest coach of the age, or nearly so, they would not have been at Salisbury at all, for the Telegraph diverged from the Salisbury road at Andover; and as "the Lunnon Coach," a perpetual source of wonder to staring rustics at work on the wayside, went to Exeter by Amesbury, Deptford, Wincanton, and Ilminster. I propose to follow this route as far as Deptford Inn, which is, or was, for its days are gone, a very celebrated house, standing about twenty-four miles from Andover, on the middle of Salisbury Plain. And then I shall leave the Telegraph to go on to Mere and Wincanton alone, and returning to Salisbury once more from Deptford (it is only eleven and three-quarter miles on the worst branch line in Europe), shall go down to Exeter by the route taken by the Telegraph's great rival, the Quicksilver, which did (I never can sufficiently impress my readers with

The Lunnon Coach.

the astounding fact) the 175 miles from London in eighteen hours, and went by Shaftesbury, Sherborne, Yeovil, Crewkerne, and Chard.

Meanwhile we have to do with the Telegraph, and the first thing that the Telegraph coach did after leaving Andover was to turn to the right, and do a three-mile stretch of collar work to Weyhill, at which place is annually held a fair, which would make those people who have never seen one stare. This festivity, which is indeed quite an un-English and out-of-the-way sight, begins on October 10th (Michaelmas Eve) and goes on for six days, during which all the country-side seems to have broken loose, and high junketings are to be seen. Besides junketings (which prevail chiefly on the last day of the fair in connection with peep-shows of the most blood-curdling description, whirligigs, merry-go-rounds, rifle galleries, and gingerbread) are also to be seen wonderful shows of sheep, magnificent cheeses, the finest hops in England displayed in the Farnham Row, great exhibits of machinery and enormous cart-horses, and, enveloping all, a Babel indescribable. The whole thing is curious in the extreme and antique into the bargain—indeed the line in *Piers Ploughman's Vision*,

> "At Wy and at Winchester I went to the fair,"

is supposed to allude to Weyhill, and I have no doubt that it does, though I leave the decision of the point to the wise.

After leaving Weyhill the Telegraph went by way of Mullen's Pond, where in the good old days there was a turnpike to give you pause (if you had no coppers), to the Park House four miles further on, in old days an inn of some importance, now a solitary beer-house, standing on the verge of desolate downs—on the verge of Salisbury Plain, in fact—across which the road runs under the side of Beacon Hill, a windy place celebrated for its hares, coursing meeting, and some time since for a march past held at the close of autumn manœuvres; then across the Bourne river into the extremely ancient town of Amesbury, which is fourteen miles from Andover and seventy-seven miles seven furlongs from Hyde Park Corner.

Over this bleak and inhospitable country, between Amesbury and

Andover, the great snowstorm of 1836 raged in a way which those who have seen a snowdrift on Salisbury Plain may best be able to realise, and the Telegraph coach passed through the very thick of it. The guard of the mail who travelled with it on that memorable December 27, 1836, from Ilminster to London, had an experience to retail when he reached Piccadilly. The snow began to fall when the coach reached Wincanton, and never left off driving all the way to London. Nor did the coachman either, to his credit be it said, though over this tract of ground we are discussing two extra pairs of leaders were put on, and could only with the utmost difficulty and after much "fanning" get, even in that reinforced state, through the mountainous snowdrifts. It must have been an awful drive that, I know; for I know the country well.

For the present however we have safely arrived at Amesbury, where we can alight at the George and conjure up a celebrity or two before we go to supper. Amesbury indeed is rich in these, from the time when Guinevere arrived here somewhat late at night, after a ride across the Plain (which is more unlike Doré's representation of it than anything I have ever seen in my life, but this by the way), up to the time when the charming Duchess of Queensberry played the Lady Bountiful in the place, and by entertaining Prior and Gay at the Abbey graced the quaint old Wiltshire town with the memories of two of the not least celebrated of the English humorists.

But indeed Amesbury is so ancient that if we cared to enter the sacred garden of the antiquary, and if Guinevere were not perhaps legendary enough, we might start the history of Amesbury further back than Guinevere. As an antiquity however I think that Guinevere may pass. After the unfortunate lady had retired from Amesbury

"To where beyond these voices there is peace,"

hither came Queen Elfrida in 980 in search of it, after her murder of her stepson Edward at Corfe; and bent, like all mediæval murderesses suffering from a temporary mental depression, on building a church. When she came to the point however, and had interviewed the architect and the abbot, she went the whole hog, and built an abbey. In 1177, I regret to say, all the ladies of this establishment were dismissed without

Old Houses on Exe Island.

a month's warning by Henry II. for staying out all night; and twenty-four nuns and a prioress from Fontevrault in Anjou, all with personal characters, filled the vacant places. Within the walls of this abbey a whole bevy of royal, hipped, and unfortunate ladies of all ages sought shelter from a wicked world. I must chronicle these, because they are all, from my point of view, memories of the Exeter road, though the Exeter road at that time was but a mediæval cart-track, and a very bad one too. At Amesbury then lived, and for the most part died, Eleanor of Brittany, sister of Prince Arthur; Mary, sixth daughter of Edward I., with thirteen ladies to keep her company. This was in 1285. In 1292, Eleanor, Queen of Henry III., died here, and Katharine of Aragon stayed for a while here on her first arrival in England in 1501.

Shortly after this came the dissolution, when a somewhat similar fate befell the old abbey as that which turned the castle at Marlborough into a posting inn and a public school. In point of fact, the abbey of Amesbury became Amesbury Abbey, and passed from the Earl of Somerset, to whom it was granted by Henry VIII., into the respective hands of the Aylesburys, Boyles, and Queensberrys, till, after the death of the fourth Duke of Queensberry, the estate was bought by Sir Edmund Antrobus, in the possession of which family it still remains.

Under the hospitable roof of the Duke and Duchess of Queensberry, when they were in possession at the abbey, the genial Gay passed the latter years of his epicurean life, "was lapped in cotton," as Thackeray has it, and "had his plate of chicken and saucer of cream, and frisked, and barked, and wheezed, and grew fat, and died." It was here that he wrote the *Beggar's Opera* (inspired by how many personal recollections of highwaymen, I wonder, gleaned on journeys between Amesbury and the capital?), and in the garden, there is shown, or used to be, a curious stone-room, built in a bank and overlooking the Avon (here famous for its trout), which is said to have been the poet's study. But I dare say that this is an allegory. The dining room would have been a more likely place for it I should have said.

The Exeter road after leaving Amesbury mounts straightway on to Salisbury Plain again, and two miles from the town passes on the right Stonehenge, which I shall not write about, because everybody has written about it, and most people have read what has been written. If anybody however who has not seen it, should chance to be in the neighbourhood I would advise them (without troubling themselves much beforehand as to whether it is Druidical, or post Roman, or built by the Belgæ) to approach it from Amesbury about sunset, when they will see what they will see, and return home—or I am in error—well-pleased with what they have seen. From Stonehenge it is a run of little more than eight miles through Winterton-Stoke to the once celebrated Deptford Inn, of which, as I have said before, nothing is to be seen now, except its site, which is an exceedingly pretty one, looking over the valley of the Wily.

An Exeter Gable.

And here I shall leave the Telegraph to continue its eagle flight, as Mr. Micawber would say, alone, merely remarking by the way that it went from Deptford to Hindon, sixty-four miles four furlongs from Hyde Park Corner, which is an ancient market-town, and was once a rotten borough contested successfully by "Monk" Lewis of *The Castle Spectre* renown and Henry Fox, afterwards Lord Holland; and unsuccessfully contested by Lord Beaconsfield; from Hindon the Telegraph went on to Mere, 101 miles 2 furlongs, noted for its Ship Inn, and a mediæval house of plain Perpendicular in one of its streets; and so on to Wincanton, 108 miles 3 furlongs, noted for its Bear Inn, for a visitation of the Black Death in 1553, and for the first blood shed in a slight skirmish in the Revolution; and thence by Holton, and Sparkford Street,

Paying Toll.

to Ilchester and Ilminster which former place was once represented by Sheridan, and the neighbourhood of which was the scene of an amusing difference between a toll-keeper and a guard, thus pleasantly told by Mr. Stanley Harris in his justly well-known work *The Coaching Age.*

"The Exeter Defiance, one of Mrs. Anne Nelson's coaches from the Bull Inn, Aldgate, went through the gate at Staines; all the tolls at the gates below were paid by the guard every Monday, amounting to about £30. It so happened that the keeper of the gate near Ilchester had got in arrear with his payments to the trustees, and accordingly their clerk served a notice on the guard of the coach not to pay him any more tolls. The gatekeeper to counteract this move, shut the gate before the time for the arrival of the coach. When the coach came in sight therefore, the guard blew his horn to no purpose, and couldn't get through till he had paid three shillings. Meanwhile with the assistance of a horse and trap, the pikekeeper reached the next toll, which the coach also found barred against it. This keeper being more obdurate than the other, the guard produced his tool-box with the object of breaking through the outwork. This led to fisticuffs between himself and the keeper, in which the keeper came off second best. The bout ending in the gate's being opened."

Ilminster, to conclude, as readers of Thackeray may remember, was graced by the presence of Barry Lyndon in 1773, who lay at the Bell (now the George or the Swan presumably, for the Bell is at Ilchester) on his third night from town. Here, as he had previously done at Andover, he engaged himself in the pleasing distraction of cracking a bottle with the landlord, and overcoming by this recipe Lady Lyndon's natural vice of pride. There is nothing after this to notice in the fifteen miles between Ilminster and Honiton, where this Wincanton route joins the mail road from Salisbury to Exeter, down which I now propose to travel.

And I think that I will not go by the Quicksilver as I said I would, though it took the shortest route by Shaftesbury, Sherborne, Yeovil, and Chard, but will go instead by the old mail road *viâ* Blandford, Dorchester, and Bridport, by which such well-known coaches as the Eclipse, the Royal Mail, and the Regulator used to travel. And I select this route not only because it is the old mail road, but because it runs

Forde Abbey, near Chard.

to my mind through a more interesting and storied country. At ten miles three furlongs from Salisbury, then, this road, to begin with, brings us to the once celebrated Woodyates Inn, and at the same time enters the delightful county of Dorset. And here we are surrounded on all sides with memories of that fatal rising which culminated on the bleak plain of Sedgemoor, and crushed for ever the daring hopes of the brilliant young nobleman who was for so long the darling of the West. The memory of Monmouth is still preserved about Woodyates. It was close to the Woodyates Inn that the giving in of the desperately ridden horses stopped the flight of Monmouth, Grey, and Buyse to the sea. Here the fugitives turned their horses loose, concealed the bridles and saddles, disguised themselves as rustics, and made their way on foot towards the New Forest; and quite close by they fell into the hands of James's troopers. Monmouth himself was taken on the Woodlands Estate near Horton, his captors failing for some moments to recognise in the gaunt figure, crouching in a ditch, dressed like a shepherd, with a beard of three days' growth, already prematurely grey, the once brilliant and graceful son of Charles II. and Lucy Walters. The ash-tree under which he was discovered still stands.

Old House at Bridport.

Three miles further down the road is Thorley Down Inn; two miles beyond it stands Cashmoor, famous in the coaching days for post-horses, victuals, rum and milk, snug bars, and general accommodation of the best old English quality for man and beast; and another seven miles and three furlongs bring us into Blandford, 103 miles 4 furlongs from Hyde Park Corner, celebrated for a disastrous fire in 1731, to which it owes its present handsome appearance, and also for having been the scene in 1760 and 1762 of some of Gibbon the historian's outings with the Hants Militia; or, as he more aptly describes it, of "his wandering life of military servitude." It was on the downs round pleasant and hospitable Blandford, in short, that "the discipline and evolutions of a modern battalion" gave the future historian of the Roman empire a clearer notion of the phalanx and the legion, or would have done, may I add, if the captain of Hampshire grenadiers had not passed so much of his time in the Crown and the Greyhound; for a page further on he speaks of the dissipations of pleasant, hospitable Blandford, in a strain of deeply philosophical regret.

Charles II.'s House at Exeter.

There is not much to be said for any place between here and Dorchester, which is sixteen miles down the Exeter road. At Winterborne, Whitchurch, however there is a church with a curious font in it, of which the grandfather of John Wesley, founder of Methodism, was vicar; but he does not seem to have had a very pleasant time of it. For either by reason of having married the niece of Thomas Fuller, author of the *Worthies*, or because he had not been properly ordained, he was much hunted up and down like "a partridge in the mountains," when the king enjoyed his own again. Four miles beyond Whitchurch, at Dewlish, there was a turnpike gate, I notice, but there does not seem to have been much else there of any interest, and so on to Dorchester (inns, the Antelope and the King's Arms), which was a posting-town of great importance, and is 119 miles 6 furlongs from Hyde Park Corner.

Dorchester has been remarkable for all time for its extreme healthiness, and was remarkable during the great Civil Wars for its antipathy to the king: two extremes in the way of qualities which may cause wonder, but which are well vouched for nevertheless. For on the first peculiarity the celebrated Dr. Arbuthnot—Arbuthnot the learned, the fascinating, the friend of Pope, Gay, and Swift—who was here in his young days, remarks, "that a physician could neither live nor die at Dorchester," commenting on his own experience; and on the second

The White Hart, Dorchester.

peculiarity, lack of loyalty, no less weighty an authority than Clarendon reports, that when the great Rebellion broke out, no place was more entirely disaffected.

Less pleasant celebrities however than the brilliant author of the *Art of Sinking in Poetry*, *Law is a Bottomless Pit*, and the *Effects of Air on Human Bodies*, haunt the streets of this almost aggressively healthy town. Recollections of Monmouth's rising spring up on all sides, terrible episodes of blood and cruelty, too, and the memory of a universally execrated monster. Dorchester was the second place Judge Jeffreys reached on the Bloody Assize.

"The court," writes Macaulay, "was hung, by order of the chief justice, with scarlet, and this innovation seemed to the multitude to indicate

Judge Jeffreys' Lodgings, Dorchester.

a bloody purpose. It was also rumoured that when the clergyman who preached the assize sermon enforced the duty of mercy, the ferocious countenance of the judge was distorted by an ominous grin. These things made men augur ill of what was to follow.

"More than three hundred prisoners were to be tried. The work seemed heavy, but Jeffreys had a contrivance for making it light. He let it be understood that the only chance of obtaining pardon or respite was to plead guilty. Twenty-nine persons who put themselves on their country and were convicted were ordered to be tied up without delay.

Charles Recognized by the Ostler.

The remaining prisoners pleaded guilty by scores. Two hundred and ninety-two received sentence of death."

Jeffreys, after this amiable display of judicial activity, retired to his lodgings in High West Street (Duffall's glass-shop), where he no doubt partook of brandy, according to his convivial wont, slept the sleep of the conscienceless carouser, and left for Exeter next day.

And by the same road that we are on now, by Winterborne Abbas, through Winterborne Bottom, past Longberry turnpike gate, 540 feet above the sea, then down a descent of two miles to the Travellers' Rest, 253 feet above the sea, and then down into Bridport, 134 miles 4 furlongs.

The Packhorse, Bridport.

The inns in Bridport proper used to be, in the coaching days, the Bull and the Golden Lion; but half a mile distant, on the quay, there is a house called the George, where Charles II. was nearly seized in

1651, by reason of an ostler recognizing his face—a compliment at the moment not appreciated by our future king, who made the best of his way to Salisbury *viâ* Broadwindsor—a very out-of-the way route surely. But main roads at the time were not Charles's fancy. He would have preferred tunnels had they been in vogue. Meanwhile we must go on to Exeter, past Chidiock, where there used to be ruins of an old manor house belonging to a family of the same name, but which now is not, thanks to Time and Colonel Ceely, Governor of Lyme in 1645. At Charmouth, which is one of the most charming places on the Southern coast, Charles II. was nearly caught, before he was nearly caught at Bridport in the manner already described; but while at Bridport the fatality almost occurred through an ostler's recognizing the fugitive's face, here at Charmouth a village blacksmith got upon the scent by observing with much curiosity that the horse's three shoes had been set in three different counties, and one of them in Worcestershire; which, considering that the Battle of Worcester was in everybody's mouth, was too near the mark to be pleasant, and caused the much hunted Charles to get instantly to horse.

At Hunters' Lodge Inn, about four miles on, the road enters the pleasant county of Devon, and then passing through Axminster (occupied by Athelstan in 938, after the battle of Branesdown, and by Monmouth in 1685, a few days after his landing at Lyme) runs through Honiton (visited by Charles I. in 1644), and thence by Fenny Bridges, Fair Mile Inn, Honiton Clyst, into the town of Exeter, which by this route is 172 miles 6 furlongs from Hyde Park Corner.

Much might be written about Exeter, its history, its site, its castle its promenade on Northernhay, its beautiful cathedral. I shall content myself however with remarking that the town has been besieged more times than I can remember; that Perkin Warbeck, one of the many claimants who troubled Henry VII.'s digestion, was in 1497 led through the picturesque streets clothed in chains as in a raiment; and with that

I shall pass on to the inns of this terminus of the great western road, and to the coaches and the great coachmen who haunted them. For I have not touched upon the coachmen on the Exeter road yet, and yet they were mighty men in the land.

The principal coaching inns at Exeter then were the Old London, and the New London, and the Half Moon, kept by a Mr. Stevens who

The George Inn, Axminster.

The Half Moon, Exeter.

immortalized himself by putting on the celebrated Telegraph, which used to leave Exeter at 6.30 A.M., breakfasted at Ilminster, dined at Andover, and reached Hyde Park Corner at 9.30 P.M. In the way of coaching this record of the Exeter Road was hardly if ever beaten; and as for the coachmen who performed this and kindred feats of different character, but all of the highest style of art, I cannot more appropriately round the Exeter Road's story than by solemnly, and in the place of honour, inscribing their great names. First then let mention be made of the incomparable Charles Ward, who drove the Telegraph out of London; and after him, let there be ranged in no narrow spirit of rivalry, but in the order which chance and my note-book dictates, the following masters of their art: Jack Moody, who worked on the Exeter Mail, an out and outer, whose fine performances on the road were interrupted at last by ill health, whose retirement was the signal for general mourning, and whose appearance and execution on the box were as superior to other coachmen as night is to day; "Pop," a coachman on the Light Salisbury, whose father hunted the Vyne Hounds; Mountain Shaw, the respectable, the scientific, who drove Monk's Basingstoke coach to London one day and down the next; Jackman of the Old Salisbury, who was a great favourite with his master, whose cattle were always of unequalled size and condition, and than whom no one in England who sat on a box-seat better understood the art of saving horses under heavy work.

Castle Arch, Guildford.

III.—THE PORTSMOUTH ROAD.

THE Portsmouth Road has been described to me by one having authority as the Royal Road; and certainly kings and queens have passed up and down it, eaten and drunken in the Royal Rooms, still to be seen in some of the old inns; snored in the Royal Beds (also in places to be seen, but not slept in), and dreamed of ruts and bogs, and blasted heaths and impassable morasses, and all the sundry and other mild discomforts which our ancestors, whether kings or cobblers, had to put up with; or those among them at all events who travelled when the weather was rainy, and there were no real roads to travel upon.

To me however the Portsmouth Road—so-called Royal—presents itself in a less august guise; so much so that if I were asked to give it a name whereby it might be especially distinguished, I should be inclined, I think, to call it the Road of Assassination. And it will be found to have claim to the title. Apart from Felton's successful operation on the Duke of Buckingham at Portsmouth in 1628, which marks the terminus with a red letter; and the barbarous doing away of the unknown sailor on September 4th, 1786, which has made the weird tract of Hindhead haunted; the beautiful country between Rowland's Castle and Rake Hill yields an especially prime horror. For here was enacted at the latter end of the last century that protracted piece of fiendish brutality known as the "Murder by the Smugglers," an atrocity which was spun out over eleven miles of ground, which out-Newgates anything of the kind to be found in the *Newgate Calendar*, and of which I shall have more to say when I get to the scene of its commission. Here meanwhile we have three good juicy murders in seventy-one miles, seven furlongs—the distance from the Stone's End, Borough, Surrey, to Portsmouth; and that is a fair average of crime for mileage, as I think most people will admit.

The old Portsmouth Road, as appears above, is measured from the Surrey side of the water; and it was from the Surrey side that old-fashioned visitors to Portsmouth started. Pepys, in 1668, having received orders to go down to Portsmouth in his official capacity, and having gone through the usual formalities of going to bed, waking betimes, &c., &c., discovered suddenly that his wife (who no doubt suspected junketings on the part of the susceptible Samuel) had resolved at an hour's warning to go too. So Samuel first of all sent her mentally to the deuce, and then to Lambeth, where she embarked in a coach. Samuel, after having adjourned to St. James's and remarked "God be with you" to a Mr. Wren (who surely ought to have remarked it to Samuel, considering the state of the Portsmouth Road), went over the water to what he calls Fox Hall, where he ingeniously intercepted the coach containing his wife; and in due course lost his way for three or four miles about Cobham, at the very moment when he was hoping to be seated at dinner at Guildford.

In 1668 the Portsmouth and Guildford Machines left London (as the South-Western Railway leaves it now, but not quite so quickly) by

The Angel, Guildford.

Vauxhall, Battersea, Wandsworth, and so on to Putney Heath; and so the route is marked in Carey's *Itinerary*. In more modern times however the Portsmouth coaches felt it incumbent upon them to appear (like everything else that was fashionable) in Piccadilly, and, starting from the White Bear, made the best of their way to Putney, without troubling to cross the Thames till they got there.

Most of us connect Putney in our minds with the Oxford and Cambridge boat-race, and attempts more or less successful to see it; but the place has a history other than an aquatic one—was indeed the birthplace of two very celebrated men, and the scene of a third one's death. At Putney was born Thomas Cromwell, blacksmith first of all, and afterwards, according to Mr. Froude, the most despotic minister who ever governed England. "Fierce laws," writes the same picturesque historian, "fiercely executed—an unflinching resolution which neither danger could daunt, nor saintly virtue move to mercy—a long list of solemn tragedies weigh upon his memory. Be this as it will, his aim was noble." He certainly made it hot for the monks, having no doubt learned the lesson in very early days at his father's forge, the site of which is still somewhat apocryphally pointed out, south of the Wandsworth Road.

At Putney also was born, "April 7th, O.S., in the year one thousand seven hundred and thirty-seven"—as he writes it in that delightful autobiography, which will always be read, I fear, in spite of Mr. Ruskin's thunders—Edward Gibbon, whom we have met already down the Exeter Road at Blandford, carousing and masquerading as a militiaman. The house in which the future author of the *Decline and Fall of the Roman Empire* was born was bought by his grandfather, who used to exercise "a decent hospitality" in its spacious gardens on summer evenings. It lies between the Wandsworth and Wimbledon Roads, and since the days of the Gibbons has been successively inhabited by Mr. Wood, Sir John Shelley, and the Duke of Norfolk. These be good tenants, but I prefer the Gibbons myself. I like to think of Edward in his young days at Putney, a fat, heavy, and huge-headed boy, voted by his neighbours uncommonly slow, but with his precocious brain already working—not on consuls and legions, and emperors and bishops, and all the rest of the gorgeous paraphernalia with which he was one day to make his name immortal—but on that

Courtyard, White Hart, Guildford.

large appreciation of creature comforts, of the good things of this good earth which his dawning intelligence felt about his father's house, and which he has thus in his autobiography so whimsically described—

"My lot might have been that of a slave, a savage, or a peasant; nor can I reflect without pleasure on the bounty of Nature, which cast my birth in a free and civilized country, in an age of science and philosophy, in a family of honourable rank, and decently endowed with the gifts of fortune. From my birth I have enjoyed the rights of *primogeniture;* but I was succeeded by five brothers—and one sister—all of whom were snatched away in their infancy. My five brothers, whose names may be found in the parish register at Putney, *I shall not pretend to lament.*"

Happy eldest son, I say. Proper predilection for primogeniture's enjoyable rights!

To finish with Putney and its celebrities (for I must be getting forward to Portsmouth as quickly as local celebrities and legends will permit)—at Bowling Green House, on the east side of Putney Heath, lived, and on the twenty-third of January, 1806, died, William Pitt, broken-hearted at the news of Austerlitz, confident that the map of Europe would be needed no more. And not far off the house where the great statesman lay dying, still stands the small inn where the wire-pullers of both parties put up their horses, while they made inquiries couched in a true spirit of Christian and political sympathy, as to how the struggle between death and the invalid was getting on in the sick chamber—alternately (as they chanced to be Whig or Tory) jubilant or depressed as the bulletins were issued; tremulous with anxiety even in their cups as to which way the political cat would jump.

Now the road runs over Putney Heath, where our ancestors (who had drunk three bottles over night and transmitted the blessings of gout to a distant posterity) showed, in a humorous age, so little lack of humour as to appear early on a frosty next morning to be skewered by a blackleg parading as a boon companion in the presence of sharps for seconds. The preliminary negotiations have been well described by the late Lord Beaconsfield, and should be commended to our cousins in France and on whatever other barbaric shores the code of the *duello* still ridiculously lingers.

"Did you ever," somebody or other says in *Vivian Grey*, "fight a duel?" . . "No? Nor send a challenge either?" (a very different thing!) "Well, you are fresh indeed! 'Tis an awkward business indeed, even for the boldest. After an immense deal of negotiation, and giving your opponent every chance of coming to an honourable understanding, the fatal letter is at length signed, sealed, and sent.

A Duel on Putney Heath.

You pass your morning at your second's apartments, pacing his drawing-room with a quivering lip and uncertain step. At length he enters with an answer, and while he reads you endeavour to look easy, with a countenance merry with the most melancholy smile. You have no appetite for dinner, but you are too brave not to appear at table; and you are called out after the second glass by the arrival of your solicitor, who

Back of Red Lion, Guildford.

Bakers' Market House. (*now demolished*).

Birthplace of Archbishop Abbot, Guildford.

comes to make your will. You pass a restless night, and rise in the morning as bilious as a Bengal general."

So slept and so rose, and in such state appeared on Putney Heath, in the history of the Portsmouth Road in 1652, Lord Chandos and Colonel Compton, when the latter was run through the body after half-a-dozen passes; in 1798 Mr. Pitt and George Tierney, M.P. for Southwark; and in 1809 my Lord Castlereagh and Mr. Canning.

The passengers in the up mail from Portsmouth must often have passed about this neighbourhood the meaning procession of principals, seconds, and leeches, making with a ghastly ostentation of indifference for the celebrated heath; the principals as yellow as Disraeli has described them, the seconds full of the importance of self-security, the leeches sniffing guineas in the morning air. The passengers on the down coaches to Portsmouth may have seen such inspiring spectacles as well—and after having remarked to one another, "another affair," passed on to Kingston (which is eleven miles five furlongs from the Stone's End, Borough), where they breakfasted.

The old inn at Kingston, which used to be called the Castle, is now, like many another such place, converted into dwelling-houses, and in the process (as is also, alas! usual) a valuable record has been lost. But there is antiquity enough about Kingston to make up for the practical disappearance of its old inn. To say that its importance as a town dates from the Saxon period has long since failed to convey any meaning to a posterity who have ceased to recognize celebrated names under the disguise of pedantic spelling; but Egbert was here discoursing on state affairs long before coaches ran to Portsmouth (though Ecgberht will be preferred by Mr. Freeman); and in the open space in front of the coachhouse is, or was, a shapeless block placed in an octagonal space, upon which eight kings were crowned.

From kings to public houses the transition is easy; and permits me the opportunity of remarking that the Griffin and the Swan have taken the place of the transformed Castle, and still retain the traditions and the ale of the old days, when I should not like to say how many coaches, chaises, and travelling waggons, passed through the old town between sunrise and sunrise.

Let a few of the more celebrated coaches suffice—for I must not in my history of the Portsmouth Road lose sight of the coaching portion of it, though the Portsmouth Road does not take a high place in the record, for speed, coaches, or cattle. Amongst the coaches then which in 1821 (to be particular in dates) passed through Kingston may be mentioned—

The Royal Mail, which left the Angel, St. Clement's, Strand, at half-past seven every evening and arrived at the George, Portsmouth, at 6.30 next morning; from the same house the Portsmouth Regulator, which departed at eight in the morning and arrived at the George, Portsmouth, at five the same afternoon; from the Belle Sauvage, Ludgate Hill, departed every morning the popular and celebrated Rocket, which same coach left the White Bear, Piccadilly, at nine, and did the seventy-one miles, seven furlongs to Portsmouth in nine hours, arriving at the Fountain, Portsmouth, at 5.30 to the minute. From the Cross Keys, Cheapside, the Light Post Coach took eleven hours to do the journey, leaving London at eight every morning. The Portsmouth Telegraph leaving the Golden Cross, Charing Cross, improved upon this performance, but still failed to beat the Rocket by half an hour.

Old Court, Guildford.

Besides these once familiar names must be chronicled the Hero, from the Spread Eagle, Gracechurch Street, which left the city daily at eight A.M. and arrived at the Blue Post, Portsmouth, at six P.M.; from the same house the Night Post Coach, seven P.M. from London, getting its passengers to the same inn at Portsmouth, sick no doubt of an all-night journey, but just in time for a good breakfast; and finally several light post coaches from the Bolt in the Tun, the Spread Eagle, and other well known inns, which ran no further than Godalming, taking about five hours to compass the thirty-three miles.

Leaving the town by any of these coaches (if we did not meet one Jerry Abershawe, whose name now, like many others of ephemeral celebrity, awakes no echo in our breasts, but who was in his day a noted highwayman much revered and feared, greatly given to robbing travellers to Portsmouth, and to drinking at a road-side house called the Bald Faced Stag, now no more to be seen on earth)—leaving Kingston and this digression behind us, I say, we should soon in the old coaching days have covered the four miles to the pretty village of Esher, and stopped of course at the Bear.

And at Esher the Portsmouth Road is connected with another great historical character, who lived near here in a fine, damp house picturesquely situated on the banks of the river Mole; and must, one is tempted to think, have often travelled from his country seat to Westminster surrounded with all the pomp and circumstance which he so particularly affected, in an age remarkable perhaps above all others in our history for splendour and pageant.

But to suppose this would be, I regret to say, an historical error; for in 1529 when Wolsey was ordered to retire to Esher, he was ordered to retire there because his royal master was bilious; and when Henry the Eighth was bilious, melancholy marked his courtiers for her own. No! there was not much magnificence about Wolsey during the short time he stayed at Esher Place. He had no steward about him, "which was always a dean, or priest; no treasurer—a knight; no controller—a squire—who always had within his house their white staves;" nor in his privy kitchen had he the master cook, "who," according to Cavendish, "went daily in satin, damask, or velvet, with a chain of gold about his neck"—though a white cap and apron would surely have been more in harmony with the surroundings. No, Wolsey, when he retired to Esher Place, had none of these things. He was closely shorn of all his magnificence, and was indeed in want of the common necessaries of life. His dejection was not mitigated by this starved condition of the larder, nor by the dampness of the house,

The Bear, Esher.

of which he wrote a sad account to Gardiner, describing it as the reverse of a desirable country residence, and as being remarkable for its moist and corrupt air. And yet it seemed to me an attractive place enough when I was there the other afternoon. A fallen minister however is not likely to be pleased with any palace; and I dare say that Wolsey from sheer *ennui* and lack of company used often to steal up to the Bear (disguised as a pedlar of course according to immemorial prescription), spend a pleasant evening on the ingle bench with the local boors, hear them discuss his own disgrace and his chances of restoration to royal favour, and then steal back again to the lonely house by the Mole—late and beery.

Not that the beer of the Bear would have done the cardinal any harm, if it was as good a tap then, that is to say, as it is now. It probably

Wolsey's Palace, Esher.

brought him a temporary return of luck, for in 1530 he was taken into favour again, and left Esher Place for the north. At Esher however the memory of the Ipswich butcher boy (who of course never was a butcher boy at all—are any of our fond historical beliefs to remain unsubverted ?) is preserved ; as also is the memory of another great man who lived in the neighbourhood, travelled much on the Portsmouth Road, rose from almost as low a grade as the great cardinal, was equally successful in making by force his merit known.

Claremont, which lies immediately at the back of the Bear, is a palace now; but I doubt whether its towers (if they can be seen) excite more interest among the inhabitants than they used to in the days when

The Old Church, Esher.

they sheltered the gloomy life of the hero of Arcot and Plassy. Lord Clive lived at Claremont during many of the latter years of his life in the present house, which he built on the site of Vanbrugh's palace.

But the Trajan of England, according to Macaulay, was more feared than admired by the simple inhabitants of Esher.

"The peasantry of Surrey," he writes in his Essay on Clive, "looked with mysterious horror on the stately house which was rising at Claremont, and whispered that the great wicked lord had ordered the walls to be made so thick in order to keep out the devil, who would one day carry him away bodily." This is what comes of being a warrior of the rank of Lucullus, and a reformer of the rank of Turgot and Lord William Bentinck—but I must get on to Guildford.

Not however before noticing the enormous pair of jack boots (on view in the entrance hall of the Bear, and redolent with memories of miry roads, ruts a yard deep, coaches hopelessly stuck in morasses, and other picturesque incidents of the travelled past), which boots are said to have been worn by the fortunate postillion who went with the pair of fortunate horses which drew the unfortunate Louis Philippe's carriage when Claremont sheltered the royal exile. I can only remark in leaving these boots that they are "very fine and large," and are obligingly shown to all visitors at the Bear by the obliging landlord; and so pass on to Cobham, three miles four furlongs down the road, on the heath, surrounding which place, had we been travellers to Portsmouth in the year of grace 1668, we should have found Mr. and Mrs. Pepys aimlessly wandering, having lost their way "for three or four miles." Travelling at a later date however we should not, I take it, have seen much at Cobham, except the White Lion, a fine old relic of old coaching days—out of the rush of life now, but alive still; where, having taken a glass of rum and milk, we should pass on to Ripley, three miles seven furlongs on, noted for its cricketers, its green on which they play cricket, its old inn, the Talbot, full of gables, long corridors, and hoary memories of gastronomic feats, performed by cramped travellers in the twinkling of an eye to the accompaniment of the guard's horn, relentlessly proclaiming imminent departure. And from Ripley it is a run of six miles

Guildford Town Hall.

Courtyard of the Crown, Guildford.

into Guildford, which is twenty-nine miles seven furlongs from the Stone's End in the Borough, the capital of Surrey, a most picturesque town, and a good place to dine at after rambling about lost on a common, as Mr. Pepys in 1668 found.

The inns of Guildford were in the coaching days the Crown and the White Hart, when the constant throb of traffic on the direct Portsmouth Road must have kept the now sleepy old place from ever even nodding; but there is not much throb of traffic about the High Street now; and Guildford sleeps on its past according to the present comfortable practice of most provincial towns, most of them equally suggestive of laudanum, mandragora, poppies, hop-pillows, and other sedatives; few of them (as to their High Street, at all events) half so picturesque. I have heard that the record of Guildford goes back to the days of Alfred, but I have not, I confess, inquired too curiously into this matter; having found a passage in the town's history to my mind more interesting, and of a trifle later date. In the upper room of the tower then, over the entrance gateway of Archbishop Abbott's hospital, the unfortunate Duke of Monmouth was lodged on his way to London after his defeat at Sedgemoor. The melancholy journey from Ringwood—where Monmouth was kept for five days after his capture—to London occupied the better part of a week, ended at Vauxhall, and thus gave another interesting personage to the Portsmouth Road. In the coach with the Duke was an officer, whose orders were to stab the prisoner if a rescue were attempted. The captive himself made no attempt however for liberty; the large body of regular troops and militia who served as guard probably convinced him of the utter hopelessness of any such attempt, if the utter prostration from which he was suffering

Fireplace in Abbott's Hospital.

had not made even an attempt impossible. Monmouth indeed was unnerved to such an extent that through the whole of the trying journey to London he made the spectators stare at his pusillanimity ; as Grey, his companion in bonds, made them stare with his incessant cheerful chatter on dogs, field sports, horses, and other subjects of general

Old Mill, Guildford.

interest, not however supposed commonly to occupy the attention of travellers going to certain death.

At the pretty town of Godalming, four miles two furlongs further on, most coaches stopped for refreshments at the King's Arms ; a house which I see scored in my note-book as famous for good dinners ; and here or at the George some of the coaches from town, as I have already observed, stopped altogether. Charles the Second used to be seen at Godalming a good deal, hunting and flirting when he ought to have been otherwise employed; and a timbered house in Bridge Street is said to have been his hunting lodge, or, to be quite accurate, *was* said to be, before it was (as usual) pulled down. A short distance west of the railway station is Westbrook, not a particularly beautiful house by any means, but long the residence of the Oglethorpes. Here a very delightful gentleman of the old school was born in 1698, and here he died in 1785. I refer to General Oglethorpe, sportsman, soldier, and kindly patron of literature: an amiable combination surely which deserved success in life, and General Oglethorpe gained what he deserved. As a patron he defended Samuel Johnson; as a soldier he was present with Prince Eugene at the siege of Belgrade; and as a sportsman he shot a woodcock in what is now the most crowded part of Regent Street. As a triple record, this, I believe, will be found hard to beat —if indeed it does not absolutely take the cake.

After leaving Godalming and Milford behind them, careful coachmen used in the old days to save their horses, especially if they had a heavy load and the roads were heavy; for it is collar work now almost all the five miles on to the top of Hindhead Hill, long before which summit was reached careless coachmen who had not followed the above prescription discovered the painful fact that "there was no life in the coach," which, being interpreted from the dark language of stage coachmen, means that they found themselves travelling slowly over deep and gravelly roads. They also found themselves, if in mood for such observation, in the face of one of the wildest bits of scenery to be found in England, and face to face with a silent memorial of murder. This takes the form of a gravestone placed simply by the roadside, with an inscription on it simple enough also, but which when read in so lonely a spot on the closing in of a November afternoon, has been known to give a chill. It sets forth its erector's and all honest men's detestation of a barbarous murder committed on the spot on the person of an unknown sailor (who lies buried in Thursley Churchyard, a few miles off); and airs also with some satisfaction the feeling then very prevalent (before Scotland Yard was), that murderers are a class who invariably fall into the hands of justice. We are perhaps not so credulous as this nowadays; but we put our trust in a large detective force when our throats have been cut, and hope for the best. The local police of 1786 however could have given many of our shining lights a lesson, it seems to me; for on the very afternoon of September the 4th in that year (which was the date of the murder) they apprehended three men named Lonegon, Casey, and Marshall, twelve miles further down the road, at Sheet (or in a public-house opposite to the Flying Bull at Rake, as some accounts say), engaged in the unwise exercise of selling the murdered man's clothes. For this, and previous indiscretions, they were presently hanged in chains on the top of Hindhead as a warning to his Majesty's liege subjects; and not much to the delectation of travellers on the Portsmouth Road I should apprehend, especially when tired by a long journey, and when the wind was favourable. On the site of the original gibbet the late Sir William Erle, Lord Chief Justice of Common Pleas, set up a beautiful granite monument, with a Latin inscription on each of the four sides, which much puzzles amiable youths rusty in their Latinity, when, accompanied by inquisitive maidens, they have breasted the steep pitch of the hill.

And now it is all down hill into Liphook, five miles from Hindhead, and here late coaches made up for lost time. The Seven Thorns inn, a little way down the road, is supposed to stand where the three counties meet; but it doesn't, for they meet in Hammer Bottom, which is some distance away. The Seven Thorns, apart from this undeserved distinction, has the reputation of being a legendary house; but I have never been able to discover what legend is attached to it; nor indeed, so far as I am aware, has anybody else. It was however the scene of an adventure in a snowstorm, which I find chronicled in the Reverend G. N. Godwin's *Green Lanes of Hampshire, Surrey, and Sussex*, and which I shall take the liberty of extracting for the benefit of my readers :—

"The snow," writes Mr. Godwin—and he is repeating the story of an old stage coachman—"was lying deep upon Hindhead, and had drifted into fantastic wreaths and huge mounds by the fierce breath of a wild December gale. Coach after coach crawled slowly and painfully up the

The Seven Thorns.

steep hill, some coming from London, others bound thither, But as the Seven Thorns was neared they one and all came to a dead stop. The tired, wearied, exhausted cattle refused to struggle through the snow mountains any longer. Guards, coachmen, passengers, and labourers attacked those masses of spotless white with spade and shovel, but all to no purpose. It seemed as if a way was not to be cleared. What stamping of feet and blowing of nails were there! Women were shivering and waiting patiently; men were shouting, grumbling, and swearing; and indeed the prospect of spending a winter's night on the outside of a coach on such a spot was, to say the least, not cheerful. At last a brave man came to the rescue. The Star of Brunswick, a yellow-bodied coach that ran nightly between Portsmouth and London, came up. The coachman's name was James Carter, well known to many still living. He made very little to do about the matter, but whipping up his

Charging a Snowdrift.

horses, he charged the snow-drifts boldly and resolutely, and with much swaying from side to side, opened a path for himself and the rest."

I do not know whether Mr. Godwin refers in this stirring episode to the great snowstorm of 1836; but if he does his story accounts for a fact which has caused me a good deal of surprise. For I find that of all the main roads of England the Portsmouth Road (far from being the least exposed of any of them) was the only one which was kept open. And in this case the credit belongs to gallant James Carter and the Star of Brunswick—and much credit it is.

From the Seven Thorns into Liphook is a nice run, not unadapted to the agreeable pastime of "springing them," which as I have before interpreted into common or ordinary English, means galloping pure and simple, a practice not at all uncommon to the Portsmouth Road in spite of the poor times made, as I shall presently show. Meanwhile we have arrived at the Anchor at Liphook, which is one of the most famous houses between London and Portsmouth, and is forty-five miles five furlongs exactly from the Stone's End, Borough. And the Anchor at Liphook not only is an historical house, but has the advantage of possessing in Mr. Peake a host, who is proud and careful of its history—a pleasant experience which I regret to say I have found far from common in my wanderings. Indeed many houses as old as the Anchor on the great roads, some too on this very Portsmouth Road that I am speaking of, have had as full a tide of history fill their state rooms and flood their broad corridors as the famous inn at Liphook can boast of. But where is this history now? It is simply gone for want of being garnered.

Not so at the Anchor; where, thanks to a decent care for memorials of the past, and to a respect for that Romance which is becoming so extremely unfashionable, we are able to meet in the imagination a whole crowd of distinguished guests of all centuries and all ranks—kings, queens, statesmen, admirals, soldiers, down to clerks in the Admiralty in the person of Samuel Pepys; who having lost his way at Cobham on his way to Guildford, as already chronicled; and having dined at Guildford and congratulated himself and his wife on having found it; lost it again coming over Hindhead on his way to Liphook, and arrived at the Anchor at ten o'clock on August 6, 1668—exceedingly tremulous about highwaymen and in company with an old man, whom he had procured for a guide. "Here, good honest people," he writes. "And after supper, to bed." I can imagine that succulent supper well, taken with an appetite whetted by a long ride in moorland air, and flavoured with an agreeable recollection of past perils safely surmounted. I can imagine also the sound sleep which fell afterwards on the amiable Samuel; and the nightmares, graphically representing coaches standing on their heads with their occupants inside them, which, to break the monotony of a too perfect repose, passed now and then under his cotton night-cap.

But more celebrated people than the theatre-loving clerk of the Admiralty (was he a dramatic critic I wonder like all Admiralty clerks now?) stayed at the Anchor, and before his time. Edward the Second was hunting in Woolmer Forest continually; and unless he liked camping out on marshy heaths, probably put up with his suite at the old hostelry, whose internal arrangement by the way he threw into some disorder by bringing his own cook with him—a very bad compliment to the house surely. And the cook, whose name was Morris Ken (no ancestor I presume of the Bishop) was not less cook than acrobat; continually pretending to fall off his horse as he rode before the king through the forest, after the manner of the clowns at Sanger's. And the Royal Plantagenet is said to have laughed consumedly at this foolish feat on the part of Ken, which had nothing to do with his cooking! and ordered twenty shillings to be given him out of the parish poor box—I mean out of the Royal Exchequer.

Of crowned heads besides Edward the Second, who have at times honoured Liphook with their august presences may be numbered—Edward the Sixth, who must at all events have come very near to the place, on the only royal progress which he had time to make in his short life—to Cowdray; Elizabeth on her royal progress from Farnham to the same fine seat (safely arrived at which, need I say, that she shot the proverbial stag?); Charles the Second on his way to Portsmouth; and indeed every English king that was ever crowned it seems to me, and who was anxious for an outing, and wanted to see his ships.

Queen Anne however came to Liphook for a different purpose, namely, to see her stags, which in those days wandered over the royal Forest of Woolmer. With which end in view she turned off the road at Liphook after luncheon, and very unwisely (as she was always

The Anchor, Liphook.

The Porch.

rheumatic) reposed on a bank, which was smoothed for that purpose, lying about half-a-mile to the east of Woolmer Pond. Thus enthroned she saw the whole herd of red deer, brought out by the keepers and driven along the vale before her, consisting then of about 500 head. After which she went back to the Anchor to dinner, no doubt well pleased with what she had seen, and I hope took some hot toddy.

To complete the chronicle of the guests at the Anchor—for I am still twenty-six miles and two furlongs from Portsmouth—may be named King George the Third and Queen Charlotte, the Duke of Clarence, afterwards William the Fourth. The allied sovereigns after the campaign of 1815, in company with Blucher and the Duchess of Oldenburg. The Queen of Spain and the Queen of Portugal. Liberty Wilkes, who used to lie here on his journeys to and from Sandown, and lastly the Duchess of Kent and the Princess Victoria. There is a *Court Circular* flavour about this list which entitles the Anchor, I think, to its epithet of Royal, and Mr. Peake thinks so too.

To leave him and his fine old house behind us, and to descend from kings to coachmen, the eight miles between Liphook and Petersfield—the next change—was the scene of a race between two coaches, or rather between three, which might have ended in a casualty of no common order, but didn't, thanks about equally, I should suppose, to good luck and good management. Mr. Stanley Harris tells this story well in his *Coaching Age*—which remains in spite of all other rivals the text-book on this great subject. And an old coachman speaks.

"It happened," said he, "that when he was driving on the Portsmouth Road there were two other day coaches on it; but as they left Portsmouth at different hours, there was no fear of their coming into contact. With the down coaches it was different, as from their leaving London by different routes, and from other circumstances, such as stopping or not stopping to dine, they would sometimes in the middle of a journey all get together, as they did one day, when on returning he overtook the other coaches at the Anchor at Liphook, where they changed horses and dined. The coachman asked him what time he intended to get to Portsmouth that evening, to which he replied much about the same as usual; and he then left."

But, alas! while this coachman, who had hitherto resisted temptation, was changing horses at the Wheatsheaf inn half a mile out of the village, the other two coaches, who had changed at the Anchor, came by at a round trot, and shot out at him the tongue of the scorner. At this the blood of the old coachman boiled; in point of fact he said,

"I will pursue," and he was fortified in this wicked determination by his fresh team being composed of four thoroughbred horses. He pursued accordingly, and soon came in sight of his rivals, one a little in advance of the other, and travelling as fast as they were able. Upon this the old coachman flung official directions and prudence to the winds and "sprung his cattle." Success soon rewarded this disregard for the safety of his passenger's neck. He overtook the Regulator, which was the name of one of the rival coaches, as it was ascending Rake Hill. The Hero however, which was the name of the other coach, he saw still about half-a-mile in front of him. Upon this "he sprang his cattle" more than ever, and the only passenger in his coach, a soldier, was tossed about on the roof like a shuttlecock on a battledore. This however was as nothing in the old coachman's eyes, who could see nothing with them but his rival, and him he overtook on the top of Sheet Hill. The old coachman and the driver of the Hero, now qualified for charioteers in the Roman chariot races at the Paris Hippodrome, by driving their respective vehicles at full gallop down a steep and winding pitch. At the bottom of it they met a post-chaise returning from somewhere or other; but they did not heed it; the petrified post-boy only saved his neck by driving at full speed into a ditch. So far so good; especially as the old coachman now thought he saw the Hero beaten. He marked a place therefore in his mind's eye on the opposite rise where he might pass her comfortably; and when he came to the place he had marked, he came with a rush. The old coachman's leaders, answering to the call gamely, were already by the front wheels of the Hero, when what happened? Why the driver of the Hero suddenly pulled his horses right across the old coachman's leaders' heads; who thus at the very moment that he thought he was going to snatch a victory, found himself driven up a bank. Fortunately no strap or trace, or buckle, was broken by this extremely ungentlemanly manœuvre, or the old coachman would at the finish have been nowhere;

but as it was he was never after able to get beyond the hind boot of the Hero, who won therefore at the Dolphin by a short length.

Time—twenty minutes for the eight miles.

Result of the race—three of the Hero's horses never came out of the stable again, and a complaint to the proprietors.

There is not much to see in the town of Petersfield, except the

The Castle Inn, Petersfield.

memories of old coaching days which linger round the three inns, the Castle, now turned into a private house, the Dolphin, the Red Lion, and the White Hart. Two miles out of the town the Portsmouth Road passes Buriton, the home for some period of Gibbon, on the left; and then, assisted by a chalk cutting, crosses Butser Hill, which is the highest of the Southdowns, and commands everything from the spire of Salisbury

Cathedral to Chanctonbury Ring, a little beyond Worthing. Here, to geologize, the chalk is entered : and here, to be historical, a gentleman was stopped by a highwayman, who presented a pistol and modestly demanded horse, money, and watch. These the gentleman handed over and returned to Petersfield exceeding sorrowful. The highwayman meanwhile made for Hindhead, hotly pursued by a hue

Racing the Mail

and cry. Seeing which condition of affairs he foolishly enough dismounted and sought consolation by grovelling in the heather—which was a fatal instance of bad judgment, and enabled him shortly afterwards to feast his eyes on the interior of Winchester Gaol.

The Portsmouth Road after passing through Horndean, which is ten miles from the terminus, runs for about four miles through the forest of Bere; in which tract of country the "old coachman" of the racing episode, enjoyed a further adventure in a thick fog, and a rime frost, upsetting his coach with a noise like the report of cannon while he was listening to the aimless babblings of a loquacious passenger. The coach was not empty on this occasion either. On the contrary there were four young ladies inside it, who must have been artless creatures indeed, for they were fast asleep when the coach was upset, and woke up when it was being restored to its equilibrium, and remarked, "What is it?" Some gipsies who were chiefly instrumental in removing the coach from its side, showed themselves more wide-awake; for mistrusting the gratitude of upset coachmen while with one set of hands they reared the upset coach, with the other set of hands they removed several baskets of game, which according to the custom of the day were hanging underneath it. And the coachman did not discover till he got to Portsmouth that his generous assistants had thus earned their reward!

And this brings me to the second of those three crimes, which, as I said in the beginning of this chapter, gives the Royal Road in my eyes so unenviable a notoriety. I do not purpose to treat the atrocity known as "The Murders by the Smugglers," at any great length, or with any detail, though a curious pamphlet which I have by me entitled, "A full and genuine History of the Inhuman and Unparalleled Murders of Mr. William Galley, a custom house officer, and Mr. Daniel Chater, a shoemaker, by Fourteen notorious Smugglers with the trials and Execution of Seven of the Bloody Criminals at Chichester," would enable me if I had the inclination to do both the one and the other. I leave however the full accomplishment of so graceful a literary labour to the young disciples of M. Zola in this country; assuring them that in the above pamphlet (which by the way is very scarce) they will find abundance of that precious documentary evidence concerning the abysms of human depravity, the spectacle and analysis of which affords them such radiant delight. In my eyes the subject is totally unfit for literary treatment.

A bare statement however of it I feel forced to make, not only because its ghastly memory still haunts this part of the Portsmouth Road (so poignantly did the atrocity touch the imagination of a generation little given to hysteria), but because the criminals formed a characteristic portion of a class of desperadoes who were the terror of travellers on this part of the Portsmouth Road in George the Third's time, and lend therefore local colour, however detestable, to this part of the Portsmouth Road's history.

All through the last century, then, it seems the country from Portsmouth, almost as far as Liphook, was infested by gangs of smugglers, of whom the poachers who still confer notoriety on some of the villages of the area may be perhaps the lineal descendants.

From time to time, after some unusually audacious outbreak against custom-house laws had taken place, violent reprisals were made; but on the whole the revenue officers seem to have had decidedly the worst of it, and the smugglers enjoyed an enviable immunity from the retribution of justice. The climax to this condition of affairs came on the 6th and 7th of October, 1747, when a gang of some sixty of these desperadoes assembled secretly in Charlton Forest; made a sudden raid on Poole; broke open the custom, where a large quantity of tea which had been seized from one of their confederates, was lodged, and made off with the booty, without encountering any resistance from the surprised authorities.

The smugglers returned to their quarters by way of Fordingbridge, and it is here that one of their future victims first makes his appearance in the history. Daniel Chater, a shoemaker of the place, was standing watching the triumphant procession as they riotously passed his house, when he recognized a man among them who had worked with him in the last harvest-time. The man thus recognized, whose name was Diamond, not altogether relishing the attention, threw Chater a bag of the stolen tea as he passed him—by way of a sop to Cerberus.

Shortly afterwards however he was unfortunate enough to be taken into custody at Chichester on a suspicion of complicity in this very Poole affair; and the fact coming to Chater's ears, he was tempted by the promise of a reward to accompany a Mr. William Galley, a custom house officer, to Chichester for the purpose of identifying Diamond. And Galley carried a sealed letter to Major Battin, a justice of the peace for Sussex, clearly setting forth the object of the journey. Never probably did a letter prove more fatal to its bearers.

The above is but the prologue to the tragedy. The tragedy itself was set in motion by the arrival of Chater and Galley at the White Hart, Rowlands Castle, in the company of a Mr. George Austin, who had found them somewhere out of their proper road, and had undertaken to set them right. No sooner had they arrived at the inn than the landlady, a Mrs. Payn, friendly ot course to smugglers and highwaymen, seems to have been struck with a sudden suspicion—that there was something in the custom-house officer's presence which boded no good to her friends. She communicated her fears to Mr. George Austin, who, by way of assuring her that they were groundless, told her that the custom-house officer and his friend were simply bearers of a letter to Major Battin at Chichester. But this ominous fact, far from comforting Mrs. Payn, only assured her that she had harped her fears aright. She knew that Diamond was in bonds at that very place, and that Major Battin was a justice of the peace. She took instant action. First she advised Mr. George Austin to leave Chater's and Galley's company at once or harm would come to him (a hint which he with pusillanimous alacrity availed himself of), and then when he was safely off the premises, she sent for seven smugglers resident in the place—by name William Steele, William Jackson, William Carter, John Race, Samuel Downer, Edmund Richards, and Henry Sheerman, and confided to them her suspicions and her fears.

They too took alarm. For some time divided counsels prevailed as to what course should be taken to provide most effectively for their own and Diamond's safety; but by and by it was generally felt that the first step to be taken was to ascertain beyond all doubt the contents of the letter which Galley and Chater were carrying to the Chichester magistrate. The smugglers at once proceeded to carry out this scheme with an assurance which was assisted from the first by the total ignorance which Chater and Galley showed of the gravity of their own situation, or of the profession and character of the men who surrounded them.

The old programme was pursued. An impromptu fight was got up; Galley, on being struck on the mouth by Jackson, called out that he was a king's officer, and could not put up with such usage. Then followed the usual pretended reconciliation, and then the drinking bout to set a seal to it.

In the midst of this, the unfortunate victims—who were already, as it were, dead men—from some smuggler's chance observation, dropped probably in incipient drunkenness, seem suddenly to have realized what kind of company they were in, and at the same moment their dire danger. They began to be uneasy, and wanted to be going. But they were prevailed upon with force to stay and drink more rum; and the drink, drugged in all probability, soon had its intended effect. Galley and Chater became unconscious, were dragged into a neighbouring room, thrown upon a bed, and their vital secret was directly afterwards in their enemies' hands.

A brief consultation now took place among the smugglers, not as to whether Galley and Chater should be murdered or not, but as to the most convenient manner of murdering them. Two ladies, Jackson's and Carter's wives, who with several more smugglers had recently joined the party, thus expressed their views: "Hang the dogs, for they came here to hang us."

This view of the case seems to have in an instant turned men into monsters. A devilish fury possessed the whole company. Jackson rushed into the room where Chater and Galley were sleeping. He leaped upon the bed and awakened them by spurring them on the forehead. He flogged them about the head with a horsewhip till their faces poured with blood. Then they were taken out to the back yard, and both of them tied on to one horse, their four legs tied together, and these four legs tied under the horse's belly.

They had not got a hundred yards from the house when Jackson, in one of those sudden accesses of fiendishness continually characteristic of the whole affair, and which seemed a veritable possession of the devil himself, yelled out—"Whip them! Cut them! Slash them! Damn them!" and in an instant the whole gang's devilish fury was wreaked on their bound and helpless enemies. Past Wood Ashes they whipped them, past Goodthorpe Dean, up to Lady Holt Park. Here they proposed to throw Galley into the well.

The wretched man, who had already fallen off the horse three or four times, in the very exhaustion of agony, welcomed death loudly as a release. Upon which his tormentors decided to spare his life for a little more torment, and whipped him over the Downs till he was so weak that he fell.

But it is not my intention to trace the red steps of this barbarity further. The details sicken. It is sufficient to say that near Rake Hill Galley fell off the horse; and was supposed to have broken his neck. He was at once buried in a fox earth, in Harting Coombe, alive presumably, since when he was found his hands covered his face as it to keep the dirt out of his eyes. Chater did not find so fortunate a release from his torments. He was kept for over two days chained by the leg in an outhouse of the Red Lion at Rake, "in the most deplorable condition that man was ever in; his mind full of horrors, and his body all over pain and anguish with the blows and scourges they had given him." All this while the smugglers were calmly debating as to how they should finally make an end of him. At length a decision was come to. Subjected all the way to treatment which I cannot describe, he was taken back to the same Harris Well where it had been originally proposed to murder Galley ; and after an unsuccessful attempt at hanging him there, he was thrown down it, and an end put at last to his awful sufferings by heavy stones being thrown on the top of him.

This last act in this unparalleled atrocity was committed on the Wednesday night or Thursday morning. The victims had set out for Chichester on the Sunday before. This four days' murder was avenged

The Jolly Drovers on Rake Hill.

at Chichester shortly afterwards, when all the principals were executed at Broyle, near the town, amidst the universal execrations of a crowd drawn from two counties. The body of Carter was hung in chains on the Portsmouth Road on Rake Hill ; the bodies of the other murderers being distributed between Rock's Hill, near Chichester, and the sea-coast, near Selsea Bill, whence they were visible for miles.

And that is the end of the story of the murders by the smugglers ; and I am glad myself that I am at the end of it. It is pleasant after such a horror to arrive at last at Portsmouth, though I have nothing much to say about the old town now that I have got there. The usual number of kings and queens visited it by sea and land, the latter sea-sick, the former inquisitive about the state of their navy. Robert, Duke of Normandy, landed here in 1101, bent on an argument with his brother Henry as to who should wear the crown. Henry however elected to wear the crown and avoid the argument, in which I think he was wise. Richard the First gave the town its first charter; and at Portsmouth in 1290 the first oranges were landed in England by a Spanish vessel as a present for the Castilian wife of Edward the First.

Besides these royalties already mentioned, Henry the Eighth was at Portsmouth once or twice. Edward the Sixth came here in 1552, not in the best of moods, and remarked that the bulwarks of the town were "chargeable, massy, and ramparted" (whatever that may mean), "but ill-fashioned, ill-flanked, and set in remote places" (which is more clear); after which he left for London; and left Elizabeth to correct the faults he had pointed out; and James the Second to inclose Gosport within its present lines.

I have described enough scenes of blood in the seventy-one miles, seven furlongs from London, it seems to me, to suit the most sanguinary taste, and a great deal more than suits my own. But still I cannot leave Portsmouth, the terminus even of the road, without reminding my readers that at what was in 1628 the Spotted Dog Inn, and what is now a gabled house known as 12 High Street, Villiers, Duke of Buckingham, the Steenie of King James, was assassinated by John Felton, a discontented half-pay officer, just as the Duke was about to sail to the relief of La Rochelle, then being besieged by Richelieu. Lingard has written the history of the episode; and the great Dumas, in the *Three Musketeers*, has written its romance; and the subject has been too well treated by both writers in their different styles to make a subject for me. It remains for me to remark that the journey of Felton to London, where he was hanged, drawn, and quartered at Tyburn, was accomplished amidst scenes of extraordinary and many-sided excitement; and coming, as it does, before a similarly mournful expedition over the same ground on the part of the Duke of Monmouth, seems to me to cast a characteristic gloom over the annals of a road—not remarkable for coaching anecdotes or coaching records—which has been called Royal, and rightly perhaps enough,—but which has yet witnessed, so far as its historical side is concerned, and so far as my knowledge goes, gloomier and more tragic scenes than any other of the great thoroughfares out of London.

Anne of Cleves' House, Southover.

An Old Sign at East Grinstead.

IV.—THE BRIGHTON ROAD.

A PECULIAR flavour of the Regency lingers about the record of the Brighton Road. It is a record, as I read it, of Bucks, with stupendous stocks, and hats with brims weirdly curly, casting deathly glances at lone maidens perambulating haplessly by the wayside; a record of "The Fancy," as I see it drawn for me in the classic pages of *Boxiana*—thronging in their thousands, and in almost as many different kinds of conveyances to witness one of the many great battles decided on Crawley Down or Blindley Heath; a record finally of the great George himself, repairing to the health resort which his royal penetration had discovered, and repairing there in a coach and four, driven by his own royal hands, at the rate of of fifty-six round miles in four hours and a half.

Indeed it seems to me that the Brighton Road might almost be called the Regent's Road. For where without the Regent would its terminus have been? Why, it would have been nowhere; or it might have been at St. Leonards, Eastbourne, or anywhere else. When once however the Regent has discovered that the air of Brighton tended to benefit his health, he made a centre of fashion out of a small health-resort, almost before he had time to finish the Pavilion; and one of the finest of the coaching roads of England out of an uncertain track, often impassable.

Regency Bucks.

For before the Pavilion was, Brighton was about as easy to get at as Cranmere Pool in the middle of Dartmoor, the moon, the North Pole, the special exits in case of fire at our principal theatres, or anything else on earth totally inaccessible. When in 1750 the genial Doctor Russell, of Lewes, found himself better for a trip to the small fishing village, and induced some of his fair hypochondriacs to go there too; how they were to get there, considering the state of the roads—if they could be called roads—was the conundrum which they generally proposed. And I have no doubt that Doctor Russell, of Lewes, prescribed oxen as a means of transit; for oxen were about the only beasts of burden which could cope at the time I speak of, with the country's wickedly deep ruts. People got into coaches to go to Brighton and only got out of them when they were overturned. Princes on royal progresses sat fourteen hours at a stretch in state carriages, without being able to get an atom of refreshment into their royal jaws. In 1749 Horace

A Snappea Pole.

Walpole cursed the curiosity which had tempted him to tour in a country in which he found neither road, conveniences, inns, postillions, nor horses! What *did* he find in Sussex? one is tempted to ask. Why, he found that "the whole country had a Saxon air" (which seems a very remarkable discovery to have made); and "that the inhabitants were savage"—which is a discovery not so remarkable, when one remembers that near Brighton not long ago one of these savages ran at a lady with a pitchfork for riding over a turnip-field. Poor Horace had no such adventure as this—so far as I can learn; but it was clear to him that "George the Second might well be the first monarch of the East Angles," and "that coaches grew in Sussex no more than balm or spices"; almost immediately after which horticultural remark he had to leave his post-chaise (for some horrid reason which he veils from posterity), and take to pedestrianism—a form of exercise which he ever particularly loathed. No doubt however he would have bewailed his wrecked post-chaise more had it resembled "a harlequin's Calash" less; and a harlequin's Calash too "which was occasionally a chaise or baker's cart"—which is the most remarkable definition of a vehicle that I have chanced on between Boadicea's chariot and a hansom cab! Who can wonder after reading it, that the man who had rested in it found Sussex "a great damper of curiosity"? I cannot wonder for one.

All these horrors of the Brighton Road the much abused George the Fourth did away, with a sweep as it were of his fat, bejewelled, and august hand! He built the Pavilion, and people from all parts of the country came straightway to see it and him. Now in building the Pavilion, there can be no manner of doubt I think in reasonable minds that the first gentleman in Europe did the "accursed thing" spoken of by the prophet; but when the crowds which this atrocity attracted are considered, almost half the sin may be forgiven him. For the crowds soon found from such miry experiences as have already been detailed, that if they *were* to come to Brighton, and to court, they had better have some decent road to come upon. And from this simple bringing home of a plain truth came into existence the Brighton Road—"perhaps the most nearly perfect, and certainly the most fashionable of all"—according to "Viator," who should know what he is talking about.

A Visit to

the Invalids.

And not one road only ; but three roads—in point of fact, according to some authorities, about five. From having practically no road to it all, there is surely no place in England which can be reached—(or rather could be in the coaching days, for we can now only go by the London and Brighton Railway)—could be reached, by so many different routes as Brighton. Of these the favourite—called the new road—went by Croydon, Merstham, Redhill, Horley Turnpike, Balcombe, and Cuckfield, making the distance fifty-one miles three furlongs ; then there was a route through Ewell, Epsom, Dorking, Horsham, and Mockbridge, making the distance fifty-seven miles five furlongs. A more favourite way than any was by Croydon, Merstham, Reigate, Crawley and Cuckfield—making the distance fifty-three miles exactly ; while the longest and the oldest route was through Croydon, Godstone Green, East Grinstead, Nutley, Maresfield, Uckfield, and Lewes—the entire distance being fifty-eight miles two furlongs from the Surrey side of Westminster Bridge, which is the point from which the Brighton Road is measured.

The Maiden's Head, Uckfield.

Of the celebrated coaches which ran by these various routes, and which all made fast time, due mention must be made, as also of their coachmen, of whom however the already mentioned "Viator" seems to have held no extraordinary opinion. Of the coaches Carey's *Itinerary* of 1821 gives me the names of some eighteen—all celebrated, and many of which I recollect hearing spoken of, by one who had travelled in most of them, long before I ever thought it would be my lot to revive their memories. There started then in the prime era of coaching—*circa* 1821—from the Angel, St. Clement's, Strand, at 9.30 every morning for Brighton, the Light Post Coach, which went by Reigate and Cuckfield; from the Bell and Crown, Holborn, the Alert (Safety) Coach, which started daily at 8.30 a.m., and arrived at Brighton at 4; from the Old Bell, Holborn, the Meteor daily at 10.30; the True Blue, from the Blossoms Inn, Cheapside, started daily at 9 a.m., and did the journey in six hours; as also did the Night Coach, from the same inn—which was extremely good travelling. Amongst other celebrated coaches whose names were once household words may be mentioned the Royal Eagle, which left the Boar and Castle Inn at midday; the Royal Clarence, from the Bull, Bishopsgate, at 8.30 every morning, and which took a still different route from any that I have yet named—going by Lindfield and Ditchling; the Life Preserver, daily at 8.45 from the Cross Keys, Cheapside; the Regent, daily at 8 a.m., from the Flower Pot, Bishopsgate Street; the Original Red Coach — *viâ* Croydon, Reigate, and Crawley — from the Golden Cross, Charing Cross, at 9 every morning; the Eclipse, at 2 in the afternoon, from the same celebrated house; and to make an end, from the Spread Eagle, Gracechurch Street, the Dart, at 2.45 p.m., and the Sovereign at 6.45 in the morning; the Royal Brunswick at 2.30 daily from the Spur in the Borough; the Rocket at 9.30 a.m., and the Tally-ho at 10 a.m. daily from the White Bear, Piccadilly; the Princess Charlotte, which left the White Horse, Fetter Lane, at 9.30, and going the favourite route through Croydon, Reigate, Crawley, and Cuckfield, reached the Old Ship at Brighton at 5 in the afternoon; and finally in the post of honour the celebrated Vivid, which did the journey in five hours and a quarter.

Of the coachmen on this celebrated road for travelling, as I have already remarked, a great authority on the subject held a poor opinion. And why? Simply because, according to "Viator Junior" (quoted by

Captain Malet in his *Annals of the Road*, to which exhaustive authority I gratefully recommend coaching fanciers), simply because the excellence of the road annihilated the breed. This severe critic indeed ranges forty-five trembling coachmen in his judicial mind's eye, and out of the whole batch is only able to select seven or eight worthy of the title of "artists;" capable, as he poetically puts it, of "hitting 'em and holding

The Village Cage, Lindfield.

em." Oh, what a fall is here! But Viator Junior proceeds to details. Not having travelled in an excursion train (he writes in 1828), he marvels how passengers can trust their necks to coachmen, utterly incompetent to take along a heavy load in safety, at the pace at which the Brighton coaches are timed—and then a ghastly vision of incompetence rises before his critical ken. "This very day," he writes, "I saw one of the awkward squad keep his coach on her legs by pure accident, in bringing her with a heavy load round the corner by the king's stables; and as his attitude was rather good I'll endeavour to describe it. His bench" [here he proceeds to attain to the irony of Sophocles], "his bench was very low: and he himself is rather a tall man; his legs tucked under him as far as possible, were as wide apart as if he was across one of his wheels; both hands had hold of the reins which, though perfectly slack, were almost within his teeth; his whip was stuck beside him (in general

The Star, Alfriston.

however it is hanging down between his wheel horses, about the middle of the footboard), and to complete the picture, his mouth was gaping wide open, like Curran's Irishman endeavouring to catch the English accent." This satiric touch is surely not unworthy of a coaching Swift—but to continue to the bitter end. "South of York," writes Viator, "I have not often seen this man's fellow; but surely Providence must keep a most especial guard over him; for I understand he has worked some years on the same coach without an accident. And judging from appearances it is a daily miracle that he gets to his journey's end."

A personal experience gave shortly afterwards to this all-seeing eye another example of incompetence in Brighton coachmen. He mounted on a coach driven by one who, had he measured tape behind a linen-draper's counter, would in Viator's opinion, have more nearly fulfilled

Fresh Teams.

the purpose for which Providence had designed him. Instead of measuring tape however, unfortunately he held the ribbons—also a cigar —*horresco referens,* between his teeth. He also had a pair of bad holders as wheelers (both thoroughbreds) to complete the situation, and the miserable slave to tobacco could not keep them out of a canter. He was more successful in putting his chain on down the hill by New

Timbers, or this tale would never have been told except at a coroner's inquest; but being too busy with the aforesaid cigar ("the march of intellect," as Viator once more crushingly remarks), he let his team get well on to the crown of the hill, just above his change, before he attempted to pull up. And what happened when this too long-deferred effort failed? Why, "away they went." And where they were going to, except to perdition, Viator for some moments was utterly unable to tell. For the incompetent one had his reins clubbed by way of meeting the emergency, and by reason of his awkward pulling and hauling, had the coach first of all in one ditch, and then in the other, till the passengers were utterly unable to say whether they were on their heads or their heels, and momentarily expected to be lying ready for burial on their backs. At the very crisis of the affair the stables of the run-away team loomed into sight, when they stopped of their own accord, in spite no doubt, of the efforts of their driver. On the next stage an opportunity of another kind was given to this miserable charioteer for retrieving his lost laurels and pocketing the half-crowns which the outside passengers had determined at the moment not to give him. For the next stage was one which required the exercise of a little "fanning"; and it was within the bounds of reasonable human hope that such an ignoramus with the reins might yet be able to use his whip the least bit in the world. But, alas! "Dominie Sampson could not have made a more diabolical attempt at hitting a near leader." And every time the fellow tried to hit his off-side wheel horse, he nearly cut off his off-side passenger's near ear! Under which delightful conditions the journey to London was done in six hours, the passengers never being out of jeopardy the whole time.

This sort of romance makes us feel momentarily thankful for railway trains, and drivers, who have to pass a severe examination, and are not supposed to take anything stronger than cold tea. Not however must the impression be permitted to remain (in spite of Viator's savage indignation) that all the Brighton coachmen were the dangerous dunces which the above experience shows one of them to have been.

On the contrary several among them were of the A 1 class—others not up to this standard quite; but decidedly fair all round. In the latter category was Sam Goodman, of the Times. Yet it were profanity to compare him to the incomparable Mr. Snow, whose perfect

Crowhurst Grange.

ease and elegant attitude on his box in turning the Dart out of the Spread Eagle Yard in Gracechurch Street was a sight for gods and coachmen. Gray, on the Regent, was "fair—inclining to steady," as the meteorologists might say; Ned Russel, when once started over London Bridge, not worse than some of his neighbours. Mr. Steven, of the Age, had the reputation of being a good coachman, which is all that Viator will say for him, except to wish him success; but young

Cook, formerly of the Magnet, but afterwards of the Regulator (having changed his coaches, from sickness, at being bandied about between Hell and Hackney, as he graphically expresses it), Young Cook, was not only a first-rate coachman, but one of the pleasantest fellows to travel with that could be met on the road. From this bead-roll of distinguished professionals (to make an end of coachmen) can the distinguished amateurs of the Brighton Road be with any justice excluded? Certainly not! For the Brighton Road, to keep up its distinctive flavour of what I call "Corinthianism," has ever been distinguished and fortunate in its choice of aristocratic whips. And of these no selection could be complete which wanted the names of Sir Vincent Cotton, who drove the Age; of the Marquis of Worcester, father of the present Duke of Beaufort, who drove the Beaufort; of the Hon. Fred. Jerningham, a son of Lord Stafford, who drove the Brighton Day Mail—who were all artists to the tips of their fingers, who never solicited fees, and yet pocketed them when offered, with as much readiness and relish as could be shown by the poorest "knights of the whip."

And what of the travellers on the Brighton Road in the days of its prime? They are as the sands of the sea for multitude, and pass before my mind's eye in a long line, beginning with the Regent and ending with Tom Cribb—if indeed the prince should be put before the pugilist. Byron was here in 1808 with another fighting man, the celebrated gentleman Jackson, and also, I much regret to have to say it, with a young lady who rode about with him in male attire, and who remarked to Lady P——, who said, "What a pretty horse you are riding," "Yes; it was *gave* me by my brother." How many times I wonder did the beautiful Mrs. Fitzherbert, the only woman that George the Fourth ever loved probably, travel from London to her lodgings in the Steyne, and from her lodgings in the Steyne to London? Those journeys must have been countless, and what heartburnings, what agonies of pride broken and hope deferred must have been suffered by the way! Not that Mrs. Fitzherbert was by any means the only wounded beauty drawn moth-like to the gracious glare eternally effulgent at the Pavilion. Perdita Robinson was constantly to be seen on the Brighton Road during her brief period of ascendency—her turn-out faultless, her postillions pictures, her luncheon bills at the Dorset Arms, East Grinstead, or the White Hart at Godstone Green, worthy of the attentive consideration of a nation who had to pay for them. But why pursue further the bevy of frail beauty who posted to and fro from Brighton in pursuit of the Royal George. It would be a scandalous research not requiring much consideration. Let us look at another side of the picture—a more intellectual side.

The White Hart, Lewes.

In 1779—three years that is to say before the Prince Regent visited Brighton for the first time — Miss Burney (than whom I have found no more entertaining companion since I first set out on the roads) came here in company with Mr., Mrs., Miss, and Miss Susan Thrale. She travelled in a coach with four horses ; the servants travelled in a chaise, and two men additionally accompanied them on horseback. The procession started from Streatham, and took the Reigate and Cuckfield route; and they were obliged to stop for some time at three places on the road. Of Reigate Miss Burney has only to remark that "it is a very old, half-ruined borough;" and that a high hill leading to it afforded a very fine prospect; after which she passed on to Cuckfield, where, instead of at once visiting Cuckfield Park, (which is a most entrancing sixteenth-century house, possessing a gloomy park, a family curse, and a general atmosphere altogether redolent of Mrs. Radcliffe at her darkest), Miss Burney contented herself with observing that the view of the South Downs from the King's Head or the Talbot (where I suppose she was taking tea) was very curious and singular.

The utter lack of feeling displayed by the most cultured people of the eighteenth century for the domestic architecture of England positively appals. I believe that Horace Walpole was the only man living who had the faintest natural tendency to the taste—and his taste naturally was affected by the vitiated atmosphere which prevailed. Here is the second fine house that Miss Burney (so far as human nature is concerned, the observant of the observant) passes entirely without observation. First it is Littlecote on the Bath Road, which she fails to perceive, and now it is Cuckfield Park on the Brighton Road. Two points only can be urged in excuse of this deplorable exhibition of wall-eyedness in one so young. Firstly, that Miss Burney was not by nature a romanticist—indeed held them rather in contempt—and so was probably watching from the landing window a comedy in real life played by two post-boys and a chambermaid in the galleried inn's backyard; secondly, that the author of *Evelina* had not enjoyed the advantage possessed by the present generation of revelling in the romances of Harrison Ainsworth. No; Miss Burney had no opportunity of reading *Rookwood* (not that she would have read it if she had had the opportunity, I fear); and so Cuckfield Park was not associated in her mind, as it is in ours, with Dick Turpin and all the adventurous, dashing figures that throng the pages of Ainsworth's first success. For Cuckfield Park is

The Gossips.

the Rookwood of the romance; and it is no undeserved compliment to its intrepid writer, who with all his faults, possessed the truly refreshing capacity for "cutting analysis and getting to the story," that his novel has thrown the glamour of an additionally romantic interest over an old manor house already instinct with romance.

At Cuckfield then Miss Burney is disappointing; but when she gets to Brighton—which she did on this occasion at about nine o'clock in the evening—she is in her element. Then she becomes rich—rich in description, humour, observation, analysis, rich in everything in short which can help to bring the terminus of the Brighton Road in 1779 vividly before our eyes. I do not think that I can do better than follow her for a day or two through the pages of the diary which so racily describes this visit.

The day then after her arrival, Miss Burney dined at the Ship Tavern—(now known as the Old Ship, by actors, authors, managers, and other distressed unfortunates, jaded with their labours and in search of change between the Saturday and the Monday). Not that Miss Burney dined in such congenial company. Far from it. She dined at the officers' mess—she forgets to say of what regiment, to which she has been specially invited by the major and captain. The next morning there arrived at Mrs. Thrale's house, which was situated in West Street, a melancholy and typical personage, who was destined to inflict upon Miss Burney several very bad quarters of an hour. This was one Dr. Dewlap. The wretched man had written a tragedy, and had also had it accepted. His attitude towards men and things may therefore be imagined; and was I need hardly say carefully noted by Miss Burney, who had herself written a comedy—accepted also. But Dr. Dewlap seems to have been a very wicked specimen of the budding dramatic author. He was commonly of course naturally grave, silent, and absent; yet when any subject with which he was conversant had once been begun, he worked it threadbare: and, wretch that he was, seemed hardly to know when all was over; or, what is more remarkable, whether anything had passed. He was thinking of his tragedy, no doubt.

Quaint Signs.

Not the least noxious point about him was that his appearance was "smug and reserved." He soon however gave Mrs. Thrale his play to read. A deed which drove Miss Burney (with a keen perception of what was in store for her too) out for a walk on the Parade. Here she found some soldiers mustering. And in what state? It pains me to say that they were half intoxicated, and laughed so violently as Miss

The Chequers, Maresfield.

Burney passed by them, that they could hardly stand upright. The wind, too, to make matters worse, was extremely high, blew Miss Burney's gown about abominably, and played the deuce with her bonnet. And the merry light infantry laughed the more. And "Captain Fuller's" embarrassed desire to keep order, made Miss Burney laugh as much.

There is an exterior of Brighton in 1779! But an interior equally graphic is also to hand. It is connected with Dewlap the inevitable. On one occasion I read (there is an end to everything) an accursed divergence of occupation called away all the gentlemen from Miss Burney's society, and precipitated the deeply dreaded hour. Dr. Dewlap remained. He seated himself next to the fair diarist. He began to question her about his tragedy—which by this time he had given her too

Sackville College.

to read. But had Miss Burney read it? That is the question. I doubt it extremely. Hear what the lady herself says—

"I soon said all I wanted to say upon the subject," she writes. "And soon after a great deal more; but not soon after was he satisfied. He returned to the same thing a million of times, till I almost fell asleep with the sound of the same words."

To leave the fair authoress of *Evelina* for ever, with many thanks for her assistance so far (and I hope that these thanks may reach her wherever she may now chance to be studying character, and regretting eternally her desertion of literature for a servile attendance on a hum-drum court); three other travellers on the Brighton Road—and immortal travellers too, as long as English is read—present themselves for notice.

About the time then when the air was full of the rumours which culminated in Waterloo, Captain Crawley, Captain Osborne, and Mr. Jos Sedley, "were enjoying that beautiful prospect of bow windows on the one side, and blue sea on the other, which Brighton affords to the traveller." Who can forget the incident? Who does not remember the sublime and here first recorded attempt of the immortal Jos to catch the warlike spirit of the times by a subtle alteration of costume? Jos, brilliant in under waistcoats, sporting a military frock coat, clinking his boot spurs, swaggering prodigiously and shooting death glances at all the servant girls who were worthy to be slain!

"'What shall we do, boys, till the ladies return?' he asked. The ladies were out to Rottingdean in his carriage on a drive.

"'Let's have a game of billiards,' one of his friends said—the tall one with the lacquered moustachios.

"'No, dammy; no, Captain,' Jos replied, rather alarmed. 'No billiards to-day, Crawley, my boy—yesterday was enough.'"

And then, after various suggestions for killing time, including Jos's, "'to have some jellies at Dutton's and kill the gal behind the counter—devilish fine gal at Dutton's'"—the determination was come to, as is generally known, to go and see the Lightning "come in"—and the advice prevailing over billiards and jelly, the trio turned towards the coach-office.

It would be impossible to leave Brighton and Thackeray behind us, without recalling another incident detailed by the author of the *Four Georges*, this time an historical one, which has to do with a wicked old celebrity, once a well-known figure on the Steyne—with posting, and with the august personage who called posting and coaching to Brighton into fashion—nay, even into life. "In Gilray's caricatures," I quote from the *Four Georges*, "there figures a great nobleman called 'Jockey of Norfolk' in his time, and celebrated for his table exploits. He had quarrelled with the Prince, like the rest of the Whigs, but a sort of reconciliation had taken place; and now being a very old man, the Prince invited him to dine and sleep at the Pavilion, and the old duke

Taking up the Mails.

drove over from his castle of Arundel, with his famous equipage of gray horses, still remembered in Sussex."

A pleasant Bacchanalian scene is then enacted, it will be remembered, which began by everybody challenging the old duke to drink (who, not forgetful of his reputation, did not decline the honour), and ended by the first gentleman in Europe proposing bumpers of brandy. Too proud to brook defeat in his especial line of art, the old duke's intrepidity did not fail him even here. He drank. Then finding that his head was failing him, he remarked that he had had enough of such hospitality, and would go home.

"The carriage was called and came, but in the half-hour's interval the liquor had proved too potent for the old man; his host's generous purpose was answered, and the duke's old gray head lay stupefied upon the table. Nevertheless, when the post-chaise was announced he staggered to it as well as he could, and stumbling in, bade the postillions drive to Arundel. They drove him for half-an-hour round and round the Pavilion lawn; the poor old man fancied he was going home. When he awoke that morning he was in bed at the Prince's hideous house at Brighton. You may see the place now for sixpence; they have fiddlers there every day, and sometimes buffoons and mountebanks hire the riding house, and do their tricks and tumbling there. The trees are still there, and the gravel walks round which the poor old sinner was trotted. I can fancy the flushed faces of the royal princes as they support themselves at the portico pillars—and look on at old Norfolk's disgrace; but I can't fancy how the man who perpetrated it continued to be called a gentleman."

It certainly is a hard nut to crack. But the above graceful scene of conviviality at Brighton reminds me that I have yet to make mention of the houses of entertainment on the Brighton Road. Horace Walpole, it will be remembered, said, in 1749, that there were no inns in Sussex. But here I fear Horace pulled the long bow of the disappointed tourist—for the guide-books of the old coaching-days tell a different tale. Amongst others the following were well-known houses

—of varying degrees of merit, no doubt, and situated on different routes.

At Croydon — the Crown ; at Godstone Green — the White Hart ; at East Grinstead—the Dorset Arms ; at Uckfield—the Maiden's Head ;

The Dorset Arms, East Grinstead.

at Reigate—the Swan ; at Hickstead—the Castle ; at Cuckfield—the King's Head and the Talbot.

Out of these, two houses are in my opinion specially worthy of mention, namely — the White Hart at Godstone Green, and the Dorset Arms at East Grinstead ; not only because the houses are fine in themselves, but because, thanks no doubt in a great measure to the interest taken by their landlords in their past history, something of that rare romance of the roads hangs about them still. The inn at East Grinstead, which is an unusually fine specimen of its class, used formerly to be called the Cat — but why it was so called it will not be well too particularly to inquire—in fact, as Mr. Silas Wegg would have said, "In Mrs. Boffin's presence, sir, we had better drop it." A token however was struck off to perpetuate this title, which I have been shown through the courtesy of Mr. Tracy, the landlord of the house; and a very rare and curious token it is, showing "The Cat"—the name of the town, and inn.

All distinguished travellers on the Brighton Road pulled up as a matter of course at the Dorset Arms. Amongst those whose names have been handed down as habitual visitors, was Lord Liverpool, who always stayed at the Dorset Arms when on his way to visit the Harcourt seat near Buxted, and who has left a record of his impatience at dawdling waiters and dinners not served up to the minute; "Liverpool's in a hurry" even now being remembered in the place. Another constant guest was Lord Seymour, who died, I believe, in 1837—mean, I am sorry to say, as regards his expenses; and yet not mean either one way, for if he didn't eat and drink much, he possessed a passion for illumination which must have produced some respectable items in the bill—thirty wax candles or more burning in his bedroom all night. Spencer Perceval too (the Prime Minister remarkable for great ability and for having been shot in the lobby of the House of Commons in 1812 by John Bellingham) must have been a familiar figure at the Dorset Arms, for the house from which he was married in 1790 to Miss Jane Wilson stands just at the bottom of the Dorset Arms' garden.

At nine miles three furlongs up the London Road, towards London, stands the other inn that I have particularly mentioned—the White Hart, now called the Clayton Arms, at Godstone Green. The White Hart claims to be a very old house. Mr. Churchill, the proprietor, who has had it for twenty-two years, and who takes a natural and gratifying pride in its history, tells me that it was an inn in Richard the Second's time, whose badge was a white hart couchant, as heralds may know. The

White Hart was open timbered then, and had quarried windows. The gable ends were added in Elizabeth's time. In the absence of documentary evidence it requires but a small stretch of the imagination to picture the long crowd of all ranks, kings, queens, soldiers, statesmen, conspirators, coachmen, and highwaymen, who must have passed the

The Clayton Arms,
Godstone.

portals of so venerable a place of entertainment as this, in the lapse of six centuries. A tradition however which associates one royalty with the White Hart is noticeable; not only from the singularity of the association, but because the particular association in question is to me a distinctive feature in the history of the Brighton Road.

It is said then that in 1815 the Regent, the Tsar of Russia, and many royal visitors stayed at the inn on their way to Blindley Heath, to be present at the fight for the championship of England. Having lost my *Fistiana,* I am unable to verify the date of this fight, or to name the combatants; but people who know their subject, in an age when boxing may be said to be revived, will not need me to tell them that Blindley Heath, which is about four miles from Godstone Green, was one of the most popular and celebrated of prize-fighting *rendezvous.* Here, to quote one example: On the 12th of June, 1821, Hickman, the gas-light man, and Oliver, fought ten rounds in thirteen minutes. Not that Blindley Heath is the only place in the neighbourhood celebrated for this classic amusement. Within a few miles are Copthall Common, where on December 10th, 1810, Cribb fought and beat Molineaux, the black, for the first time; and Crawley Down, which has witnessed more mills than I have time or memory to catalogue.

The processions from town to these fights however afford too remarkable an illustration of contemporary manners for me to pass over so lightly: an illustration of manners continually to be studied in this neighbourhood on the Brighton Road. And I think that an extract from *the* classic authority will give a better idea than I can of the scenes to be witnessed on the road immediately before a celebrated "mill."

"The *Fancy* were all upon the alert soon after breakfast" (I quote from *Boxiana's* description of the Grand Pugilistic combat between Randall and Martin, at Crawley Down, thirty miles from London, on Tuesday, May 4, 1819) "on the Monday, to ascertain the seat of action; and as soon as the important *whisper* had gone forth, that Crawley Down was likely to be the place, the *toddlers* were off in a *twinkling.* The gigs were soon brushed up, the *prads* harnessed, and the boys who intended to enjoy themselves on the road were in motion. Between the hours of two and three o'clock in the afternoon upwards of a hundred gigs were counted passing through Croydon. The Bonifaces chuckled again with delight, and *screwing* was the order of the day. Long before eight o'clock

The Judges' Houses, East Grinstead.

in the evening every bed belonging to the inns and public-houses in Godstone, East Grinstead, Reigate, Bletchingley, &c., were *doubly*, and some *trebly* occupied.

"Five and seven shillings were charged for the stand of a horse in any wretched hut. But those customers who were *fly* to all the tricks and fancies of life, and who would not be *nailed* at any price, preferred going to *roost* in a barn; while others possessing rather more *gaiety*, and who set sleep at defiance, blowed a *cloud* over some *heavy wet*, devouring the

The Grange, Lewes.

The Sign of the Swan, Southover.

rich points of a *flash chaunt;* and thought no more of *time* hanging heavily than they did of the *classics. Chaunting* and *swiping* till many of the young *sprigs* dropped off their *perches;* while the *ould ones* felt the influence of the *dustman*, and were glad to *drop* their *nobs* to obtain forty winks. Those persons whose *blunt* enabled them to procure beds, could not obtain any sleep, for carriages of every description were passing through the above towns all night. Things passed on in this manner till daylight began to peep. Then the *swells* in their barouches and four, and the swift trotting fanciers, all hurried from the metropolis, and the road exhibited the bustle of the *primest* day of Epsom Races. The *brilliants* also left Brighton and Worthing at about the same period, and thus were the roads thronged in every direction. The weather at length cleared up, and by twelve o'clock the amphitheatre on Crawley Down had a noble effect, and thousands of persons were assembled at the above spot. It is supposed if the carriages had all been placed in one line they would have reached from London to Crawley. The amateurs were of the highest distinction, and several noblemen and foreigners of rank were upon the ground."

Regent and emperor putting up at a wayside inn to witness a fight for the championship! Young sprigs chaunting and swiping till they dropped off their perches! The swells in their barouches and four hurrying from the metropolis! The noblemen and foreigners of rank crowding round the twenty-four foot ring! What can give us a better idea of the Brighton Road in its prime than these facts? What paint more vividly what I call its "Regency flavour", its slang, its coarseness, its virility—in a word, its "Corinthianism"?

St. John's Hospital, Canterbury.

V.—THE DOVER ROAD.

Such rich crowds of historical figures throng the long reaches of the Dover Road that one really hardly knows where to make a beginning and where to make an end with them. Indeed, when I think of the record of this seventy-one miles, one long, confused, grotesque procession of all ages, and all periods of English history, files before me. I see as many sights as Tilburina does in the *Critic*, and a few more. Kings returning from conquest. One king returning from exile. Many queens on their way to weddings—("unfortunate chiefly, I regret to say," as Mr. Pecksniff might have remarked)—one queen on her way to a wedding, which, fortunately for her, can hardly be said to have completely come off; grave archbishops tremulously proceeding to installation; our earliest dramatic genius on his way to London, glory, and a violent death, his "unbowed, bright, insubmissive head," already full of *Faust.* I see too another English man of letters as immortal as Marlowe, with keen, kindly eyes, overlooking from Gad's Hill the dusty track along which he, and so many of his creations, travelled; and the latest of the ingenious race of footpads at his adroit business on Blackheath; and one of the last of the old coachmen (with whom I have had the honour of shaking hands), calm in the emergency of "chain snapped and coach running on wheelers on a frosty morning," descending the Dartford side of Shooter's Hill.

Perhaps it may be thought that it would be well for me, with such material in hand, to begin at the beginning. But the beginning of the history of the Dover Road, I fear, would be the beginning of the history of the Watling Street—for the two terms are in a large measure identical—and this would lead me into a long dissertation on chariot wheels suddenly flying off, to the intense discomfiture of centurions; to details concerning the stern tramp of the legions; to the heart-quaking sound of "Consul Romanus," according to De Quincey; and to other classic items, foreign, even in my extended view, to gossip about the great coaching roads of England.

And so I think that (this being an age in which many people talk of Chaucer without having read him) I cannot do better than start from the Old Tabard in Southwark—as it stood in Edward the Third's time—in the company of a certain body of pilgrims who set out thence for Canterbury on a certain May morning. In the company, to wit, of a "verray parfight gentil knight," in cassock and coat of mail; his curly-headed squire; the brown-faced yeoman bow in hand; the abbot, a mighty hunter from his youth up; the friar, mediævally typical of our street singers, abhorred by literary men; the prioress, possessed of a charming French lisp, and having *Amor vincit omnia* characteristically graven upon her brooch; in the company too (in case the Tabard whisky—malmsey, I mean—should prove cumulative in its effects) of a doctor of physic, who had been making hay while the sun shone and the plague was rampant; in the company, lastly, of the clerk from Oxford, whom much study had made—not mad—but as lean and leaden-eyed as Eugene Aram ever was.

Not that I intend to travel with this famed company all the way to Canterbury. They did not hurry themselves enough; sat too long

The Old Tabard, Southwark.

telling discursive stories by the way-side, which may be read to advantage in editions carefully prepared for ladies' colleges and the young. And here I may perhaps remark with advantage—to myself (in case it may appear that I am on history bent rather than on coaching)—that the purely coaching record of the Dover Road is a thing only to be touched on briefly. For in point of fact it is "thin", as dramatic critics would say, in the extreme. The following copy of a time bill marks probably the beginning of its development.

"LONDON EVENING POST. *March* 28. 1751.

"A STAGE COACH

"WILL SET OUT

"For Dover every Wednesday and Friday from Christopher Shaws the Golden Cross at four in the morning to go over Westminster Bridge to Rochester to dinner to Canterbury at night and to Dover the next morning early; will take passengers for

"Rochester, Sittingbourne, Ospringe, and Canterbury—and returns on Tuesdays and Thursdays.

By { Thos : Hartcup.
Robt : Legeyt.

By { Richd : Stradwick.
Cath : Pordage."

And I wish the four could have got up some better grammar and punctuation amongst them.

To advance from this barbaric attempt of our ancestors to induce credulous people to go to Dover, the fastest coach which ran on this road in the golden age of coaching was Chaplin's Tally-ho, which was driven by Clements—the fine old coachman whom I have already mentioned, and whose interesting personal experiences given to myself I shall deal with when I get to Canterbury, where he lives. The Tally-ho used to run from the Spread Eagle in Gracechurch Street to Sittingbourne—forty miles—every day, including Sunday, and (as Mr. Stanley Harris tells all who will learn how their forefathers travelled in *The Coaching Age*) was largely patronized by the Kentish farmers, who could leave their homes at five or six o'clock on Sunday afternoon, get their night's rest—acrobatic, somewhat, I fear—and be on the spot for the early markets in London.

To get along on our way to Rochester the Dover Road (which is measured from the Surrey side of London Bridge) after going through New Cross, where in coaching days there was a turnpike, runs into

Deptford, where there has been some history. For here, to begin with, in 1581, Elizabeth went on board Drake's ship, the *Golden Hind*, in which that greatest of English seamen had circumnavigated the globe. On board the *Golden Hind* the queen dined, and after dinner knighted the captain. I read that the ship was afterwards laid up in a yard

The Toilet.

here, and converted into a sort of dining-house for London visitors; in which case all I can say is that I hope that they recollected in what sort of sanctuary of heroism they were dining, and drank the health reverently of the great man who made English commerce possible, and so, indirectly, enabled them to pay the bill.

Eleven years after Elizabeth had dined at Deptford the greatest perhaps of our Elizabethan dramatists was killed here in a tavern brawl. The death of Christopher Marlowe at the age of thirty makes most of us wonder with Mr. Matthew Arnold at the prodigal way in which nature plays with the lives of the most gifted of her sons. As the author of *Doctor Faustus* however had permitted himself the licence of certain criticism quite uncalled for and extremely distasteful to the clergy,

Hall Place, Bexley.

our view of his premature cutting off was not shared by his contemporaries. Beard, on the contrary, in his *Theatre of God's Judgments,* thus urbanely comments on Marlowe's death from his own dagger. "But see what a hooke the Lord put in the Nostrils of this barking dogge;" an effort in criticism which makes us hope that there are such things as literary amenities among us after all.

The poet's birth at Canterbury; his education there at the King's School, gives him to the Dover Road as perhaps its brightest ornament. When we are tired it may be of erecting tablets to third class authors

(English and others), adorned with inscriptions which for unintelligibility would not misbecome the tomb of Cheops, it may occur to us that one of the greatest of our poets is unrepresented in our pedantic Pantheon. Till which time comes Mr. Swinburne's fine eulogy will take the place of a bad statue. "This poet," he writes, "a poor scholar of humblest parentage lived to perfect the exquisite metre invented for narrative by Chaucer, giving it (to my ear at least) more of weight and depth, of force and fulness, than its founder had to give; he invented the highest and hardest form of English verse, the only instrument since found possible for our tragic or epic poetry; he created the modern tragic drama; and at the age of thirty he went

"'Where Orpheus and where Homer are.'

"Surely there are not more than two or three names in any literature which can be set above the poet's of whom this is the least that can in simple truth be said. There is no record extant of his living likeness; if his country should ever bear men worthy to raise a statue or monument to his memory, he should stand before them with the head and eyes of an Apollo, looking homeward from earth into the sun: a face and figure, in the poet's own great phrase,

"'Like his desire, lift upward and divine.'"

To leave Marlowe for a while—and before leaving Deptford—it may not misbecome me to remark for the benefit of those who still read Scott in an age which has turned aside after brazen images with feet of clay—that at Sayes Court—long since pulled down—are laid some of the most brilliant scenes in *Kenilworth.* It is here that Blount and Raleigh first appear in the pages of perhaps the finest historical novel in the world; it is here that Tressilian, milksoppy to the verge of nausea even for one of Scott's heroes, brings Wayland Smith to cure Sussex of Leicester's broth; it is to Sayes Court that Elizabeth herself comes when she is least expected, finds it watched like a beleaguered fort, and makes a rapid exit, "having brought confusion along with her, and leaving doubt and apprehension behind."

I confess that it does me good when in the course of these disjointed rambles along the great roads of England I can find some spot haunted by the, to me, charmed figures which throng the pages of the Waverley Novels. Hitherto I have not reaped much of a harvest of joy in this direction it must be confessed; but Deptford has given me my first

Cobham Hall, Rochester.

opportunity; and the Dover Road, a little further on, will give me my second; with which remark I think I may leave Deptford altogether, lamenting that all that can be seen of Sayes Court is now a parish workhouse, which stands on its site; and marvelling at the imperial relaxation of Peter the Great who stayed here in 1698 (at the Court, not at the workhouse), and who was wont to unbend a mind wearied with shipbuilding, by being driven through the world-famous hedges of the garden in a wheelbarrow.

Immediately beyond Deptford we come to Blackheath, seven miles from London Bridge, famous in these days for football matches, and for

A Clandestine Interview.

villas built for credulous people simple enough to believe in fine air as a remedy for that mysterious disease which, to quote the terrific advertisement, is "stealing upon us all." But the villas, I regret to say, in which these deluded persons seek for that health which passeth understanding, and can only be procured at the vendors of patent medicines, are by no means equal to the aristocratic residences for which Blackheath was once famous. The manners of their inhabitants are however much improved. At least I hope so. For Montague House, now pulled down, did not, I apprehend, shine conspicuously in this desirable respect. The reverse indeed was the case; Montague House having been, in the days I speak of, the residence of the unfortunate Queen Caroline, and the scene of the delicate investigation —which reminds me that I am on delicate ground. From the same house that delightful combination of the devil and the three graces, my Lord Chesterfield, wrote some of those amazing letters to his son. At Blackheath also lived, at intervals, the conqueror of Quebec, and from his villa here his remains were carried to Greenwich for burial.

Besides a queen devoted to junketings, a letter-writing father, bent on directing his son to the deuce, and a great warrior, rebellion has in the good old days (when people who wanted a purse simply took one on the nearest common, without starting a subscription in the newspapers)—rebellion has raised its head on this celebrated spot; and it raised its head in the person of Wat Tyler, who was here in 1381 at the head of one hundred thousand other heads (which was wise of him seeing that he had previously cracked a poll-tax collector's head at Dartford, after drinking too much ale, I suppose, at the celebrated Bull Inn). Another rebel was here, at Blackheath 1497. Lord Audley to wit, who went through the somewhat aimless exercise of bringing troops all the way from Cornwall, pitching their tents, and immediately afterwards suffering defeat at the hands of Henry the Seventh.

Here we have found history enough in seven short miles from

London—and yet not half the history yet which can be directly associated with Blackheath. For this celebrated spot occupied in the annals of England much the same sort of position apparently as Rotten Row occupies in the annals of contemporary fashion. It was the place where kings and ministers met casually on their way to or from London, and babbled of the weather, the price of corn, the latest hanging, the odds on the next bear-fight, the state of the unemployed, or any other

The Leather Bottle, Chobham.

kindred subject which might suggest itself to mediæval brains, in an open space, where it was not too windy. Here then, to notice a few of such meetings, in 1400 Henry the Fourth met Manuel, Emperor of Constantinople, who came to ask for aid against the Sultan Bajazet; and sixteen years later the Emperor Sigismund was received here and conducted in state to Lambeth. Henry the Fifth, after one long triumphal procession the whole way from Dover, was met here on Blackheath by the mayor and five hundred citizens of London, and hailed Victor of Agincourt. The mayor and aldermen had "got them all on" on this occasion (I refer to their scarlet robes and red and white hoods), and were doubtless prepared, with the help of conduits running wine, pursuivants-at-arms, cloth of gold, and emblazoned trappings, to give the conquering hero the reception he deserved. But Henry on this occasion seems to have borne his honours with exemplary modesty; and whether he was surfeited by the sweets of a triumph which had already lasted sixty-four miles, or whether he was bilious from the Channel passage and a long ride on horseback, he nipped all the worthy mayor's preparations in the bud. In point of fact, according to Holinshed, "the king, like a grave and sober personage, and as one remembering from Whom all victories are sent, seemed little to regard such vaine pompe and shews as were in triumphant sort devised for his welcoming home from so prosperous a journie; insomuch that he would not suffer his helmet to be carried before him, whereby might have appeared to the people the blowes and dints that were to be seene in the same; neither would he suffer any ditties to be made and sung by minstrels of his glorious victorie, for that he would have the praise and thanks altogether given to God." A pious decision, but one which must have been extremely unsatisfactory to town councillors who had launched forth in the way of dress and decorations, and to the thousands of Londoners who had flocked out to Blackheath to see the show.

The next royalty I find on Blackheath is Henry the Eighth, whose name is constantly cropping up in Kent and Sussex, and curiously enough, generally in connection with the one of his six wives whose appearance he from the first particularly abhorred. I refer to Anne of Cleves, whose sad fate should be a lasting warning to young ladies about to marry, of the danger of flattering portraits. It was here on Blackheath that the already muchly married king publicly received his fourth wife, with all due decency and decorum, having already made up his royal mind to put her away privately. For Henry on this occasion did not play fair; and though he pretended to Anne of Cleves herself that it was at this meeting on Blackheath that he had first seen her—in saying so, he said that which was not; for he had already privately inspected her at the Crown Inn at Rochester. It was on this occasion it may be remembered that the bluff Tudor gave way to a regrettable license of speech at first sight of the goods the gods had provided for him, and said many things unfit for publication; which shocked the onlookers, and made Cromwell put his hands to his head to feel if it was still on his shoulders.

It was not there long after. The match-maker expiated his unfortunate choice on Tower Hill; and Anne of Cleves was content to forego the dubious joys of married life for the possession of the several manors in Kent and Sussex that her grateful late lord bestowed upon her. The number of these manors exceeds belief, and at the same time gracefully gauges Henry's conception of the magnitude of the matrimonial peril past. Indeed, it seems to me that the king's brain must have been quite turned with delight at the retiring attitude of the Flanders lady; and that whenever he had nothing villainous on hand, and was disinclined for tennis, he gave Anne of Cleves a manor or two simply to while away the time.

But though on either of these great occasions that I have named, Blackheath must have been a sight worth seeing, it was in 1660 no doubt that the grandest of its historical pageants was to be seen: when the long reaction against Puritanism had suddenly triumphed, and all England went mad on a May morning at the Restoration of her exiled king; when through sixty-one miles as it were of conduits running wine, triumphal arches, gabled streets hung with tapestry—through battalions of citizens in various bands, some arrayed in coats of black velvet with gold chains, some in military suits of cloth of gold or silver—Charles, who had slept at Rochester the night before, rode on to Blackheath between his brothers, the Dukes of York and Gloucester.

And on Blackheath he saw on one side the stern array of the great army which he had seen last (and seen too much of) at Worcester; and on the other, according to Walter Scott, a very favourite family group, well known to readers of the Waverley Novels. In point of fact, Sir Henry Lee, of Ditchley, arrived at the uttermost limits of a noble old age, "having a complacent smile on his face and a tear swelling to his eye, as he saw the banners wave on in interminable succession, and heard the multitude shouting the long-silenced acclamation, 'God save King Charles!'" And round the old man's chair stood a delightful group, it will be remembered, of all the pleasant characters of *Woodstock*—Colonel Everard and Alice, now his wife; Joceline Joliffe, of quarter-staff renown, and Mrs. Joceline Joliffe, *née* Phœbe; then Wildrake too, the incomparable of Squattlesea Mere, in the moist county of Lincoln, much given to singing "Rub-a-dub," and requesting the moon and stars to catch his hat. This morning he blazes in splendid apparel, but his eyes, I regret to say, have been washed with only a single cup of canary. And last, but not least, Beavis, the wolf-hound, dim also as to his eyes, stiff as to his joints, a ruin of his former self, but having lost none of his instinctive fondness for his master.

It will be remembered that when Charles from the midst of a maze of pursuivants and trumpeters, and plumes and cloth of gold, and waving standards and swords gleaming in the sunlight, saw this group, he had the tact to remember it, the urbanity to dismount, prevent Sir Henry Lee from rising, and ask for his blessing. Having duly received which, the king went on to London, and his very faithful servant, having seen the desire of his eyes, was gathered to his fathers.

After Blackheath and Scott (so literary is this part of the Dover

Road), comes Shooter's Hill and Dickens. And Dickens is the veritable genius of the road. His memory burns by the way—as all but the wicked man who has not read *Pickwick* and *David Copperfield* will remember—and indeed *A Tale of Two Cities.* For in the second chapter of that wonderful book the very spirit of the Dover Road in George the Third's time is caught as if by magic. Who (having eyes)

Walking up the Hill.

cannot see "the Dover Road on a Friday night late in November in the year of our Lord one thousand seven hundred and seventy-five—the Dover Road, lying beyond the Dover Mail, as it lumbered up Shooter's Hill"? The coachman (whose name was Tom) towelling the tired horses —especially the near leader, much given it will be remembered to shaking its head and everything upon it, as it were denying that the coach could be got up the hill at all. The passengers wrapped up in rugs and in a mortal distrust of each other, trudge through the slush by the coach's side—Mr. Jarvis Lorry, of Telson's bank, among them. A steaming mist rises out of all the hollows; the hour is "ten minutes, good, past Eleven"—learning which the coachman remarks, "My blood!" and then, "Tst! Yah! Get on with you!" The last burst carries the Mail to the top of the Hill. Then comes some dialogue often heard on the old coaching roads when George the Third was king. The passengers are in the act of re-entering the coach.

"'Tst! Joe!' cried the coachman in a warning voice, looking down from his box.

"'What do you say, Tom?'

"They both listened.

"'I say a horse at a canter coming up, Joe.'

"'I say a horse at a gallop, Tom,' returned the guard, leaving his hold of the door, and mounting nimbly to his seat. 'Gentlemen, in the king's name all of you.' With this hurried adjuration, he cocked his blunderbuss, and stood on the defensive."

Then to the Dover Mail as it stood on the top of Shooter's Hill entered Mr. Jerry Cruncher; remarkable for his leaning towards pursuits of an agricultural character, carried on in churchyards at one in the morning with the assistance of a sack, a crowbar of convenient size, a rope and chain, and other fishing tackle of that nature; remarkable also, on his domestic side, for a wife much given to flopping herself down and praying that the bread and butter might be snatched out of the mouth of her only child. Mr. Cruncher was not on a body-snatching expedition on this occasion however; though Mr. Lorry's answer, "Recalled to life"—a verbal answer to the letter of which Jerry was bearer—struck him as ominous decidedly.

Who does not remember all these things? Who has not read them again and again? I declare that I think this second chapter of *A Tale of Two Cities* a picture of the old coaching days more perfect than any that has been painted. Every detail is there in three pages. Every colour, every suggestion, from "the mildewy inside of the old Mail, with its damp and dirty straw, its disagreeable smell, and its obscurity," to the guard's arm-chest where the blunderbuss lay recondite; to that smaller chest too in which there were a few smith's tools, a couple of torches, and a tinder-box. "For he was furnished with such completeness that if the coach lamps had been blown and stormed out, which did occasionally happen, he had only to shut himself up inside, keep the flint and steel sparks well off the straw, and get a light with tolerable safety and ease (if he were lucky) in five minutes." I can see the passengers hiding their watches and purses in their boots (still fearful that the messenger who had stopped the Mail was a highwayman), their hearts beating loud enough to be heard, and the panting of the horses communicating a tremulous motion to the coach—as if it too were in a state of agitation. Which fancied peril passed—if we had been in the Dover Mail on that memorable night with Mr. Jarvis Lorry—we should have probably taken our watches gradually out of our boots as we passed Welling, Bexley Heath, and Crayford, in order that on arrival at the Bull Inn at Dartford, we might walk to the bar comfortably to take a drink.

And the Bull at Dartford looks, at the present time of speaking, much as it must have done to the passengers by the Dover Mail in 1775. It is indeed one of the finest inns on the Dover Road. Here at the Bull at Dartford we have a galleried courtyard (not however rendered more interesting to artistic eyes by the addition of a glass roof, under which local corndealers try to get the best of a bargain). We have also the low archway decorated with game suspended, the kitchen on one side, the bar on the other, and a general atmosphere of deliberate travelling and sleepy comfort. Also a reminiscence of antiquity—for the Bull, according to local legend and Mr. Harrison Ainsworth, was a flourishing concern five centuries ago. In front of the old house the impetuous Wat Tyler began his historical record in the fifth year of

Richard the Second by incontestably demonstrating to an incredulous crowd that the local poll-tax collector had brains. In truth he spread them *coram populo* upon the Green. Much history has passed in front of the old inn of course since those exhilarating days; in 1822 perhaps scene the last. For then while the great Fourth George was majestically

The Bull, Dartford.

reposing in his royal post-chaise in front of the old archway he experienced an unpleasant surprise. A very ungentlemanly man named Calligan, a working currier who ought to have known better, suddenly projected his head into the carriage window, and observed in a voice of thunder, "You're a murderer!" an historical allusion to the king's late treatment of Queen Caroline, which made the royal widower "sit up". Upon which a bystander named Morris knocked the personal currier down, and the window of the post-chaise was pulled up, and the post-boy told to drive on as quickly as possible.

But I cannot leave Dartford without visiting Place House, a delightful record of the Middle Ages, standing in immediate juxtaposition

Place House—Anne of Cleves' Manor House.

to an iron-foundry and a railway station, and approached by a narrow lane rich in black mud. We are indebted for Place House, as well as for much that is picturesque in England, to the monks—or rather in this case (I beg the ladies' pardon) to the nuns. For the house founded by Edward the Third was a priory of Augustinians to which all the noble ladies in Kent, who had discovered that life is not worth a potato, retired serenely from a tedious world. After the dissolution, Henry the Eighth saw in it a desirable residence for Anne of Cleves—Place House indeed was one of the first manors granted to this little-married but much dowered lady. In after times the manor was given with many others by James the First to Robert Cecil, in exchange for Theobalds (the Stuart king's Naboth's vineyard), and here its history ends; but it is a charming place to feast the eyes upon still, and is best looked at from the farmyard.

There is nothing much now to see or describe in the eight miles which separate Dartford from Gravesend. Cardinal Wolsey however was down this part of the Dover Road in 1527, with his usual brobdingnagian retinue. The cardinal in his prosperous days must have been a deuce of a person to ask to one's country-house—as Sir John Wilshyre, of Stone Place, discovered on this identical occasion. For Stone Place was not big enough for Wolsey's nine hundred followers, and so most of them had to put up at Dartford, and Sir John had to pay the bill.

People now go to Gravesend to embark in the P. and O. steamers for the uttermost parts of the earth, and so it is still a busy place. But it was always busy even in the old times, and was then additionally picturesque. At Gravesend distinguished visitors to London made up their minds as to whether they would approach the capital by the river or the Dover Road. And if they decided on the river, there wa generally a gorgeous sight to be witnessed on

"The clear Thames bordered by its gardens green"

—the Thames that is to say of the sixteenth century, and Mr. William Morris. The present Lord Mayors' Shows give us no conception I fear of the gorgeous processions which attended the passage of distinguished visitors up the river in the days when the Thames looked as Mr. Morris has described it, and the Lord Mayor of London was the important personage that French dramatists still believe him to be. Cardinal Pole came by this route on his return from exile, and the Poet Laureate in *Queen Mary* has put a fine passage into his mouth descriptive of his experience. With "royal barges" however, "thrones of purple on decks," "silver crosses sparkling before prows," "ripples

The Precinct Gate, Rochester.

twinkling in their diamond dance," "boats as glowing gay as regal gardens," we have nothing to do, so had better get on to Rochester *viâ* Gad's Hill.

The New Leader.

Here Falstaff's horse was removed by Prince Hal, an operation which caused its owner to "fret like gummed velvet." Here he was desired by his unfeeling companion to lie down and lay his ear close to the ground in order that he might hear the tread of travellers—a formality which he declined to comply with, unless somebody promised to help him up. Here he was called opprobrious names—"Fat Guts" amongst others. Here he robbed the travellers who were carrying money to the king's exchequer, in order that he might divert it to the King's Arms. And here he was robbed of what he had robbed by his graceless confederates childishly bent on a practical joke.

Here too from his house on Gad's Hill (and a very hideous house it is) Charles Dickens, having a full view of the scene of this Shakesperean interlude, gave novel after wonderful novel to an astonished world, which was never sated with a humour and an observation of life which were indeed Shakesperean; but kept craving and calling for more, and for more—till the magician's brain was hurt, and the magic pen began to move painfully and with labour, and the chair on Gad's Hill was found one June morning to be empty for ever.

I remember the shock of that announcement well. It was as if some pulse in the nation's heart had stopped beating. There was as it were a feeling that some great embodied joy had left the world, and silence had fallen on places of divine laughter. So men must have felt, I think, when Rabelais died—Rabelais, the man who first taught a monk-ridden world how to shake its sides: so men must have felt, I think, when the day destined for the departure came to Swift and Fielding and Sterne—Sterne so much maligned by Coleridge and Thackeray and others, yet of all his contemporaries the most profound, the most misunderstood. Yes, the feeling was general, I think, that English literature had suffered an irremediable loss by Dickens's death; and time has confirmed the fear. We have abandoned laughter in these days for documentary evidence, psychology, realism, and other prescriptions for sleep, and have entered on a literary era which has lost all touch and sympathy with Dickens, and is indeed divinely dull.

The above may appear perhaps in a coaching article, a literary digression, but it is in truth but a resurrection pie of thoughts which occurred to me—and would occur to any real lover of Dickens—in the

The Nuns' Houses, Rochester.

course of that two mile seven furlong walk on the Dover Road between Gad's Hill and Rochester, which the great author used to cover nearly every other day of his life. For Rochester is as closely associated with Dickens as Chaucer is with Canterbury, or Shakespeare with Stratford-on-Avon. In that great cycle of imaginative prose beginning with the *Pickwick Papers* and ending with *Edwin Drood,* Rochester is written almost on the first page, and almost upon the last. Is it a wonder then that in the picturesquely beautiful old town reminiscences of the departed genius should haunt one at every step ?

The Bull and Victoria, Rochester

"The principal productions of Rochester," wrote Mr. Pickwick, "appear to be soldiers, sailors, Jews, chalk, shrimps, officers, and dock-yard men." But I think the description is truer of the three other towns of Stroud, Chatham, and New Brompton, which are included in the category ; for when I was at Rochester I saw few of these articles of commerce, and nothing whatever I am bound to say of the historic conviviality of the military. But I saw the cathedral and the castle, which are both fine, especially the castle ; and I heard as it were in the air the voice of the immortal Jingle observing, "Glorious pile—frowning walls—tottering arches—dark nooks—crumbling staircases—old cathedral too—earthy smell — pilgrims' feet worn away the old steps — confessionals like money-takers' boxes at the theatre ;" after which I looked at the bridge over which David Copperfield saw himself coming as evening closed in footsore and tired, and eating the bread that he had bought for supper ; after which I went to the Bull and Victoria Hotel and had supper myself.

"Good house—nice beds," according to Mr. Jingle, who however did not put up here himself, if my memory serves me, but he dined with the Pickwickians and recommended broiled fowl and mushrooms—if he

Courtyard of Bull ana Victoria, Rochester.

might be permitted to dictate. But why prolong the description of that immortal night? It is sufficient to say that at the Bull—which is as fine a specimen of the inn of old days as I have seen on my travels——everything connected with the stay of the Pickwickians is preserved and cherished as the apple of his eye by the courteou and cultivated proprietor. All is shown to those who are interested and reverent. The long room where the ball took place, "with crimson covered benches and wax candles in glass chandeliers; the elevated den in which the musicians were securely confined;" the corner of the staircase where the indignant Slammer met the victorious Jingle returning after escorting Mrs. Budger to her carriage, and said "Sir!" in an awful voice, producing a card; the bedroom of Winkle "inside that of Mr. Tupman's," an arrangement which enabled Mr. Jingle to restore his borrowed plumage "unbeknownst" at the conclusion of the ball. All the first part of Pickwick is to be seen I say at the Bull and Victoria—with surroundings eloquent of the old world past; and which the author has in some other of his works thus graphically described:—

"A famous inn! The hall a very grove of dead game, and dangling joints of mutton; and in one corner an illustrious larder, with glass doors developing cold fowls and noble joints. And tarts wherein the raspberry jam coyly withdrew itself, as such a precious creature should, behind a lattice work of pastry."

But to leave the Bull and *Pickwick* (for the Bull is not the only inn in Rochester to be described, nor is the *History of Pickwick* by any manner of means its only history)—the Crown, which stands at the foot of the bridge, is a modern house now, but it is built on the site of a venerable place with gables and barge boards, which stood in 1390, and was pulled down (without a drawing having been made of it, it is needless to remark) so late only as 1863. A portion of the original stable still stands, which is a remarkably interesting fact, since it was here that that scene with the carriers took place in *Henry IV.*, Act II., Scene I, which was an introduction to the robbery on Gad's Hill. To the Crown in its old shape came as visitor Henry the Eighth to have a private peep at Anne of Cleves. He came; he saw; he pronounced her a Flanders mare. He departed, using strange words.

The White Hart, another inn at Rochester almost opposite the Bull and Victoria, now presents the appearance of a small public-house; but it can boast some antiquity in its way, having been built in the reign of Richard the Second, and in 1667 sheltered the inquisitive head of Mr. Samuel Pepys—an incident which, remembering that Samuel was no enemy of good cheer, makes it probable that in those good old days it was the best inn in the place. Pepys was at Rochester on some business connected with the Admiralty and dockyards. He went to the Cathedral, but left before the service, strolled into the fields, viewed Sir F. Clark's pretty seat, and then retired to a cherry garden, where he met with an adventure in the shape of a young, plain, silly shopkeeper, who had a pretty young woman as his wife. Mrs. Pepys not being present, on this plain shopkeeper's pretty wife the susceptible Samuel threw deathly glances. He also kissed her, I am sorry to have to say, and they then ate their dinners together, and walked in the fields till dark. An hiatus here occurs in the *Diary*. But the paragraph on emerging from mystery ends in the usual way—"and so to sleep."

Besides Mr. Pepys there came to Rochester in 1573 Queen Elizabeth, and in 1606 James the First and that exceedingly jovial boon companion, the King of Denmark; but they appear to have been both in decent and sober frame—indeed, something in the penitential mood—for they underwent a sermon in the Cathedral. James the Second was at Rochester too, but not in the best of spirits I apprehend, or in the mood for viewing any ruins except those of his own life. For he came here under a Dutch guard, after his first attempt to escape, and after a week's detention was probably allowed to do so. He embarked on board a tender in the river from a house which is still standing, and was landed in due course at Ambleteuse.

But the most interesting events connected with royal visits to Rochester surround the stay of Charles the Second at Restoration House, in the course of his triumphant procession to London. The present owner of this house, which was built about 1587, Mr. S. J. Aveling, has kindly obliged me with some details about this royal and memorable visit which are full of interest and have been most religiously preserved.

The king arrived at Rochester on the Monday following his landing at Dover. The first thing he did was to refresh himself; the second to go and see the *Royal Sovereign*, then lying at Chatham. After which he returned to Restoration House, and was immediately presented with a most dutiful and loyal address from Colonel Gibbons, then in temporary possession of the place; and also from the regiment of Colonel Gibbons stationed at that time in Rochester. John Marloe, the mayor of the city, now had his opportunity for displaying loyalty, and went to the length of a "faire piece of plate, value one hundred pounds," being a basin and ewer gilt. The king must have been tired that night, and no doubt he slept well. He should have done so, at all events, for he slept in a delightful room which I have had the pleasure of seeing, containing amongst other curiosities a secret panel which opens into passages communicating with the garden and with the roof.

Restoration House, Rochester.

The first half of the Dover Road—that part of it as far as Rochester at all events—is so closely associated with the memory of Dickens, that another reminiscence of him may fittingly round its story. There is a passage then in *Great Expectations* referring to this very Restoration House, a place which always took his fancy, and well it might.

"I had stopped," thus the passage runs, "to look at the house as I passed, and its seared red brick walls, blocked windows, and strong green ivy clasping even the stacks of chimneys with its twigs and tendons, as if with sinewy old arms, made up a rich and attractive mystery."

This mystery held him to the end. On the occasion of his last visit to Rochester, June 6th, 1870, he was seen leaning on the fence in front of the house, gazing at it, rapt, intent, as if drawing inspiration from its clustering chimneys, its storied walls so rich with memories of the past. It was anticipated, it was hoped, that the next chapter of *Edwin Drood* would bear the fruits of this reverie. The next chapter was never written.

The Dover Road after leaving Rochester, runs through Chatham, celebrated for its dockyard, for its lines, in which Mr. Pickwick playfully chased his hat till it introduced him to the Wardles, and gave a new start by doing so to his adventures; celebrated also for a gentleman of David Copperfield's acquaintance who used to live here in a low small shop, which was darkened rather than lightened by a little window, and who was wont to remark, "O my lungs and liver! what do you want? O Goroo! Goroo!" to any one who offered him for sale an old waistcoat.

I went, when I was at Chatham, to see whether tradition could still point out the residence of this peculiar man of genius whose strange exclamation has added as far as I know another gem to the English language, and whose remarks on his constitution are so pregnant with melancholy meaning to people who live sedentary lives; but my search was unsuccessful; the home of the author of "Goroo! Goroo!" is no longer pointed out to dyspeptic travellers; so I set my face for Canterbury, finding nothing in Chatham to interest me further.

The Dover Road after leaving Chatham is simply the old Watling Street with modern improvements and nothing more. It runs consequently in nearly as straight a line as can be imagined, through a fine rolling country, commanding here and there fine views, and here and there no

Summerhill.

Town House, Ightham.

views at all. But that plethora of historic incident which marked the Dover Road as far as Rochester still occurs; till, at the end of twenty-five miles one furlong we reach Canterbury, which is a sort of historical reservoir in itself.

We are not there however yet. By no means. And on the way there (after passing through Rainham and Moor Street) Newington, six miles from Chatham, first gives me pause. For here a very dolorous event occurred in what we are pleased to call the dark ages. And it occurred in a priory for nuns, I am sorry to say, which was founded shortly after the Domesday Survey. There was a difference of opinion among the ladies on a rainy afternoon, and the next morning the prioress was found strangled in her bed. The catastrophe striking even the mediæval authorities as something out of the ordinary course of nature, they took decisive measures for staying the scandal by burying all the nuns alive in a chalk pit; a curious instance of an adroit dealing with a difficulty, which may be seen (the chalk pit, not the difficulty) to this day.

Gateway, Leeds Castle.

After which heavy business we had better get on to Sittingbourne (thirty-nine miles six furlongs from London) for a little refreshment. And Sittingbourne is, or rather was, in the old coaching days, a good place for a dinner. At all events, here many of our English kings dined, Henry the Fifth amongst the number, who was sumptuously entertained at the Red Lion on his return from Agincourt at the cost of nine shillings and sixpence ("Are visions about?") Here also George the First and George the Second refreshed repeatedly on their way to Hanover at the George or Rose, but, as I apprehend, at a more extended tariff. The George and the Rose both stand still—but as inns, alas! no more. They are fallen from their previous divinity, and now cast a shade, and

Old Hospital, Canterbury.

an extremely dismal one too, one as a shop, and the other as a lecture-hall—which is a good instance of the sort of degraded disguise in which so many of the once famous hostelries of the great roads of England coyly hide themselves from the historian's inquiring eyes.

Sittingbourne is not exactly the sort of place now, in spite of its august past, to make a weary traveller dance, and sing, and rejoice, and play the lute—as Mr. Chadband would have it. Far from it, if the truth must be told. It is indeed depressing to a distinct degree, and was the birthplace of a once celebrated critic. Here Theobald was born towards the end of the seventeenth century. He edited Shakespeare, and said nasty things of Pope, who marked, learned, and inwardly digested them, and thus in the *Dunciad* remembers him kindly:

> "Here to her chosen all her works she shows,"

sings the little man of Twickenham, describing a pastime of the great goddess Dulness.

> "Prose swell'd to Verse, verse loitering into Prose:
> How random thoughts now meaning chance to find,
> Now leave all memory of sense behind:
> How Prologues into prefaces decay,
> And these to notes are frittered quite away:
> How index-learning turns no student pale,
> Yet holds the eel of science by the tail;
> How, with less reading than makes felons 'scape,
> Less human genius than God gives an ape,
> Small thanks to France, and none to Rome or Greece,
> A past, vamp'd future, old, revised, new piece,
> 'Twixt Plautus, Fletcher, Shakespeare, and Corneille,
> Can make a Cibber, Tibbald, or Ozell."

Which last, though far from a good rhyme, enshrines, I fear, our critic's name for ever. For by "Tibbald", I much regret to say, Theobald is meant. And when Theobald read it, I've no doubt he wished that Sittingbourne had never seen him.

After leaving which town, forward the long reaches of the Dover Road stretch past Bapchild, past Radfield, past Green Street, where in the days of the Road at the Swan the London coaches changed horses; when all such coaching rites were celebrated as "throat-lashing," "taking out the leaders," &c., &c., &c. And so on to Ospringe, where at the Red

Lion horses were also kept, and a Camera Regis in a Maison Dieu as well, for the use of such kings on this truly royal road as had got galled in the saddle and felt disposed to lie on their royal faces for a night. This Maison Dieu was founded by Henry the Second, and came afterwards into the hands of the Knights Templars. By them it was no doubt administered according to their debonair wont. Barmaids, hot soup, old Malvoisie, and no change given over the counter, put fresh life into the old place, and dimly heralded the profuse hospitality of the coaching days; made many knights and squires of high estate linger on their pilgrimage, and forget whither they were going. For they were going to Canterbury we must suppose; and from Boughton Hill, about four miles on, the spire of the great cathedral was first seen from the backs of war-horses, mules, from the top of stage coaches, or from other points of view obtainable by travellers on the Dover Road of all ranks, and at various periods in its history. None but pedestrians or bicyclists get this view now, because the railway after leaving Faversham makes a *détour* which does not command it.

Butchery Lane, Canterbury.

At Faversham I should like to have paused if I had any business there at all, for it was a most picturesque place, and enshrines among its traditions a most picturesque murder, redolent of gloom, premeditation and the sixteenth century. The Dover Road proper however avoids Faversham altogether, so I must avoid it too, and passing over Boughton Hill, and shortly afterwards passing by "Courtenay's Gate" (where in May, 1838, Sir William Courtenay, Knight of Malta, an amiable man,

Taking out the Leaders.

believing himself to be somebody who he wasn't, was shot, after his remarkable pilgrimage), pass into Canterbury itself, which as a cathedral town stands alone—like its cathedral. And everywhere in Canterbury—at the Falstaff Inn beyond the West Gate, in the incomparable High Street, a very coloured vista itself of mediævalism—on the grand cathedral's dreaming close, "the Middle Age is gorgeous upon earth again," as a modern poet very felicitously puts it. On all sides, at every turn, history, romance, legend, spring beneath our feet. For the moment, in face of such a treasure house of the fantastic past, all recollections of coachmen and coaches, and wheelers and leaders, and time-bills, and Carey's *Itinerary* and Paterson's *Roads*, and other data for horsey history, vanish as a tale that is told. Only for a moment however, for the

Falstaff, West Gate, Canterbury.

coaching tale of the Dover Road has not been told yet at all, and very shortly has to be.

Meanwhile the history of Canterbury—and by its history I mean not only its coaching history, with its accompanying casualties, shoes cast, bolting horses, chains snapped, &c., &c. ; but also its long list of historical visitors who reached it by the Dover Road, and not by the London, Chatham, and Dover Railway—calls for instant telling. For its list of historical visitors is long and distinguished, and the visitors

A Cast Shoe.

must be made rotate in the order of their rotation, as a game-keeper speaking of undisciplined beaters at a battue once geographically remarked.

To avoid then a too profound plunge into the past, I shall skip such uncomfortably early visitors as King Lucius, Ethelbert, and

Augustine, who are so antique that they would be very likely to get me into trouble if I meddled with them, and mention Becket, who has been much overdone, only to point out that so many skulls have been attributed to him, that the modern inhabitants have sunk into a horrid state of incredulity as to any of them. The latest skull had been discovered (by the *Daily Telegraph*, I believe) when I was at Canterbury last; but the burghers of Canterbury when I spoke of it looked at me with a pitying smile, and directed me to the nearest house of refreshment. Skulls or no skulls however, it is certain that the fracture of Becket's at Canterbury at five o'clock on December 29, 1170, was the magnet which drew most visitors to the town; and it is equally certain that the church in which Becket was murdered in the glorious choir of Conrad (the Prior, not the Corsair) was entirely burnt down in 1174. The early inhabitants were much annoyed at this catastrophe. They held no local inquiry according to our more modern custom, but they beat the walls and pavements of the church and blasphemed, with equally satisfactory results. After which they sent for another architect, and William of Sens appeared upon the scene. All went well with William till one day there was an eclipse of the sun, upon which he fell off a scaffolding raised for turning the vault, and found himself so extremely unwell when he got to the bottom that he had to return to France—*viâ* Dover of course.

The cathedral, in spite of these mishaps, was completed in 1184. To Becket's shrine, "blazing with gold and jewels," came amongst others, Richard Cœur de Lion, on shanks's mare—barefoot too, and from Sandwich, which seems a curious place to have come from; but Richard at the time was fresh from an Austrian dungeon, and could not be expected to know what was what, or what was the best port in his own country. After Richard came Edward—he with the long legs, who knew, as he proved in the case of Wallace, what to do with a patriot when he caught him. Edward approached the shrine with a kingly gift—with nothing more or less indeed than the crown of Scotland, which next to his own crown, which he kept on his head, was about as costly a thing as he could have thought of. At Becket's shrine knelt Henry the Fifth, "his cuises on his thigh, gallantly armed," but his beaver off on this occasion, I trust, though it was fresh from the splendid shocks of Agincourt. In 1520 Henry the Eighth knelt here with a much greater man—that is to say, with Charles the Fifth. The two young kings rode together from Dover, and entered the city through St. George's Gate. They sat in the same coach—I mean under the same canopy, and Wolsey, who was going strong at the time, was not far off. In point of fact he rode in front, which was the right place for him if intellect took precedence in the processions of the age. Canterbury looked its best, I should imagine, on that Whit-Sunday. The old streets lined with clergy in full ecclesiastical costume; the best blood of England thronging about bluff King Hal; the bluest blood of Spain acting as duly phlegmatic escort to the young monarch of Castile and Arragon, Granada, Naples, Sicily and Milan, Franche-Comte and the Netherlands, Peru and Mexico, Tunis and Oran, and the Philippines, "and all the fair spiced islands of the East."

The Chequers of the Hope, Canterbury.

Archbishop Warham met this distinguished pair at the west door of the Cathedral, and no doubt performed with due dignity the ornate duties of his distinguished office. But it was not only in such purely

Watering the Horses.

official exercises as these that this good archbishop shone. He was as good at a feast as at a reception—as he had proved sixteen years before. On the occasion indeed of his installation, which must have been a very trying time, this primate gave a foolish trifling banquet in the archbishop's palace built by Lanfranc, which, from what I can read of it, would have made some of our most redoubtable, seasoned aldermen stare, and

The Flying Horse, Canterbury.

on the morrow seek medical aid. I should not like to name the number of courses, or hint at the number of "subtylties" which appeared between each course. "Subtylties" meanwhile strike me as good. But were they good for one? That is the question! I doubt it, considering the quaint mediæval precautions that had been taken for dealing with the morrow. The high steward, the Duke of Buckingham, indeed (who served the bishop with his own hands, entered the hall on horseback, and had his own table decorated with "subtylties"), was especially prepared for ensuing fatalities. For he had the right, in recognition of his services, ot staying for three days at the archbishop's nearest manor for the purpose of being bled! So that really, so far as I can see, when our ancestors banqueted they banqueted, and looked upon apoplexy as a naturally culminating epilogue to a merry feast.

Archbishop Warham, on this magnificent occasion, had as guests the king and queen themselves, so that I suppose courtly conversation took up most of his time, and enabled him to make a show of eating while others gorged. But from this sweeping accusation I am pleased to be able to except the clergy, who fed on lampreys one and all, and withstood subtylties as they withstood all that is evil.

But the truth is that so many kings of England visited Canterbury that one becomes tired of naming them. They were all here more or less—and those who were not here ought to have been. They were all here mostly for "drams or prayers," except Charles the First, who came here to be married. He carved some pheasant and some venison for Henrietta Maria with his own royal, white, and extremely beautiful hands, and retired to rest with his royal bride in the room over the gateway of St. Augustine's College. His son was at Canterbury too of course at the time of the Restoration; but with the second Charles's connection with the Dover Road I have already fully dealt.

The mention of St. Augustine's College reminds me of a more famous Canterbury seat of learning. The King's School was established by Henry the Eighth at the Dissolution. It possesses a Norman staircase which is quite unique, up which Christopher Marlowe, who was educated here, must often have passed, rebellious more generally than not I suspect, and having the lowest possible opinion of his instructors. And after Marlowe, and some distance behind him, comes Lord Justice Tenterden, who was on the contrary a very studious and grateful boy—so much so that in after life and with all due solemnity he used to declare "that to the free school of Canterbury he owed, under the Divine blessing, the first and best means of his elevation in life." The future judge's grandfather used to shave people for a penny in a small shop opposite the west front of the cathedral. And the last time the good judge came down to Canterbury he brought his son Charles with him,

The Rose, Canterbury.

and showed him the spot, and read him a small homily, which Charles I hope digested.

It will not be forgotten that Canterbury as a cathedral town was graced for a short but stirring period in his life by the presence of Mr. Micawber. "I am about, my dear Copperfield," he wrote, "to establish myself in one of the provincial towns of our favoured island (where the society may be described as a happy admixture of the agricultural and the clerical) in immediate connection with one of the learned professions." Which connection it will be remembered led the writer into the society of Uriah Heep, which society led him into that painful slough of despond which compelled him to describe himself as a "foundered barque," "a fallen tower," and "a shattered fragment of the temple once called man."

We all know, I should hope, how the great man rose superior to this lamentable state of affairs—how in this very town of Canterbury, supported by David Copperfield and Traddles, he bearded Heep in his den, "or, as our lively neighbour the Gaul would have it, in his bureau;" how with a perfect miracle of dexterity or luck, he caught the advancing knuckles of Uriah (bent on ravishing away the compromising document) with a ruler, and disabled him then and there, remarking at the same moment, "Approach me again, you—you—you Heep of infamy, and if your head is human I'll break it." All these great landmarks of literature are to me as it were everlasting mile-stones on the old Dover Road, and I but mention them to fix their site.

Fifteen miles or so separate Dover from Canterbury. Near Bridge, which is about five miles on, lived Hooker, to whom the living of Bishopsbourne was given in 1595. Hooker's library and the sanctity of his life were so remarkable that travellers to Dover in those days turned off the road to improve their minds and eyes; after which they ascended Barham Downs, a very windy plateau about four miles long, where many people have gathered together in a highly nervous state, from the days of Julius Cæsar to that less distant period of history when Napoleon's camp threatened Kent and Christendom from the opposite heights of Boulogne. To name two instances of martial gatherings out of many between these whiles: King John's army of 60,000 men was encamped here in 1213, when Philip Augustus thought of invading England, but thought better of it afterwards, and left the business to his son; and after

John's days, in the time of Henry the Third, the Downs were turned temporarily into an armed camp by Simon de Montfort, who hourly expected a visitation from Queen Elinor of France. A less martial spectacle was to be witnessed here on the 10th of May, 1625, when Henrietta Maria, on her way from Dover to Canterbury—on her way to

"*Springing 'em.*"

church in fact—selected Barham Downs as the scene of her first drawing-room—and a very draughty drawing-room it must have been. Low dresses and plumes were however not *de rigueur* in 1625, in addition to which the court ladies who were present to pay their respects to their sovereign were provided providentially with a tent. After which nothing much occurred on Barham Downs till the muster

M M 2

for Napoleon's invasion already mentioned, except wind and snowstorms, and frantic struggles of overdue mail coachmen to make up lost time, by "springing" tired cattle, and the stopping of mail coachmen so struggling by a gentleman named Black Robbin, who rode a black mare and drank a great deal meanwhile at a small inn between Bishopsbourne and Barham, whose sign still perpetuates his name.

And so into Dover, which is seventy-one miles exactly from the Surrey side of London Bridge, and bears very few traces about it now of the Coaching Age, either in its inns or its atmosphere. Attacked on two sides by the demon steam—by land and by sea, with steam packets roaring at one end of the pier and tidal trains at the other, the very memories of old-fashioned travel seem to have folded their wings and fled. There is no touch perceptible of the Dover of 1775—of the Dover, that is to say, of Mr. Jarvis Lorry and the old Dover Mail. Where is the drawer at the Royal George who opened the coach door "as his custom was"? Who used to cry into the ears of still half-awakened passengers the following programme of peace "Bed room and breakfast, sir? Yes, sir! That way, sir. Show Concord!" [The Concord bed-chamber was always assigned to a passenger by the Mail.] "Gentleman's valise and hot water to Concord. (You will find a sea-coal fire, sir.) Fetch barber to Concord! Stir about now there for Concord;' and so on. Where is this drawer now to be found at Dover, I ask? Where is Concord, with its vision of comfort and a sea-coal fire? Where is the Royal George indeed? Its place is no longer known among Dover inns —or it may be the Lord Warden Hotel, for aught that I know.

And the customs of the inhabitants have as much changed of course as the sea view of their town. Dover no longer "hides itself away from the beach, or runs its head into the chalk cliffs like a marine ostrich; nor do the inhabitants stroll about at the dead of night and look seaward; particularly at those times when the tide made and was near flood." Or if they do they are looking for a Channel Steamer, and no for smuggled brandy. Nor do small tradesmen with no business unaccountably realize large fortunes; nor does everybody in the town loathe the sight of a lamplighter; for the pier lamps are lighted every evening!

No! Dover and its inhabitants are indeed changed, and the only memory of the old coaching days left in the place are its long bills. Long I regret to say they were. Long they remain; and long no doubt

A Roadside Inn, Hollingbourne.

they will remain so. A sea-port cannot be the exodus of an empire without some such natural tendency to extravagance.

Of the coaches on this Dover Road I have refrained from speaking, not because I was reserving the best thing till the last, but in point of fact for an exactly opposite reason. An indisputable authority on the subject tells me that, considering its importance as the principal route for travellers between England and France, there were not many coaches

Mote House, Ightham.

The Chapel.

running on the Dover Road. I fancy that most people who had the wherewithal and wanted to catch a packet when the tide set, posted, and congratulated themselves. Mr. Jarvis Lorry I know was not amongst this number, but then he travelled by the Dover Mail, which was always an institution, kept good time, and carried in its day historic matter.

Fatherly Advice.

Of the other coaches on the Dover Road I shall make no mention. For once in the way, a catalogue will not be missed, especially when that catalogue, if made, would contain no sounding names in coaching story, would register no records in the way of speed, catastrophes, or drivers especially cunning, sober, or drunk. Yet one coach besides the Dover Mail on this road I will mention, because next to the Mail it took high rank—in some estimations a rank above it; because with its coachman in its best days, I have had the pleasure of shaking hands. Yes! I have shaken hands with a classic coachman! No tyro he when

The Chequers, Tonbridge.

coaching was the fashion, but an artist to the tips of his fingers—one of the old school, whom I have heard described, by one who knew them well, as Grand Gentlemen; parties capable of giving *Fatherly advice* to bumptious pretenders—parties who at the end of a trying journey, &c., over heavy roads took their ease at their inn with an air, disembarrassed themselves of their belchers, and sat down to a pint of sterling port.

Yes, in Mr. William Clements, who still enjoys a hale old age at Canterbury, I have chanced on a type now almost extinct, and which another generation will only read of in descriptions more or less fabulous, and wonder whether such people have ever been. Mr. Clements, who still takes a sort of paternal interest in those revivals of the coaching age which delight our millionaires during the prevalence of what we are pleased to call our summer months, lives in a snug house of his own, surrounded by memories of his former triumphs. A duchess might envy the Chippendale furniture in his drawing-room, and the bow window commands an extensive view of a rambling block of buildings which in days gone by housed the treasures of a choice stud.

As I listened to this man, it seemed to me that I came into direct personal contact with the very genius of coaching days and coaching ways—felt the impulse which throbbed in the brains of our ancestors to be at the coaching office early to book the box seat: sat by the side of a consummate master of his craft; was initiated in an instant into all its dark mysteries of "fanning," "springing," "pointing," "chopping" and "towelling." I went through snowdrifts, I drank rums and milk; hair-breadth escapes in imminent deadly floods were momentary occurrences; I alighted at galleried inns; waiters all subservient showed me to "Concords" in all quarters of the empire. I revelled in the full glories of the coaching age in short in a moment! For had I not touched hands with its oldest, its most revered representative?

The Green Man, Waltham.

VI.—THE YORK ROAD.

THERE were two main roads to York in the old coaching days. The first of these was measured from Shoreditch, and went by way of Ware, Tottenham, and *Waltham;* Hatfield and Stevenage; the second was measured from Hicks's Hall, and went by way of Barnet. At the Wheatsheaf Inn at Alconbury Hill, down in Huntingdonshire, these two roads to York became one and the same road; but the Ware route was four miles one furlong the shorter of the two.

When we want to go to York now we breakfast at half-past eight, if we are wise, and catch the ten o'clock Scotch express from King's Cross. Our grandfathers did not breakfast at all; not because they had no appetite at half-past eight, but because they had to start from High Holborn at half-past six.

According to the faculty, early rising is a healthy thing, yet I have known it bring strong men to their bier ; and besides, however enjoyable, though perilous, it may be in summer, I think that few of us care to leap from our beds at half-past five on a raw January morning.

Yet this is what our ancestors had to do who wanted to catch one of the crack northern coaches.

Shall we follow them in the spirit on one of these ghastly expeditions ?

Our coach—we will take the Regent for choice—starts at 6.30 from the George and Blue Boar, but we are not there yet. We are in bed in Berkeley Square, Marylebone Lane, or where you please.

Our sleep has been fevered with grim visions of the coming strife. It is broken by a loud knocking at the outer door, as in *Macbeth.*

Our servant, who has overslept himself according to immemorial receipt, now comes to tell us that it is half-past five, and that the hackney coach ordered overnight to take us to the coach office is already at the door.

Unless on these occasions you ordered a hackney coach overnight, you were utterly undone.

We now use strange words, and ask what sort of a morn it is. We are told that it is foggy, and we soon see that it is yellow. We have thoughts of not going to York, but we recollect that we have already bought our ticket. At the same time knocking from the hackney coachman below tells us that time flies.

We now fly into our boots and hat and other things. A horrible attempt at preparing breakfast has been made in the interval by the penitent valet; an impromptu effort in the way of a dingy table-cloth, a tea-urn, a loaf and a pat of butter, which causes us to shy on one side, as a thoroughbred shies at a traction engine. We seize our portmanteau, and hurry out into the eager morning air. The eager morning air is yellow, and in it the hackney coachman, his horse, his coach, our servant, who helps us in, all look supereminently the same colour.

In the fulness of time we arrive at the George and Blue Boar, Holborn. On his legal fare being tendered to the hackney coachman, he throws down his hat and offers to fight us for five shillings. We decline the stirring invitation and hurry into the inn yard. All here is bustle and animation in a sort of half gloom.

The Stamford Regent stands ready for her flight; four chestnuts with a good deal of blood about them seem anxious to be off; ostlers making noises after the manner of engines letting off steam in underground stations, are giving the finishing touches to the toilet. Afar off in a dim doorway the celebrated Tom Hennesy draws on his gloves, and says sweet nothings to a pretty housemaid, with her black hair out of curl. Ostlers are thrusting luggage into the boot. The boot seems to have an insatiable appetite for luggage. It swallows everything that is thrown at it, and makes no sign. The two inside passengers now appear upon the scene. One of them is an Anglo-Indian, who has whiskers brushed as if by a whirlwind, a voice like a bull, and a complexion in harmony with his surroundings. A sort of Jos Sedley going to York. The other is a lady of uncertain age, who wears her hair in curl papers, and pretends to a rooted antipathy to travelling alone with a man. This antipathy she communicates to the guard in a faded whisper. The guard grinning all over his face communicates this faded whisper to the Bengal Civil Servant. He receives it with matutinal curses.

"Confound it, sir," he roars, "then let her ride outside."

With which he hurls himself into the coach. From this point of vantage he shakes his fist at a wretched native in a turban, who, safely out of distance, salaams till his head almost touches the coach court-yard, and confesses that he has indeed omitted to provide the Sahib with his umbrella.

While a terrific volley of objurgations in Bengalese pours from one door of the coach, the lady with the faded manner enters it by the other. At the same time the incomparable Tom Hennesy languidly mounts

Filling the Boot.

on to his box. He chews a piece of sweet lavender given by the pretty housemaid—assumes the whip as a marshal does his *bâton,* and darts a deathly glance over his left shoulder at the lingering fair. "Let 'em go," he says, "and look out for yourselves." The ostlers fly from the chestnuts' heads—the four horses spring up to their collars—the guard performs "Oh, dear, what can the matter be?" on his bugle in a manner which would elicit an enthusiastic *encore* at an evening concert, and we are out of the coach-yard almost before we know it, stealing down Holborn Hill with that "fine fluent motion" which De Quincey described as characteristic of the Bristol Mail—but which indeed could be experienced on any crack coach which was finely driven.

An Old Corner, Smithfield.

And Tom Hennesy is a master of his art. His manner on the box—all great artists are mannerists—is so calm, so quiet—as to be almost supercilious. But he has to keep a sharp look-out, for he is driving through Egyptian darkness. The weather indeed reminds us of Homer's Hell; and as for the cold, it would make a snipe shiver in an Irish bog. Up Cow Lane we steal, through Smithfield. The wheelers appear like phantom chestnuts; the leaders are hardly seen; the houses on each side of the way loom grim and ghostly. And through the gloom the Stamford Regent steals along, like some ghost of a coach itself. We on the box seat feel like unembodied joys. We have already lost the use of our hands and feet. Deep draughts of yellow fog complete our discomfiture.

Suddenly shouts are heard ahead, and large herds of cattle throng the streets; they seem to spring out of the foul air as everything does besides, but they come from Smithfield of course, or are going there. Drovers—looming phantom-like, like everything else, prove by a graceful flow of expletives that they are after all, but men. Our near side leader now mistakes a strayed bullock for some monster of mythology and swerves on one side after the manner of Balaam's ass, upon which our coachman, who has up to now sat perfectly upright with hands still, the very statue of an accomplished charioteer, immobile as fate, turns his wrist under, and lets his thong "go" in such a way that the near side leader's hind leg is nearly severed from his body. Which duty done Tom Hennesy remarks "that there are some of 'em as never could hit a horse." And we feel, almost as poignantly as the near side leader has done, that he Tom Hennesy is not to be included in the category.

And now the Peacock at Islington (where in old days "The Queen's Head," pulled down in 1829, was the topping tavern, with its wood and plaster walls, its three stories projecting over each other in front, its porch propped by Caryatides)—and now the Peacock at Islington begins to loom through the fog. Or rather the horn lantern of the old ostler, whose province it is to stand outside the inn and announce the names of the coaches as they drive up to the door, with the voice of an asthmatic trumpet. All the northern coaches made a point of stopping at the Peacock, on their way north; though why they did so I have never been able to discover. The fact remains that there were twenty or more drawn up at a time here at seven o'clock in the morning. And such an outcry attending their arrival, such a clattering of hoofs, clanging of bugles, slamming of doors and stamping of feet on splash boards, as never was heard, well, out of Islington; and through all this din the raucous voice of the ostler continuously sounds, like the cry of a mediæval herald with a cold in his head announcing the entry of distinguished competitors to a tournament. And he announces famous names though they are recognized as such no longer. They made our fathers' blood boil at times if we are to believe De Quincey. These names—the York High-

The Queen's Head, Islington.

flyer, the Leeds Union, the York Express, the Stamford Regent, the Rockingham, the Truth and Daylight—made our fathers' blood boil as these famed coaches carried northwards the heart-stirring news of Vittoria, or of Waterloo! But times are changed—such national telegrams (when we have them to transmit) are transmitted silently and decorously, by the telegraph. There is no advertisement possible in the way we travel now, except on the walls of railway stations—and of this latter form I regret to say Mr. Ruskin does not approve.

But to return to ourselves and the Stamford Regent. The announcement of the Truth and Daylight coach makes us hope that we too, shortly, may see the sun. We see it in due course, as our steaming team breasts the ascent to Highgate archway. The sun springs lurid from a cloud of yellow mist. The great city lies before us, the coverlet of the fog but half withdrawn from her disturbed sleep. The dawn from Highgate is doubtless a grand sight. But it unfortunately inspires my next neighbour

The Two Brewers, Ponders End.

on the box seat with the idea that he is a Constable—this always occurs. He determines to paint the salient landscape—this always occurs too. I ask Tom Hennesy at what point we may discern the bourn of the next public house. He says that the Green Man at Barnet is the first change, and expatiates on the soothing joys of rum and milk as applied to a constitution that has relished a winter's dawn breakfastless. The Green Man at Barnet is now to me like the star, seen, or not seen, by the mariner, and in due course I see it, and alight at the first opportunity. But not before Tom Hennesy. In front of the Green Man at Barnet his languidly sedate manner goes. For here too, alas!

for the historic inconstancy of coachmen! he is a great favourite with the fair. Looks quite the coaching Lothario, as he lounges against the

At the Cross Roads.

bar, his beaver adjusted rakishly, his melting glances fastened, now on his next team already fuming in the traces, now on the Barnet Hebe as hopelessly, alas! in the toils.

"Take your seats, gentlemen, please."

And Barnet is soon a memory on the great north road. A memory however which shows some claim to "recollection dear", fixing as it does the site of a great battle, and of a highwayman's exploits, which have occupied almost the same space in history—I mean fiction —No! I mean history. To come to details:—On Hadley Green, half-a-mile to the north of the town, was fought on a raw, cold and dismal Easter Day, in the year 1471, the famous battle between the Houses of York and Lancaster which ended in the death of the king-maker, and established Edward IV. upon the throne; and behind an oak tree, which still stands opposite the Green Man at the junction of the York and Holyhead Roads, the immortal Dick Turpin used to sit silent on his mare, Black Bess, patiently waiting for some traveller to speak to. The battle has been celebrated by Lord Lytton in *The Last of the Barons*, perhaps as fine an account of a mediæval "set to" as can be found out of Scott. The noble author lived at Copped Hall, near Totteridge, and often used to pay visits to the scene. The Highwayman has been immortalized by Harrison Ainsworth. Did he not write in one night's sitting the whole series of chapters—I don't know how many there are—should not like to say how many there are not—in which is set forth in such stirring form the celebrated ride to York? Certainly he did, and Macaulay as certainly denied that such a thing ever took place, according to the invariable practice of Whig historians, who are always heavy when they handle volatile matter.

And Turpin's ride to York reminds me that there is another road to it, besides the one I am on; namely the road by Ware, which, according to the prophet Ainsworth, Turpin took, though why he should have gone to Ware when he was already in Barnet is a matter which will ever remain one of conjecture to the curious. I think however that we will follow this Ware route for a few miles, just to get us clear of London, when I shall go off the York Road, so far as its history is concerned, and tell

The George and Vulture, Tottenham.

The Bell, Edmonton.

here of some great northern coachmen, and some great northern catastrophes.

The York Road then, which goes by way of Ware, runs through Shoreditch, Stoke Newington, Stamford Hill to Tottenham, and so into Edmonton, through which place John Gilpin, Esq., passed at the rate of sixty miles an hour. The world has made itself acquainted with that famous ride. But now Edmonton gains as much fame perhaps from having been the residence of Charles Lamb as from Cowper's humorous poem.

A few miles further on and we are at Enfield Highway, and in the neighbourhood of that celebrated Chase where once our kings and queens used to disport themselves, but where now the jerry builder and the credulous agriculturist who believes in small holdings labour day by day. James I. was here hunting on an extremely wet day, on his royal progress up to London, and curiously, as it seems to me for such an acute sportsman, was much disconcerted by the showers. I had thought that a southerly wind and a rainy sky realized the hunter's ideal; but I suppose that James's padded saddle got wet, certain it is that he broke up the hunt long before he had a chance of breaking up the stag, and retired to London in the worst of moods. And I hope the Earl of Northumberland, who rode on his right hand, and the Earl of Nottingham who rode upon his left, properly appreciated their positions.

The first of the Stuarts (so far as England is concerned) was in Enfield Chase again in 1606, but he had a better time on this occasion. He was entertained at Theobalds by Cecil, and was in the company of a first-class boon companion in the person of the King of Denmark. These two often, I apprehend, woke the night owl with a catch in Cecil's lordly halls, which the King already had his eye upon. They passed into his possession shortly afterwards by a process of exchange and mart similar to that advocated in our society journals. Cecil gave up Theobalds for Hatfield; and I am not sure that he had the worst of the bargain.

I read that when the Princess Elizabeth was residing at Hatfield in charge of Sir Thomas Pope, Enfield Chase used to be favoured a good deal too with that prospective royal presence. The future Queen of

England always knew what a wardrobe meant, and carried her love of finery with her to the hunting field; to the considerable disgust I should say, of her twelve ladies in waiting, who found themselves pursuing

The Falcon and the Four Swans, Waltham.

the flying hart, arrayed in white satin, and seated on ambling palfreys.

Fifty archers, too, had to be careful what they had on their backs (though details as to trimming of tunics is not given); but they had gilded bows in their hands, and scarlet boots on their feet, and yellow caps on their heads—and presented, I should say, a sufficiently startling *ensemble*, which the stag they were after must have admired a mile off.

To leave hunting subjects behind us and get to graver matter. At Camelot Moat, situated in one of the most delightful and least desecrated parts of the Chase, is laid the last scenes of the *Fortunes of Nigel.* Here Dalgarno waited impatiently for his rival, in order that he might wipe out a long score in a quiet glade; here, as he shaded his eyes with his hands and gazed eagerly down an alley, he received a shot which, grazing his hand, passed right through his brain, and laid him a lifeless corpse at the feet, or rather across the lap of the unfortunate victim of his profligacy. A very fitting close to a consummate scoundrel's career, and in most picturesque, in almost too picturesque surroundings.

It is not however by romance alone that Enfield Chase earns fame as a trysting-place for people whose characters are doubtful. More sinister associations cling to it, associations linked with one of the most lurid episodes of a nation's history. The old house of White Webbs, which in 1570 Elizabeth granted to Robert Huicke, her physician; was pulled down in 1790. A portion of the grounds of Middleton, however, still marks its site; and its position about a mile to the left of Enfield Wash, going north, gives to my gossip about the great roads of England its first batch of conspirators, in the authors of the Gunpowder Treason. For here, at this lonely house, then in the middle of Enfield Chase, nearly all the actors in the dark catastrophe, imminent at Westminster, at one time or another gathered. Over and over again the ten miles between Enfield Wash and London must have rung to the sound of their horses' hoofs, as they rode fiercely through the night—always through the night we may well believe—between White Webbs and London. That Catesby was here ten days before the meditated explosion is evident from Winter's confession:—

"Then was the parliament anew prorogued until the fifth of November, so as we all went down until some ten days before, when Mr.

Catesby came up with Mr. Fawkes to an house by Enfield Chase, called White Webbs, whither I came to them, and Mr. Catesby willed me to inquire whether the young prince came to the parliament; I tolde him I heard that his grace thought not to be there. 'Then must

The Green Dragon, Cheshunt.

we have our horses,' said Mr. Catesby, 'beyond the water, and provision of more company to surprise the prince, and leave the duke alone.'"

That a more important factor in the deadly design—if the latest judgment of posterity is to be believed—even than Catesby himself was frequently at the old house in Enfield Chase is shown in the examination of James Johnson; that is to say in the examination of Guy Fawkes.

It was stated by him that the place had been taken of Dr. Huicke by his master, Mr. Meaze, of Berkshire, for his sister, Mrs. Perkins (*alias* Mrs. Ann Vaux); that Mrs. Vaux had spent a month there, and mass had been said by a priest whose name deponent did not know.

And as Mr. Meaze, of Berkshire, was none other than Henry Garnet, the Provincial of the English Jesuits, the importance of the testimony becomes apparent. And the fact gives birth to a fancy. It is interesting to me to think that Mr. Meaze, of Berkshire, with his candid blue eyes, his fair curling hair, his polished, courteous manners, his form tending to an *embonpoint* by no means suggestive of asceticism; it is interesting to me, I say, to think that Mr. Meaze, of Berkshire, may have been a well-known and respected figure about Enfield Wash. That he may have been recognized as Father Garnet, for the first time as he stood absolutely under the beam on that May morning—"the morrow of the Invention of the Cross"—on the great scaffold at the west end of old St. Paul's; that he may have been recognized there by some Enfield yeoman, who had ridden in from Enfield to see the show, little expecting to see in the last victim, in the most distinguished of all the victims perhaps, to a justly outraged justice, the courteous, handsome stranger, whom he had so admired and respected down in his quiet Enfield home!

And here I shall leave the historical part of the great north road and take to coaching. Of the great Tom Hennesy, with whom we have already made a driving acquaintance, an anecdote may first be told. The scene of it is laid of course on the Barnet route to York, on which route the great Tom drove. Between Hatfield and Welwyn then, Tom aforenamed nearly got into hot brandy and water. And in this wise—A young gentleman, named Reynardson, who in the matter of coaching

P

was at quite an early age a devotee, and has lived to write a book of his various experiences *Down the Road,* was seated at Tom Hennesy's side on one of his numerous journeys from London to Huntingdon. He—the young gentleman—burned as usual to be Jehu. Upon which Tom Hennesy, who seems to have been an extremely agreeable and vivacious box companion, said "Now then, sir, you must take them a

The Roebuck, Knebworth.

bit." Mr. Reynardson did not refuse the contest. Far from it. He changed seats with Mr. Hennesy, "took them a bit," and all went well between Hatfield and Welwyn. Arrived at this place (where the coach changed horses) Tom Hennesy remarked that he had better take them down the hill. And why did he think it necessary to depose his young *protégé* at the very apex of his triumph? Because he had the fear of a "three-cornered old chap named Barker" before his eyes. "Who would kick up a devil of a row if he saw you working!" Thus spoke Tom Hennesy, with great disrespect to the proprietor of the White Hart at Welwyn who horsed the coach. Thus he spoke and prepared to take the reins from the unwilling hands of the unwilling neophyte when lo! he looked ahead and saw the very "three-cornered old chap" spoken of advancing up the hill to meet them. The situation was now summed up in three words, "Here's a go!" At the same time Mr. Hennesy disdained to attempt disguise at a time when disguise was useless, and told Mr. Reynardson to drive on and not look at him—by him meaning Barker.

Perhaps he hoped to escape by a quick change at the inn below. But not so. Before the fresh horses had been put in, entered to them Mr. Barker, not wearing upon his face the most pleasant expression in the world. In fact it was so unpleasant that Tom saw that it meant mischief, and adopting the method prescribed by the best pugilists "opened fire" at once. In point of fact he remarked "Good morning, Mr. Barker, sir! Did you ever see a young gentleman take a coach steadier down a hill?" Mr. Barker showing no immediate inclination or capacity for answering this question, the glib Tom continued, "'Pon my word, sir, he could not have done it better. He's a pupil of mine, and I'm blessed if he didn't do it capital! Don't you think he did, sir, for you seed him?"

What could the three-cornered Barker answer to this appeal? Nothing! And this is practically what he answered, muttering something about "against the rules," and "don't do it again." And so Tom and Mr. Reynardson got off very lightly from what might have been, had it not been less directly handled, an awkward dilemma—and Tom should have been grateful to Barker for once. But his gratitude, I am sorry to say, did not take a very grateful form. "Well, he was wonderful civil for him," he said as soon as they got off. So far so good, but now comes the fall. "But as I said before he's a cross-grained, three-cornered old chap at the best of times, and if I could only catch him lying drunk in the road, I'd run over him and kill him, blessed if I wouldn't"—and then comes the cause of so sanguinary an indignation—"What business had he to be walking up the hill? I suppose he thought he should catch me shouldering."

And "shouldering" in the tongue of coachmen and guards meant taking a fare not on the way-bill and unknown to the proprietor.

A Coachman's Courtship.

This same Tom Hennesy had a celebrated whip—it was a crooked one—and in his practised hands inflicted deadly execution on lagging wheelers, and on leaders given to dropping going down declines, on coach horses meriting justice generally. But perhaps the most remarkable thing about this whip was that it was not Tom Hennesy's own.

No! He had "conveyed it", as the wise call it, from a brother coachman, whose weakness it was to borrow stray whips with no fixed intention of returning them.

The end of this accomplished artist in his own line—clearly, from what I can learn, one of the most distinguished box figures on the first eighty-nine miles out of town of the great north road—is melancholy in the extreme to contemplate. But it is typical at the same time of the remorseless destiny forced on men who were really fine men in their way by the Nemesis of a new invention. It is a marvel to me when I read the record of their fall that stage coachmen did not form themselves into an amalgamated society, with branches everywhere, for smashing locomotives. Never surely was such a fall seen since the days of Lucifer, who is rather out of fashion, as the fall of the great stage coachmen before the demon steam. The observed of all observers at one moment! In another, heeded by no one; buried away in obscure corners of out-of-the-way counties; driving 'buses; hanging about inn-yards, where formerly their very footfall produced clumsy reverences from drunken postboys; melancholy, blue-nosed phantoms of their former selves. Seldom surely has there been so cruel a revolution!

The Falcon, Huntingdon.

Why, this man Tom Hennesy, the dandy of the Stamford Regent!

the knight of the crooked whip, the adored of barmaids, the idol of schoolboys, horsily inclined, for eighty-nine miles of the finest coaching road in England, came down from mere natural force of circumstances —circumstances in a real sense over which he had no control—to what? To driving a two-horsed 'bus from Huntingdon to Cambridge.

Nor is the hope permitted that others of his craft as distinguished as he, fared better at the end of laborious lives when fortune should have shone kindliest upon their efforts. John Barker indeed—the Daniel Lambert of the north road—not a swell coachman, but as strong as the man of Gath and as safe as the Bank of England, was saved the painful experience of seeing his empire ravished away from him by the Great Northern Railway Company; but he was only saved from this humiliation by a mortification setting in after an accident to his right foot, and what the ultimate fate of Cartwright was, and what the last engagement of Leech, I scarcely like to consider. Yet few, not excepting even Hennesy, could show greener laurels than they.

For the first of them, Cartwright—who drove the York Express from Buckden to Welwyn and back—about seventy miles every day—was described by Peter Pry in the *Sporting Magazine*, and Peter Pry knew what he was describing, as almost everything that a fine coachman should be—"under fifty years of age, bony, without fat, healthy looking, evidently abstemious; moreover not too tall, but just the proper size to sit gracefully." So much for a general view! And to descend to detail—"His right hand and whip were beautifully in unison;" at which point Peter Pry appears to me to rise into the regions of metaphor in the description of his favourite. But he continues his eagle flight undaunted.

"Cartwright's perfections," he cries, "end not here! His manner of treating his leaders is equally fine. His system is stillness, and to drive without using the whip; his personal equipment, not that of a dandy, but modest, respectable, in confirmed good taste."

Well this it seems to me is the description of an artist's salient traits—the sort of critical effort which we expend now on young actors who bound upon the stage without experience; on authors who write African romances without having read their Dumas! And I could quote twenty more examples of a coachman's fine points as carefully considered,

Huntingdon Bridge.

had I the space to do so or the inclination. Cartwright's great rival, to take one instance, has been as carefully weighed in as crucial a balance and not found wanting. He drove the Edinburgh Mail from Stamford to Doncaster, about seventy-five miles. Not so polished a man as Cartwright quite; but of his method—quietness itself. Under his urbane direction, no hurry, no distress, no whipping, the pace ten miles an hour, including stoppages seemed nothing to do. And a team of four bay blood mares did this nothing from Barnby Moor to Rossiter Bridge in exceptionally gratifying style.

Peter Pry in this neighbourhood, or, to speak more accurately, in the neighbourhood of Sutton, was witness of a local custom from Leech's box-seat which filled him with an ingenuous surprise. This was the annual offering of extremely indigestible firstfruits to guards and coachmen, not excluding passengers, by the honest-hearted farmers and cottagers of the roadside.

When I say that upon a tray covered with a beautiful damask napkin, plum cakes, tartlets, gingerbread, exquisite home-made bread, and biscuits, profusely appeared, my readers may understand what sort of a digestion was needed to cope with them on a May morning after sundry rums and milks. The deadly list however is not concluded; ales, currant and gooseberry wines, rounded the homicidal whole; ales and currant wines only more instantaneously fatal from the pleasing appearance which they presented in old-fashioned glass jugs embossed with jocund figures.

But was Peter Pry's figure jocund after he had partaken? "Eat and drink you must," he says. "I tasted all." Wretched man, let him describe in directly simple words his own miserable subsequent state! "My poor stomach," he writes, "not used to such luxuries at eleven in the morning, was in fine agitation for the remaining fifty miles of the ride."

And who can say justly that this agitation was to be wondered at!

It must not be thought however that perils such as these, springing from an unreasonable hospitality were the only perils to be encountered in the coaching days on the great north road. Catastrophes abound in the record; and this very Stamford Regent which I have been speaking of used frequently to get into cold water when the floods were out and the weather rainy.

Mr. C. T. Birch-Reynardson who has much to say about the northern

A Morning Draught.

coaches in his *Down the Road*, commemorates one of these contingencies, which occurred in this wise—At a place called St. Neot's, fifty-six miles from London, the Regent coach used to leave the main road, every now and then, for some reason which remains occult, and go round by some paper mills, which were naturally situated on the flat. The river Ouse has a habit, as is well known, of playfully overflowing its banks, and the consequence was that the road lying before the Regent coach lay sometimes for half a mile under water. Now an extra pair of leaders were put on, and ridden by a horsekeeper, who made the best of his way through a situation which was novel not to say precarious. The water was often up to the axle-trees; and on the particular occasion of which Mr. Reynardson writes, went beyond this limit and invaded the inside of the coach. For a moment or two the Stamford Regent was afloat, also two old ladies who were inside of it, with their goods and chattels. Their cries and laments when they found the coach gradually being converted into an Ark were heartrending in the extreme. They gave themselves utterly for gone, and prepared for the most comfortable, but noistest of all deaths. Nor were the outside passengers in very much better plight. For though they were not sitting absolutely in the water, as I am sorry to say the old ladies were; still they were sitting in wet clothes, which is the next thing to it—and in this situation commanded as fine a prospect of water above, below, and around, as has been seen by travellers I should say since the flood. In addition to this not altogether gratifying panorama of flood effects, unseen dangers were on every side; to wit, a large ditch on one side, and a series of huge heaps of stones on the other; both pleasantly invisible by reason of the great waters, but both clearly there for a specific purpose; the stones to overturn the coach; the ditch to receive it when it had been overturned. It must have been a truly critical five minutes for the Regent, Tom Hennesy, the passengers, the horses and everybody else, but they all got safely through and thanked their stars.

At Wandsford, thirty miles or so further down the road, this same coach nearly came to an overturn without the aid of water, through the combined efforts of a smart set of red roans who were fit for any gentleman's drag, a young coachman too full of valour, and a very awkward, old and narrow bridge. The roans were fresh, and declined to face it. The coachman (young Norval, I mean young Percival, was his name) dropped into them. Upon which the roans committed themselves to a succession of sudden antics, too rapidly consecutive to be followed. What principally followed however was that in the twinkling of an eye the people on the Regent coach found themselves once more at the door of the Haycock Inn. A place of entertainment which they had a moment previously left, but with this radical change in the general position of affairs. The horses' heads pointed to London instead of to Stamford.

Young Percival having no explanation to offer as to how such a phenomenon could have occurred, handed the reins to old Barker, much to the relief of the outside passengers, who had seldom felt so like humming tops in their lives, and by reason of the altitude at which they had been set spinning, were feeling very low in their minds. And old Barker, safe as the Bank of England, as he always was, quieted the four roans, and negotiated the bridge without further revolution of anything, except wheels.

And here I think that I may leave the coaching side of the York Road. When I leave it, I leave by no means the most important or the most picturesque side of its story. I have still something to say of the York Road's grand inns, as fine specimens of their class of building as are to be found anywhere in England. Witness the great hostelries at Huntingdon, Stamford, Stilton, and Grantham. And these fine houses are not only interesting in themselves, picturesque as the quaint towns, of which they are the centre, but they are alive with history, fragrant with memories of those good old times, when the Mail performed the whole 199 miles in two days and three nights, if God permitted, and complaints were made about so extraordinary a velocity, which had caused several intrepid travellers on reaching London to die suddenly of an affection of the brain.

But before I deal in detail with the York Road's great inns, I think that a ride over the distance will be advisable, if only to give some sort of idea as to how the land lies. And we have been in coaches and Flying machines so often, that I think that a turn on horseback may

Bridge at St. Neots.

be a welcome change. And so I propose to go to York with Dick Turpin, though he was pronounced by Macaulay to be a myth.

I find then, on referring to the prophet Ainsworth, that Dick Turpin started for his celebrated ride from the Jack Falstaff at Kilburn—an inn I do not find in my Paterson's *Roads*. Here, after having regaled a cosmopolitan company with several flash chaunts, generally prefaced by some such remark as "Let me clear my throat first! And now to resume!" the gallant Turpin's impromptu oratorio was interrupted by the rapid entrance of those who—"in point of fact' wanted him. Upon which he "got to horse" upon his mare Black Bess, shot his friend Tom King by mistake (who observed to a lady opportunely standing by him, "Susan, is it you that I behold?")—and then rode off to the crest of a neighbouring hill, whence a beautiful view of the country surrounding the metropolis was to be obtained. Here his bosom suddenly throbbed high with rapture; he raised himself in the saddle, and prefacing his declaration with a profanity, said that he would do it. And by "it", he meant his ride to York.

He at once shaped his course for "beautiful, gorsy, sandy Highgate." No doubt he would have admired the scenery more (he was a great admirer of scenery was Turpin, and that is one reason why I am going with him to York) if "the chase had not at this moment assumed a character of interest"—whatever that may mean. Turpin however saw nothing favourable in the phenomenon, and made over Crackskull Common to Highgate. He avoided the town, struck into a narrow path to the right, and rode leisurely down the hill. His pursuers at this point somewhat aimlessly bawled to him to stand—seeming to forget in their flurry that he was on horseback. The gallant Dick answered their demands by unhesitatingly charging a gate, and clearing it in gallant style. He then scudded rapidly past Highgate, "like a swift-sailing schooner with three lumbering Indiamen in her wake." And so through Du Val Lane —(what tender recollections must here have possessed that manly breast) into Hornsey—where the turnpike fellow closed the toll-bar in his face, and the "three lumbering East Indiamen" (the metaphors here become a trifle mixed—but no matter) cried aloud, "The gate is shut! We have him! Ha! Ha!"

But not so! though the old Hornsey toll-bar was a high gate, with *chevaux de frise* in the upper rail! Not so! though the gate swung into its lock; "and like a tiger in his lair the prompt custodian of the turnpike, ensconced within his doorway, held himself in readiness to spring upon the runaway." Not so! For what did Dick do? He did four things.

1. He coolly calculated the height of the gate.
2. He spoke a few words of encouragement to Bess.
3. He stuck spurs into her sides.
4. He cleared the spikes by an inch.

The next event which followed in this order, was the narrow escape of the toll-bar keeper, who, tired of crouching like a tiger in his lair,

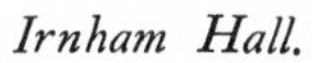

Irnham Hall.

rushed out of it, and was nearly trampled to death under the feet of the three lumbering East Indiamen—that is to say under the feet ot Paterson's (chief constable of Westminster's) horse.

"Open the gate, fellow," he (Paterson) cried.

But the man said "not at all" unless he got his dues. He'd been done once already; and he was prepared to be struck stupid if he was done a second time. By which ingenious block, while Paterson was feeling in his pocket for a crown piece, our friend Richard was enabled to take advantage of the delay and breathe his mare—after which he struck into a bye lane at Duckett's Green, and cantering easily along came at Tottenham (four and a half miles from London), for the first time in his ride, into the Great North Road.

At Tottenham the whole place was up in arms. The inhabitants shouted, screamed, ran and danced. They also hurled every possible missile at the horse and her rider. And what did Dick do under these

Driving to Catch the Mail.

sufficiently embarrassing circumstances? Why, he "laughed at the brick-bats that were showered thick as hail and quite as harmlessly around him." After which he proceeded at his best pace to Edmonton (seven miles from London). Here too, as at Tottenham, the ingenuous natives turned out to a man to see him pass. But they did not throw brick-bats at him: far from it! They supposed that Dick was riding for a wager, and received him with acclamations. But now came borne on the wind's wings the pursuers' ominous cries, "Turpin! Dick Turpin!" upon which in an instant the good Edmontonians ratted, and hissed; and no toll-gate, twelve feet high, with *chevaux de frise* in the upper rail, being handy, a man in a donkey cart, somewhat ostentatiously drew himself up in the middle of the road. And Turpin went through the usual formula above categorically set down "and cleared the driver and his little wain with ease." This feat brought down the house or rather the street. "Hark-a-way, Dick!" resounded on all hands.

Pursued and pursuers, I now observe with pain (for a change of metaphor is always embarrassing), "fly past scattered cottages along the Enfield Highway" (nine and a half miles from London) no longer "like a swift-sailing schooner with three lumbering Indiamen in her wake," but "like eagles on the wing." To descend from these aerial regions to the hard high road—they were all going well and strong. Coates's party not having lost ground, but perspiring profusely, Black Bess not having turned a hair. It was at this period in the journey, somewhere about Waltham Cross, that is to say, that Dick said, "I'll let 'em see what I think of 'em," and turned his head. This was surely an unnecessary step. But the lighting of the pipe, while Black Bess was still at full stretch, was a worthier effort in the way of showing contempt, and caused one of the enemies who pursued, whose name was Titus, who rode "a big Roman-nosed, powerful, flea-bitten Bucephalus," to call out on his "mother who bore him," and thump the wind out of his horse with his calves. Shortly after which extraordinary manœuvre the pursuers lost sight of Turpin altogether, till, encouraged by a waggoner's assurance that they would find the great highwayman at York, they caught a glimpse of him just outside Ware (twenty-one miles from London measured from Shoreditch Church), standing with his bridle in his hand coolly quaffing a tankard of ale.

Here the pursuers changed horses, either at the Bull or the Fox and Hounds, and again "pursued their onward course. Night now spread her mantle over the earth; still it was not wholly dark. A few stars were twinkling in the deep, cloudless heavens, and a pearly radiance in the eastern horizon heralded the rising of the orb of night," after which atmospheric eccentricities, it appears to me that we had better get forward as quickly as possible—as Turpin did. Whether from the atmospheric eccentricities already alluded to, or from some occulter cause, peculiar physical symptoms might at this moment have been detected in Turpin himself, had a medical man been riding by him armed with a stethoscope. His blood "spun through his veins; wound round his heart; and mounted to his brain." Where it next went to is not on record; but the possessor of this peculiar circulation went "away," away! Hall, cot, tree, tower, glade, mead, waste, woodland, and other etceteras to travel are seen, passed, left behind—vanish as in a dream. To be plain, Turpin rode as hard as he could, I suppose, through Wades Mill, Puckeridge, Buntinford, Royston, till the limits of two shires have already been passed, and as he surmounts the "gentle hill that slips into Godmanchester," he enters the confines of a third country—in point of fact the merry county of Huntingdon.

The Fox and Hounds.

"The eleventh hour was given from the iron tongue of St. Mary's spire as he rode through the deserted streets"— of Huntingdon, which, as Huntingdon is fifty-eight miles and three-fourths from London, and as Turpin left the metropolis at seven o'clock, shows a record I believe of nearly sixty miles in fo r hours.

I am sorry for one thing that Turpin did not stop in Huntingdon, because in the George he would have found a very fine inn there; but I suppose he heard his pursuers behind him, for he was gone like a meteor almost before he had appeared. Shortly afterwards he found himself surrounded by dew-gemmed hedges and silent, slumbering trees, also with broad meadows, pasture-land, drowsy cattle, and low-bleating sheep.

The George, Huntingdon.

"But what to Turpin at that moment was Nature, animate or inanimate?" It was nothing! He was thinking only of his mare—and of himself. And here I am sorry to say the light-hearted highwayman fell almost into the weeping mood at the mawkish thought that no bright eyes rained their influence upon him; no eagle orbs watched his movements; no bells were rung; no cup awaited his achievement; no sweepstakes; no plate. But at about Alconbury Hill, sixty-four miles from London, where the two roads to York meet, he recovered himself happily from this degraded dejection—asked himself what need he had of spectators, reminded himself that the eye of posterity was upon him, and midway between Alconbury Hill and Stilton (the intersecting dykes, yawners, gullies, or whatever

Down the Hill on a Frosty Morning.

they are called, beginning to send forth their steaming vapours) burst suddenly from the fog upon the York stage coach.

It being no uncommon thing for the coach to be stopped, the driver drew up his horses. Turpin at the same moment drew up his mare. I had always hoped that he was going to leap over the York coach too! But no! An exclamation was uttered by a gentleman on the box-seat—"That's Dick Turpin!" he exclaimed. The name of Turpin acted like magic on the passengers, according to advertisement. One jumped off behind; another having projected a cotton nightcap from the window drew it suddenly back. A faint scream in a female key issued from within; there was a considerable hubbub on the roof; and the guard was heard to click his horse-pistols. All which preliminaries having been adjusted, two horse-pistols having been discharged point-blank without any outward and visible effect, and some violent dialogue having been

St. Mary's, Stamford.

carried on between Dick and a Major Mowbray, who was perched on the box-seat of the coach, relating to an obscure and wicked baronet resident somewhere in Sussex, the York mail went aimlessly on its way to London, and Turpin rode through Stilton (which is a place I shall have a great deal to say about in a minute), through Norman's Cross, through Wansford turnpike gate, till eighty odd miles had been traversed, and the boundary of another county, Northampton, passed, when he deemed it fitting to make a brief halt.

He drew up, it will be remembered, at a small hostelry with which he was acquainted, bordering the beautiful domain of Burleigh. "Burleigh House by Stamford Town" that is to say. Here he called for three bottles of brandy, a pail of water, a scraper, a raw beefsteak, and other adjuncts to the toilet. Which order having been executed, the most sedulous groom could not have bestowed more attention upon the horse of his heart than Dick Turpin now paid to his mare. He performed, in fact, a complete variety entertainment of strange tricks common to ostlers, concluding the display by washing Black Bess from head to foot in the diluted spirit; not however, I am glad to be able to say, before he had conveyed a thimbleful of the liquid to his own parched throat. The effect of these blandishments on Black Bess may better be imagined than described—"her condition was a surprise even to Dick himself." Her vigour seemed inexhaustible, her vivacity not a whit diminished, and suddenly "she pricked her ears and uttered a low neigh."

"Ha!" exclaimed Dick, springing into his saddle; "they come!"

A very short time after having made which remark, Dick Turpin and his mare were "once more distancing Time's swift chariot in its whirling passage o'er the earth," in which agreeable exercise Stamford (89 miles from London) and the tongue of Lincoln's fenny shire on which it is situated, are passed almost in a breath. Rutland is won and passed and Lincolnshire once more entered. The Black Bull on Witham Common used to mark the borders of the counties, and at the same time the hundredth milestone from London.

At about this point of the journey Dick's blood was again on fire. "He was giddy as after a deep draught of kindling spirit." This disagreeable symptom passed off, my readers will be glad to learn—"yet the spirit was still in the veins"—"the *estro* was working in the brain." Subject to this somewhat complicated condition of circulation is it surprising that Dick gave vent to his exaltation in one wild prolonged halloo? or that Bess, catching the spirit of an example so contagious, also bounded, leaped, and tore up the ground beneath her? And so "as eddying currents sweep o'er its plains in howling, bleak December," the pair pass over what remained of Lincolnshire—left the town of

Calling for the Squire's Mailbag.

Grantham (110 miles), to which I shall also return in a moment or two, behind them, and in due course, that is to say when they had covered another mile and three quarters, they were rising the ascent of Gunnerby Hill. From here there is a fine prospect—on the right Lincoln Minster, and on the left Belvoir Castle. The prospect however which interfered so far as Turpin was concerned, with these scenic surroundings, took the form of a gibbet on the round point of hill which is a landmark to the whole plain of Belvoir: and to complete the disillusionment, two "scarecrow objects covered with rags and rusty links of chains depended from the tree." I need not mention I hope that on being confronted with this *coup de théâtre* prepared for him on a highway, Turpin looked up

Newark Castle.

with an involuntary shudder, and remarked, "Will this be my lot, I wonder?" any more than I need recount with detail the immediate springing from beside a tuft of briars that skirted the blasted heath, of a crouching figure who observed, "Ay, marry, will it." Such facts in romances are every-day experiences, without the aid of which their surprising worlds would not go round. Besides, such matters have nothing to do really with the ride to York. Time also presses—as the novelist almost immediately afterwards remarks—and we may not linger on our course.

With a view of obviating which undesirable contingency the prophet Ainsworth proceeds to pass full forty miles in a breath of the Great North Road, and having left Dick admiring highwaymen hung in chains on Gunnerby Hill, just out of Grantham, proceeds to pick him up again as he rides through Bawtry, which is 153 miles from London, as measured from Hicks's Hall, and is also where the Great North Road enters Yorkshire. But it may be well to mention that before Turpin got

The Crown, Bawtry.

to Bawtry he went through Newark, $124\frac{1}{4}$ miles from London, and $2\frac{1}{2}$ miles over the Nottinghamshire border—past Scarthing Moor inn (a posting-station in old days, but where is it now?), through Tuxford, where the Red Lion was a famous inn in the coaching days—now as the Newcastle Arms, and posting-house not unknown to fame—and so on past East Retford and Barnby Moor inn $147\frac{3}{4}$ miles from Londcn to the bourne where we left him.

And from Bawtry the roads to York diverge—the main and mail road going by Doncaster, Ferrybridge, and Tadcaster into our terminus: the lower road going by Thorne, Selby and Cawood. And Turpin took the lower road. And here the first signs of calamity began to overtake him. His mortal pursuers seem long since to have abandoned all idea of performing this feat. One of them named Titus, was resting like a wise man at the Angel at Grantham—having had as he poetically remarked, "a complete bellyful of it," the rest were pursuing still no doubt —but nearly a county separated them from their prey. Yes, it was at such a crisis of affairs, when all promised to end prosperously for Richard

Making the Yard Ring.

Turpin, Esquire, that, as I say, calamity began to overtake him. As he was skirting the waters of the deep-channelled Don, Bess began to manifest some slight symptoms of distress. This was bad enough; but it "was now that gray and grimly hour ere one flicker of orange or rose has gemmed the East, and when unwearying Nature herself seems to snatch brief repose." Under such a depressing condition of affairs, I cannot wonder for my part, that Bess's slight symptoms of distress were communicated to her master, and that our gallant highwayman began to feel extremely low in his mind. "Hope forsook him, the reins also forsook his chilled fingers, his eyes, irritated by the keen atmosphere, hardly enabled him to distinguish surrounding objects,"—and it was owing probably to this latter circumstance that Bess suddenly floundered and fell, throwing her master over her head. Turpin instantly recovered himself.

But his practised eye soon told him that Black Bess was in a parlous plight. Her large eyes glared wildly. "She won't go much further," said Turpin, "and I must give it up! What! . . . give up the race just when it's won? . . . No! . . . That can't be . . . Ha! Well thought on!"—with which he drew from his pocket the inevitable phial, without which romances could never be brought to their end. "Raising the mare's head upon his shoulder, he poured the contents of the bottle down her throat"—and lo! in the twinkling of an eye he was once more at a gallant pace traversing the banks of the Don and skirting the fields of flax that bound its sides!

Snaith was soon passed, and our hero was well on the road to Selby, when dawn put in an appearance with the usual accompaniments of sparrows twittering, hares running across the path, and mists rising from the earth. It became extremely foggy, and Turpin, I am sorry to say, was so weak as to be influenced by the climate and became foggy too.

He became aware of another horseman riding by his side. "It was impossible to discern the features of the rider; but his figure in the mist seemed gigantic, neither was the colour of his steed distinguishable." And Dick having taken note of these phenomena, came somewhat hastily to an amazing conclusion. "It must be Tom," thought he; "he is come to warn me of my approaching end. I will speak to him."

But why Tom? Indeed it was not Tom at all as Turpin discovered by and by when the atmosphere had become clearer. "Sir Luke Rookwood by this light!" was the exclamation which sounded the depths of this conundrum and proved the grim personage who rode at our hero's right hand to be none other than the obscure and aimless baronet, resident somewhere in Sussex, and already mentioned in the encounter with the York Mail.

After a brief mysterious dialogue with this mysterious and aimless personage, principally dealing with such fanciful subjects as oaths, affianced

Bootham Bar, York.

brides contracts sealed with blood or not sealed, as the case may be, Turpin rode down to the Ferry at Cawood—189½ miles from London. Nine miles only separated him from his goal. But the ferryman accidentally happened to be on the other side of the river, and at the same moment a loud shout smote his ear—(Turpin's ear, not the ferryman's). This shout was the halloo of the pursuers. The only thing to be done now was to ford the river, and this Dick Turpin did. Once on the other side, he had a fresh start—in other words, "Once more on wings of swiftness" Black Bess bore him away from his pursuers. But Major

Mowbray, who was one of them, saw that all this parade of victory was only an expiring flash. "She must soon drop," he observed. Bess however held on past Fulford—"till the towers of York (199¼ miles from London) burst upon him in all the freshness, the beauty and the glory of a bright clear autumnal morn. The noble minster, and its serene and massive pinnacles, crocketed, lantern-like, and beautiful; Saint Mary's lofty spire; All Hallows' tower, and architectural York generally, to make a long list short, beamed upon him; shortly after which another mile was passed; shortly after which Dick shouted "hurrah!" shortly after which Black Bess "tottered—fell. There was a dreadful gasp—a parting moan—a snort; her eye gazed for an instant on her master with a dying glare; then grew palsied, rayless, fixed. A shiver also ran through her frame." And there was an end of the celebrated ride to York. And I hope that those who can believe in it will.

And now I come to a less legendary side of my subject. Turpin has taken us to York: and faster than we could have gone there in the Coaching Age—faster a good deal—but he has not stopped for us at any of the inns, and to one or two of these inns on the great North Road I wish particularly to introduce my readers. For they are hostelries in the true sense of the word, and call up even now I know not what coloured reminiscences of the full life of the Coaching Age—reminiscences of the late arrival of fagged travellers on snowy nights before ample porches, their induction thence, their immediate induction half-frozen as they were, into snug parlours adorned with prints of coaches at full gallop, revealed by the light of a fire blazing half-way up the chimney; —reminiscences too of table comforts considered prodigious in these degenerate days—with good liquor to round the story, and a dreamless sleep between lavender-scented sheets.

The scenes of such comfortable hours spent by ancestors long since buried, still throng the now almost deserted reaches of the Great North Road; and some of these old inns, situated in places through which the northern railways pass, still live, careless of the changed condition of things, and tender the same hospitality to passengers alighting from the Great Northern Railway, as they used to tender in days gone by to passengers alighting from the Great York and Edinburgh Mail. At Stamford, for instance, the George still stands where it stood, though with main entrance altered—a huge reservoir in itself (had its record

The George, Stamford.

been in some way or other preserved) of a whole sea of travel continually ebbing and flowing between the Metropolis and the North. Royalty itself was entertained at this house in the person of Charles the First. The King slept here on his way from Newark to Huntingdon on August 23, 1645. And besides royalty, who I should like to know, can tell the list of its distinguished guests in all branches of all the arts, either of war or peace? Walter Scott was frequently at this house on those numerous jaunts of his up to London, when he was a welcome guest at the Prince's table—a valiant bottle companion and entrancing *raconteur*—always the same genial, kindly gentleman of genius, though not known yet as the author of surely the most delightful novels in the world. To pass from the pen to the sword, at this house stayed the Butcher of Culloden on his way up to London : and I do not doubt that the George's best Burgundy flowed in red seas down fierce gullets in loyal celebration of that shameful shamble. But, as I have said in another place, the list of distinguished visitors at such great hostelries on the main roads of

Stamford Town.

England, must be looked for in the letters and diaries of four generations. All were here we may be well assured, at such noted halting-places on the main artery of travel between two countries—all and of every rank, in a motley assemblage of confused travel—kings, queens, statesmen, highwaymen (the North Road about Stamford was celebrated for these gentry), generals, poets, wits, fine ladies, conspirators, and coachmen.

All were in such houses as this George at Stamford at one time or other in the centuries, and ate and drank, and robbed, or were robbed, and died, and made merry.

But if so much can be said, and indeed it is no exaggeration to say so much about the inn at Stamford, the great inn at Grantham twenty miles further north should be able to claim even a fuller tide of story. For the celebrated Angel at the latter place, now much resorted to by hunting men and women who can start from its doors to meet about four packs of hounds, is nothing more nor less than one of the three mediæval hostels remaining in England. And this means a good deal if one comes to think of it. It means, indeed, the survival of the best kind of thing in its way to be seen. For a very superlative kind of comfort was needed, I surmise, after however brief an experience of mediæval roads. And if what inns there were between London and York, when people had to ride the whole distance over often impassable morasses, had not been A 1, people would not have ridden so frequently between York and London.

To give an idea of the age of the Angel at Grantham (to come to details), the Knights Templars are supposed to have been at the foundation of the whole affair. This however I think is an allegory—but what is quite certain about the place is that it was undoubtedly one of those *Maisons du Roi*, as they were called, which in days gone by, when the roads still had life in them, were placed at the special service of kings and their retinues as they passed here and there through England on royal progresses or quelling insurrections. Perhaps indeed as well-known an historical event as can be chronicled—(not an important historical event because they are as a rule not well known)—took place in the three fine sitting-rooms, which were then one room, over the entrance gateway of this celebrated inn. For here, on October 19th, 1485, Richard the Third signed the death warrant of the Duke of Buckingham. This in itself is an appetizing fact to an imaginative traveller. It is not often I fancy that one can smoke the pipe of peace under a floor which creaked four hundred years ago to the unequal strides of a hunchbacked and irritable

The Angel, Grantham.

king. I thought I heard Richard's voice myself when I was last at Grantham, and the beautiful moulding in the oriel window of the Angel smoking-room gave life to the illusion.

It will be seen then perhaps from what I have said, that at Stamford and Grantham are two as fine specimens of the old hostelries of the great roads of England as can be found, which, fed as they are by great lines of railway, keep a generous life throbbing in their old hearts still. But whether the inns at Grantham and Stamford are as representative of the Coaching Age in its prime, as I suppose them to be, or no, it is very certain that no place more representative of the "Coaching Age Decayed," than Stilton, is to be found on Earth.

Oriel Window in The Angel, Grantham.

For here the Great Northern Railway has diverged from the line of the old road, and by doing so has turned a vast coaching emporium into a corpse of a town—if town indeed Stilton could by any stretch of language ever have been called. It was rather, in its best days, a village clustering about two magnificent inns, the Angel and the Bell, which still stare at each other stonily across the great North Road. At the Angel, well known in the coaching days as the house of the famed Miss Worthington (stout, smiling, the christener of Stilton cheeses made miles away, but so called because they were sold at her hospitable door), over 300 horses were stabled for coaching and posting purposes. Vast barracks indeed stretching at the back of the old house—one wing of which alone is now open to travellers—tell of the bustle of post-boys, of the hurrying to and fro of fidgety passengers over-eager to be off, the harnessing and unharnessing of horses, of all the many-voiced Babel of travel in fact which fifty years ago surged and swayed round this teeming coaching centre, now lying silent and deserted as the grave. I am told—and from its central position on the great North Road seventy-five miles from

London, I can well understand the fact—that at Stilton in the old days the ebb and flow of traffic never ceased. All day coaches and postchaises continually poured into the place and out of it. And by night the great mails running from John o'Groat's almost, into the heart of London, thundered through the splendid broad thoroughfare, visible mediums as it were of an empire's circulation. And other wayfarers besides postillions and coachmen seemed never off the road—huge flocks of geese destined for the London market, and travelling the seventy-five miles with uncommon ease; enormous droves of oxen, not such roadsters born. Each beast was indeed thrown and shod at Stilton to enable them to bear the journey. And to show the huge press even of this kind of traffic, this business of shoeing oxen was a trade almost in itself, as I have been told by the present landlord of the Angel Inn, who used in his youth to do the office himself, and to whose still active memory I am indebted for most of the foregoing details.

And to cross the road (the breadth of the great North Road at Stilton at once seizes the imagination, it is royal, the breadth of it, and looks like the artery of a nation), to cross the road from the Angel, and to come to the Angel's great rival, the Bell, is to bridge a whole period in the history of English travel; to pass in twenty yards from the age of crack coaches and spicy teams to times long antecedent, when Flying Machines were not; when the great roads were hazily marked over desolate heathy tracks; when men travelled on horseback and women rode pillion, and people only felt secure when they went in large companies; when solitary travellers went in fear of their lives when the gloaming overtook them, and "spurred apace to reach the timely inn."

The date of Charles the First's execution is to be seen on one of the gables of the Bell. But this dream in stone must date far further back than 1649 (when no doubt a slight restoration was here commemorated), must date far back I should say into the early days of the Tudors; must have seen much of the gorgeous life of that period of pageant pass and repass its hospitable doors. There is an inn at Tuxford, sixty-two miles further on the road to York, which stands on the site of an old house called the Crown, which must very greatly have resembled the Bell at Stilton. I make mention of it here because some of the Crown's history has been preserved, and the Bell must have had as full and very similar a record. To this Crown then at Tuxford (it

Courtyard of the Bell, Stilton.

was destroyed by a violent tempest in 1587) came Margaret Tudor on her journey to the north. "She was met by the vicar and churchmen near where the rebel stone is now standing, the bells rang merrily till midnight, and large fires kept burning in the market-place." The Virgin Queen slept in the room over the south-east angle, and proceeded on her journey on the early morning of July 12th, 1503. All the neighbours of the place came in on horseback, and a great train of persons on foot to see the Queen at her departure from the town. These all fell into the procession and the minstrels commenced their avocations and "played right merrily." Having descended the hill, they again with difficulty

"Can I have a Night's Lodging?"

began to ascend. The road at that period was anything but a road, and but barely passable even at that period of the year. Having arrived at the summit, the towers of Lincoln Minster presented their noble proportions in the distance, whereupon honour was done to this ancient temple of Jehovah. The whole *cortége* stopped as with one consent, and

Johannes and his company, the minstrels of music, and the trumpeters again made the welkin ring with their notes of praise, and the thanksgiving of the goodly company. Passing down the hill onward to Markham Moor (then consisting of only a few thatched cottages scattered here and there) the procession left what is now the route of the Great North Road, and proceeded through West Drayton, up to near Ecksley, the bells of which church merrily welcomed the daughter of the King of England. Passing slowly and heavily across the forest on the Old London Road, the cavalcade arrived at Rushey inn, then a noted resting-place for travellers, and an agreeable retreat from the gnats and flies, which then infested the ling, gorse and furze on each side the margin of the road as far as the eye could reach. In due course Margaret Tudor arrived in Edinburgh, August 2nd, and was married August 8th, 1503.

The Sign of The Bell, Stilton.

Here is a picture of mediæval travel such as I think must have often been witnessed from the windows of such old houses of entertainment as the Bell at Stilton, when the Tudors ruled England. And often sterner episodes of history must have passed beneath its magnificent copper sign than wedding processions of royal princesses, even in those days, when England was called merry, and was merry England indeed. During the year 1536 the Bell at Stilton was no doubt often visited by one of those medley cavalcades so common at the time, consisting of abbots in full armour, waggon-loads of victuals, oxen and sheep, and a banner borne by a retainer on which was worked a plough, a chalice and a Host, a horn, and the five wounds of Christ—the well-known badge which marked the fiery course of the Pilgrimage of Grace. This great rising which began in Lincolnshire ran much of its course along the Great North Road—who knows how much of it passed through the now-deserted rooms and corridors of the great Northern inns such as this Bell at Stilton! It was in an inn at Lincoln at all events that on a night of October there was present a gentleman of Yorkshire whose

The Bell, Stilton.

name (Robert Aske) a few weeks later was ringing through every English household in accents of terror or admiration.

But indeed standing before such a monument of days gone by as this is, it is not a question of this or that romantic episode rising to a fanciful man's mind as the pageant of a whole nation's history passing in a sort of ghostly procession. And what episode of that pageant, or of such part of it at all events as passed on the Great North Road, has not this great deserted house of entertainment seen, fed, sheltered within its now crumbling walls? Gallants of Elizabeth's day, Cavaliers of Charles the First's, Ironsides on their way to Marston Moor, Restoration Courtiers flying from the Plague. And in days more modern, King's messengers spurring to London with the tidings of Culloden—and

Cumberland himself fresh from his red victory, and the long line of Jacobite prisoners passing in melancholy procession, their arms pinioned behind them, each prisoner's horse led by a foot soldier carrying a musket with fixed bayonet; each division preceded by a troop of horse with drawn swords, the drums insulting the unhappy prisoners by beating a triumphal march in derision.

Why, scenes beyond number such as these must have passed before the long gabled front of this old Bell at Stilton; passed, faded, been succeeded by hundreds more stirring, which in their turn too, vanished like some half-remembered dream. And the old house still seems to keep some mysterious memory of these scenes locked in its old withered heart; as gaunt, ghost-like, deserted, but half alive, it stares night and day on the lonely North Road.

A Quaint Bay,
St. Albans.

VII.—THE HOLYHEAD ROAD.

THE history of the New and Direct Road to Holyhead by St. Albans, Redbourn, Dunstable, Brick-hill, Towcester, Dunchurch, Coventry, Birmingham, and thence to Shrewsbury, begins, as I read its record, two hundred years before the Holyhead Mail showed fair claim to be one of the fastest coaches in England, or the Shrewsbury Wonder's supreme punctuality regulated the watches of dwellers on the roadside. It is true that in November, 1605, roads as we now understand them did not exist; but this same route, or at all events tracks across uninclosed heaths, even then connected the above-mentioned places with each other and the capital, and marked the shortest way for those riding post to reach Northamptonshire, or the Counties beyond its borders.

Early then in the November of 1605, certain elaborate preparations which had been made for rapid travelling between London and Dunchurch, 80 miles down in Warwickshire was the common talk of ostlers and loafers at the chief posting-houses at St. Albans, Dunstable, Towcester,

U

and Daventry. At each of these places a Mr. Ambrose Rookwood, a young Catholic gentleman of fortune, well known on the road for his splendid horses, had placed heavy relays. The heaviness of these relays excited continual discussion. The confused rumour of the tap-room, fed by chance travellers on the road, decreed presently that these heavy relays were to carry Mr. Ambrose Rookwood down to a great hunting party, to be shortly assembled at Dunsmoor. But when this hunting party was to take place, no one seemed to know, or why the young Catholic gentleman should have made such elaborate preparations to reach it so hurriedly.

And so the few intervening days passed till the 5th of November, 1605, dawned grayly over London — amidst torrents of driving rain and wild gusts of a west wind which had gathered strength as the night waned, and by daylight had grown into a hurricane—dawned on a city distracted. Narrow streets were already crowded with excited groups, who whispered, gesticulated, at street corners. Some men but half dressed rushed from their houses as if the rumour of some monstrous imminent doom had startled them suddenly from sleep. Others with drawn swords in their hands counselled all men to arm in one breath, and, as now and again a woman's shriek rose above the press cried in another, that there was no cause for fear. Consternation was everywhere,—but no fixed rumour prevailed. Only each man eyed his neighbour suspiciously, only a vague feeling as of some nightmare had seized upon London that the past darkness had brought forth a portent.

In the dim twilight of that November dawn Mr. Ambrose Rookwood, the young Catholic gentleman, whose relays of fine horses had excited such discussion on the North-western Road—came out into these distracted streets, in company with a friend—one Mr. Thomas Winter. The two gentlemen walked aimlessly here and there for some time, listening attentively to all that was said on all sides, now joining themselves to a group and adding questions on their own part, to the sort of universal interrogatory which prevailed—now shuddering and passing, on their way quickly as the unformed phantom of the people's fear began to grow gradually into defined shape. Then as if fearful any

At the Stable Door.

longer of uncertainty, they made with extraordinary coolness towards the Parliament House.

The sun had not yet risen; but in the middle of King Street, Westminster, the two found a guard standing. Permission to pass was peremptorily refused. Then as Mr. Rookwood's friend stood parleying with the guard a white-faced citizen passed by hurriedly, exclaiming in panic-stricken tones, "There is treason discovered! And the king and lords should have been blown up."

The two gentlemen turned without a word, and made for their horses. The heavy relays on the North-western Road were now to be put to their proper use. But great caution had to be exercised. The appalling news had circulated in the city with the rapidity of poison

Saddling Up.

Barricades were being hastily erected at the ends of the streets; passengers were being stopped and questioned; any appearance of hurry would have led to instant arrest. It was eleven o'clock therefore before the two gentlemen got clear of London—and they were but just in time; for rumours were already in the air of a proclamation forbidding anybody to leave the town for three days. Once clear of London they rode desperately.

Few incidents I think in history seize the imagination so forcibly, as that wild flight of the Gunpowder Conspirators northward. Thomas Winter made for his brother's house at Huddington in Worcestershire; but Rookwood rode fiercely down the North-western Road to bear the fatal news to the conspirators already assembling on Dunsmoor. Catesby, Piercy, John and Christopher Wright were he knew on the road in front. But the relays already placed for him, and the desperate fear which urged him forwards enabled Rookwood to overtake the others as they were rising the ascent at Brickhill.

In a few words he told them what had happened in London—that Fawkes had been arrested and lodged in the Tower—that at any moment torture might make him give up their names—that the whole scheme had fallen through, and that their only chance of safety lay in instantly joining their friends. From this moment the flight became a stampede. "They devoured the ground," shouting as they rode through startled towns and villages that they were carrying despatches from the King to Northampton, flinging off their large cloaks, heavy with the rain that still poured remorselessly, that they might add wings even to their precipitate flight. Rookwood rode thirty miles in two hours on one horse. At six in the evening the fugitives arrived at Catesby's house at Ashby St. Ledgers, about three miles from Daventry. They had ridden the eighty miles from London in seven hours.

Here after a brief consultation with Robert Winter, who was staying in the house (it still stands in all its gloomy suggestiveness, this home of England's most desperate conspirator), they rode off hastily on the same tired horses to join Sir Everard Digby and the pretended hunting gathering on Dunsmoor Heath which the direct road to Holyhead still crosses at the eighty-fifth mile-stone from London.

Their further wild course through Warwickshire to Holbeach on the Staffordshire border calls here for no telling, as it is no longer associated with the Road. But so intimately associated with the Gunpowder Treason does the way to Holyhead seem that though its history is closed so far as the directest route is concerned, the earlier

Catesby's House, Ashby-St.-Ledgers.

route by Chester has another link to add to its story. A short distance from Newport Pagnell (fifty-one miles from London), stands Gayhurst,—the fine Elizabethan house once the home of Sir Everard Digby. Of him a sympathetic historian writes, "His youth, his personal graces, the constancy which he had exhibited whilst he believed himself a martyr in a good cause, the deep sorrow which he testified on becoming sensible of his error, seem to have moved all hearts with pity and even admiration; and if so detestable a villainy as the Gunpowder Plot may be permitted to have its hero Everard Digby was undoubtedly the man."

The gray walls of his beautiful Buckinghamshire home were indeed witnesses at all events of some of the most suggestive incidents in the heart-quaking scheme. Fawkes was a frequent guest here—meditating through the prolonged rains which heralded the approach ot the destined day, on the state of the powder, by now safely placed under the Parliament House; riding to and fro frequently from London; often an unexpected, always a welcome guest. From Gayhurst, besides, set out that Pilgrimage to St. Winifred's well, in Flintshire, the motive of which was so much discussed after the discovery of the Conspiracy. Motives apart however, what is more important from my point of view is that the company of about thirty persons—all relations of the conspirators; some of the actual conspirators among these, travelled in coaches—proceeded by Daventry to John Grant's house at Norbrook, a fine, melancholy, moated manor once (where is it now?), thence to Robert Winters, at Huddington, and so to Flintshire by Shrewsbury.

The fact that the pilgrims travelled in coaches brings me by quite a natural stage from the historical to the coaching side of the Holyhead Road. And it was from all I can learn the coaching road *par excellence*. Celebrated, thanks to the immortal Telford, for its 260 miles of superb surface, so masterfully laid down that, though the last 107 miles from Shrewsbury to Holyhead ran through mountainous country, no horse was obliged to walk, unless he particularly wished it, between Holyhead and London; celebrated too for its coachmen, a long list of historic names shining calmly through many a story of poles snapped; coaches overturned in the twinkling of an eye; runaway teams nearing closed toll-bars; desperate races for a slight pre-eminence, ending in desperate collisions;

Seeing them Off.

celebrated consequently and finally for its time records, which never were beaten.

Not even on the Exeter Road by the Quicksilver or the Telegraph.

For though the former covered the 175 miles between London and Exeter in eighteen hours, and though the latter covered the 165 miles in seventeen hours, yet on the Holyhead Road, the Holyhead Mail, which ran through Shrewsbury, was timed at ten miles and a half an hour through the whole journey, including stoppages; while the celebrated

Through the Toll-Gate.

Wonder did the 158 miles between London and Shrewsbury in fifteen hours and three quarters; and the Manchester Telegraph, travelling some distance at all events on the Holyhead Road, did the 186 miles in eighteen hours eighteen minutes, leaving the Bull and Mouth at five in the morning, reaching the Peacock, Islington, at 5.15., and Northampton at 8.40, where, according to Mr. Stanley Harris, twenty minutes were allowed to eat as much as you could, with tea or coffee (of course too to hot drink).

And I think that the performances of these last two coaches are so remarkable that I cannot emphasize them more firmly than by here subjoining their respective time-bills; voiceless proclamations these of great feats in the past, pasted long since most of them into the scrap-books of old-fashioned travel, or hanging in melancholy neglect and astounding frames on the smoke-begrimed walls of once celebrated posting houses.

Here then is the time-bill of the Wonder coach from London to Shrewsbury:—

Despatched from Bull and Mouth at 6.30 *morning.*

„ „ *Peacock, Islington, at* 6.45 *o'clock.*

Proprietor.	Place.	Miles.	Time Allowed.	Should Arrive.
			H. M.	
Sherman . . .	St. Albans	22½	2 3	8.48
J. Liley . . .	Redbourn	4½	0 25	9.13
	(Breakfast)	—	0 20	—
Goodyear . . .	Dunstable	8¼	0 48	10.21
Sheppard . . .	Daventry	29¾	2 54	2.15
Collier	Coventry	19	1 47	4.2
	(Business)	—	0 5	—
Vyse	Birmingham	19	1 39	5.46
	(Dinner)	—	0 35	—
Evans	Wolverhampton	14	1 15	7.36
	(Business)	—	0 5	—
	Summerhouse	6½	0 35	8.16
J. Taylor . . .	Shifnal	6½	0 35	8.51
H. J. Taylor .	Haygate	8	0 43	9.34
J. Taylor . . .	Shrewsbury	10	0 56	10.30
		158	15 45	

And here the time-bill of the Manchester Telegraph :—

Leave Bull and Mouth at 5 *a.m.*
,, *Peacock, Islington, at* 5.15.

Proprietor.	Place.	Miles.	Time Allowed.	Should Arrive.
			H. M.	
Sherman . . .	St. Albans	19½	1 54	7.9
Liley	Redbourn	4½	0 22	7.31
Fossey	Hockliffe	12½	1 10	8.41
	Northampton			
	(Breakfast)	—	0 20	—
Shaw	Harboro'	47½	4 30	1.31
	Leicester			
	(Business)	—	0 5	—
Pettifer . . .	Loughboro'	26	2 27	4.3
	Derby			
	(Dinner)	—	0 20	—
Mason	Ashbourne	30	2 48	7.11
Wood	Waterhouses	7½	0 43	7.54
Linley	Bullock Smithy	29½	2 46	10.40
Wetherall & Co.	Manchester	9	0 50	11.30
		186	18 15	

Desperate travelling this! But by no means representing solitary records of sustained speed on these fine North-western Roads. By no means. For the Mail to Holyhead *viâ* Chester (the old route), though not keeping the same pace as the Mail from London to Holyhead *viâ* Shrewsbury, still did its nine miles and a half an hour, including stoppages, travelling on not nearly such good roads too, and by night; while on May Day, 1830 (May Day being the great day for coaches to race against time, some of them with that object in view carrying no passengers), the

Saracen's Head,
St. Albans.

Independent Tallyho, running between London and Birmingham, covered the 109 miles in seven hours thirty minutes—a feat which altogether beats the record in Coaching Annals; though on May Day, 1838, "the Shrewsbury Greyhound came a good second by travelling the 153 miles two furlongs at the rate of twelve miles an hour, including stoppages. And as an irreproachable coaching authority represents that eleven miles an hour, including stoppages, stands for galloping at least the greater part of the way, an easy calculation may be made as to what extent the coachmen of the Tallyho "sprung their cattle."

Flying Machines these, indeed! Of a different kind though to those which in the year of Grace 1742 had already made the North-western Roads famous for headlong speed, when the Oxford Machine used to leave London at 7 a.m. (the weather, Providence, and a variety of other factors permitting), arrived at Uxbridge (fourteen miles seven furlongs) from Tyburn turnpike at midday, and at High Wycombe (twenty-eight miles seven furlongs) at 5 p.m., where they inned for the night, and proceeded desperately to Oxford next morning. Nor when George the Second was king was the Manchester Telegraph of 1836 without a prototype. For it came to pass in 1754 that a company of Manchester merchants, having considered how Time flew, and to what a degree the success or non-success of commercial speculation coincided with the flight of Time, bethought them how most nearly in their passage to and from London they might fly themselves. To which end they started a new sensation called a "Flying Coach." And they carefully put forward in a well-weighed prospectus the claims of their invention to the title, stating that there was no nonsensical pretence about the thing this time, but that in point of honest fact they seriously contemplated running their machine at the accelerated speed of five miles an hour; and that however incredible it might appear, the coach would actually, barring accidents, arrive in London four days and a half after leaving Manchester!

To set out ourselves on the roads on which these prodigies were perpetrated, it may be well to state at this point that there were three routes to Holyhead in the prime of the coaching days; firstly, the direct and old road, *viâ* Chester, and measured from Hicks's Hall, going *viâ*

Barnet, St. Albans, Dunstable, Hockliffe, Woburn, Newport Pagnell, Northampton, Hinckley, Tamworth, Rugeley, Nantwich, and Chester; secondly, the road measured from Tyburn Turnpike, and going *viâ* Southall, Uxbridge, Beaconsfield, High Wycombe, Oxford, Woodstock, Chapel House, Shipston, Stratford-on-Avon, Henley-in-Arden, and Birmingham; and, thirdly, the new road ("new old" though, as it turns out) *viâ* Barnet, St. Albans, Dunstable, Brickhill, Stony Stratford, Towcester, Daventry, Dunsmoor, Coventry, Birmingham, and thence to Shrewsbury, as route No. 2, *viâ* Wednesbury, Wolverhampton, Shifnal, Haygate, and Atcham.

It was this latter route which was taken by the Wonder, the Holyhead Mail, and other crack coaches; and it is on this route that I purpose to travel, permitting myself as heretofore the graceful licence of running off it, on to one of its branches, whenever the desirability of a change suggests itself, or an anecdote or an accident calls for diversion.

And the accidents on the North-western Road begin early; before indeed, it branches from the great North Road, which it does, or did, at Barnet Pillar (the stone put up to commemorate the celebrated battle), six furlongs beyond Barnet town. But as I say the first casualty to be noticed on the North-western Road occurred before this spot is reached, so near to London indeed as Finchley Common (which is about a mile and a half beyond Highgate Archway), though the cause of the accident, the first cause, originated at a place called Redbourn, twenty-one miles down the road. And in this wise: Owing to an obstruction below Dunstable—in point of fact to heavy snow-drifts—four or five coaches started together thence. They all went at a fair pace, not racing, but passing each other at the different stages, till they reached the Green Man at Finchley, where according to immemorial prescription the four coachmen alighted for a drink, or rather for four. And now "a change came o'er the spirit of the scene." In other words, one "Humpy," so called either from his driving the Umpire (but I hope not) or from his having a hump on his

Courtyard of the George, St. Albans.

back, which is more probable, was discovered to have taken too much spirits. For he was very noisy and shouted and hallooed at the top of his voice, though at what it is impossible to conjecture. However, the old coachman who tells the story (the same who, it may be remembered, upset his coach when driving on the Portsmouth Road, with a noise like the report of a cannon, and had consequently gained caution from experience), the old coachman, I say, suspected that something would happen. So he kept behind, and waited to see what he would see. He first of all saw one of the three coaches by a fence opposite a public-house (no uncommon spectacle on the roads I fancy). But what did he next see when he arrived himself at the public-house (sign, the Bald-faced Stag)? Why, he saw a coach lying on its side—the Manchester Umpire in fact—the coach of the too demonstrative Humpy. And things were pretty considerably mixed up with the Manchester Umpire. The forepart of the coach was broken, the luggage was scattered all over the road, also the passengers, who, thus agreeably circumstanced, improved the shining hour by bewailing their bruises and cursing the conduct of Humpy. This was rather unchivalrous of them as it turned out, thus to rail against the unfortunate; for Humpy was also on his back, perfectly helpless, "like a large black beetle," moaning and groaning most hideously, and certainly more injured than anybody else. He had indeed, with a curiously misdirected ingenuity, upset the coach upon himself, and materially injured his hip-joint. From Humpy himself therefore no explanation of how things had occurred was naturally forthcoming. But there were not wanting men unkind enough to allege that this complete turnover resulted from no more intricate a fact than that of the miserable Humpy having his leaders' reins wrongly placed between his fingers, which was done when he took them from his box-passenger, after the last, the fatal, brandy and water. The natural but very embarrassing consequence was that when Humpy suddenly discovered that he was too near the fence, he pulled the wrong rein, and there they were—on their backs in the road.

A more serious accident than this, inasmuch as one of the unfortunate passengers was killed, happened to the Holyhead Mail, a little further down the road, a mile indeed on the London side of St.

Albans. This arose from the exciting but highly dangerous pastime of racing. The Holyhead Mail, *viâ* Shrewsbury, attempted to pass the Chester Mail by galloping furiously by on the wrong side of the road. The coachman of the Chester Mail resented the indignity, and pulled his leaders across his rival's—a heap of stones conveniently placed by the roadside did the rest of the business,

The George and Red Lion, St. Albans.

and in a moment converted two spick and span turn-outs, full of passengers more or less alive and alarmed, into a mass of struggling horseflesh, splintered wood and groaning wounded. The inquest on the victim of this rivalry among coachmen was held at the Peahen inn in St. Albans, and a verdict of manslaughter was returned against both artists. Abundant subsequent opportunity was afforded them of meditating on their sins, for they were kept in irons in St. Albans for six months before they were tried at Hertford—in which town they enjoyed a further twelve months' imprisonment in the county gaol,

A snow effect is the next coaching incident to be chronicled in this neighbourhood of St. Albans, richer surely in its agreeably diversified crop of casualties than any other place in England. The North-western coaches at all events seem to have got the full benefit of the historic snow-storm of 1836. This visitation lasted the best part of a week and has never been equalled in England before or since. The drifts in some hollows were said to be twenty feet deep—which caused some passengers not unnaturally to report that they were "mountains high," and some coachmen to state that the snow in some places was higher than their heads as they sat on the box. "Never before," writes a correspondent of the *Times* of that day (quoted by Captain Malet in his *Annals of the Road*) —"never before within recollection was the London Mail stopped for a whole night at a few miles from London, and never before have we seen the intercourse between the southern shores of England and the metropolis interrupted for two whole days." In spite of which assertion I read a few sentences on "that the roads leading to Portsmouth and Poole were the only ones kept open during the storm!" Yet Portsmouth and Poole are on the "southern shores of England" surely,—and this is but one instance of the incurable slovenliness which marks the compilation of so much of coaching history—and makes the truthseeker ask what is truth, and wonder where he has got to.

For the present however we are at St. Albans, where during the prevalence of this great snowstorm of 1836, many mails and coaches remained hopelessly stuck, able neither to get up the road nor down it

—a state of affairs which must have caused many passengers to use strange words, and the landlords of the Angel, White Hart, and Woolpack to make hay while the snow fell. And some people were not so fortunate as to be stuck fast in a picturesque place where there was something to eat, as Burdett, the guard of the Liverpool Mail, was able to testify. For on Tuesday, December 27, of this memorable year, this guard from his vantage point, beheld a chariot buried in the snow and without horses, safely at anchor at about a mile on the London side of St. Albans. And he had no sooner seen it—and two elderly ladies inside it, who rent the welkin with clamorous cries for help—than he found, by being suddenly precipitated head first into twelve feet of snow, that his coach had got into a drift too. Having recovered his perpendicular, and emptied his mouth, a natural curiosity prompted Burdett to cross-examine the ladies on their somewhat forlorn position. They told him that their post-boy had left them for St. Albans to get fresh cattle, and had been gone two hours—no doubt having elected to get brandy for himself instead. Meanwhile there they were—and in a very deplorable plight surely. But will it be believed that this heart-moving vision of beauty in distress did not move the guard of the Liverpool Mail in the least! No! He proceeded stolidly in the plain path which is duty's—a fact which tends to the suspicion that the ladies cannot have been beauties. But whether they were or no, Burdett, after having heard their story, turned a deaf ear to their appeals for help. He just helped his coachman, his passengers,

Old Inn, St. Albans.

and his four horses on to their feet—(for the horses too had assumed a recumbent position)—and having extricated his mail, by the help of his tools, curses, and other expedients not mentioned in the text, pursued his journey to London, leaving the chariot and the ladies to their fate.

Twelve miles further on brought coaches in the old days to Dunstable in Bedfordshire, where the Priory Church is very fine and interesting, and where the Sugar Loaf Inn used to be celebrated for its dinners. Here follows a typical menu, to be dealt with in twenty minutes—

"MENU AT THE SUGAR LOAF, DUNSTABLE—

"A Boiled Round of Beef; a Roast Loin of Pork; a Roast Aitchbone of Beef; and a Boiled Hand of Pork with Peas Pudding and Parsnips; A Roast Goose; and a Boiled Leg of Mutton."

It sounds rather formidable; but there were such people as trenchermen in the Coaching Days.

Immediately beyond Dunstable, or, to be quite accurate, three miles six furlongs beyond it, is Hockliffe, immediately west of which place there used to be some inconveniently steep hills, greatly calculated to bring overladen coaches to grief, but which were cut down, and the valleys at the same time raised, when the new mail road to Holyhead was opened—improved and shortened by the Parliamentary Commissioners. At Hockliffe the mail road to Manchester, Liverpool and Chester branched off from the direct road to Holyhead *viâ* Shrewsbury; and at Hockliffe, on December 26th, 1836, the Manchester, Holyhead, Chester and Halifax Mails stuck fast in a snowdrift, within snowballing distance of each other —all the North-western Mails, that is to say, at one fell swoop. Report says not what happened to the Manchester and Halifax Mails, so I presume they remained where they were till the snow melted; but an attempt to drag the Chester Mail out of the drift with waggon-horses ended in the fore axle giving way and the coach being left behind.

Upon which the bags were forwarded by a post-horse—with a man on his back I presume. As for the Holyhead Mail, it was even more awkwardly situated, though I confess to not seeing clearly how such a state of things could be. However, the horses were almost buried in an attempt to pull the coach out of a drift; and the coachman, with all the hardihood of extreme imbecility, venturing himself to alight, disappeared in the twinkling of an eye into the drift into which he had alighted. At this crisis of affairs a waggon fortunately appeared upon this wintry scene—a waggon fortunately also with four horses in it. The four horses were at once pressed into the service of the Mail, and succeeded after incredible exertions in getting it out of the hollow in which it was sunk.

Porch at Dunstable.

The Holyhead Road enters Buckinghamshire at Brickhills, seven miles six furlongs further on, and forty-five miles from London.

But I must not leave these forty-five miles behind me without noting a curious sight which was often to be seen on this stretch from the tops of coaches before the legislature forbade the use of dogs as animals of draught. This sight was an old pauper, born without legs but with a sporting turn of mind. This natural bias led him to contrive a small waggon—very light, as may well be imagined since it had nothing but a board for the body. It was however fitted with springs, lamps and all necessary appliances, and was drawn by a new kind of team in the form of three fox-hounds harnessed abreast.

In this flying machine of his own contriving, Old Lal, for such was the name of the old pauper born without legs—no name having been given him by his Godfathers and Godmothers at his baptism—Old Lal used to make the most terrific times. His team were well matched in size and pace, cleverly harnessed, and he dashed by coaches making even their twelve miles an hour like the shot out of a gun, and with a

Old Inn, now Farmhouse, Brickhills.

slight cheer of encouragement to his team; but not in any spirit of insolence or defiance, as Captain M. E. Haworth (who in his *Roaa Scrapings* has preserved this episode of the North-western Road) is careful to tell us, but merely to urge the hounds to their pace.

This pace in the end proved fatal to Old Lal, after having lived for many years on the alms of passengers by coaches between the Peacock at Islington and the Sugar Loaf at Dunstable. For one winter, when according to the ostler of the Sugar Loaf's version, "the weather was terrible rough, there was snow and hice, and the storm blowed down a-many big trees, and them as stood used to 'oller and grunt up in the Pine Bottom so that he'd heerd folks say that the fir-trees was a-rubbing themselves against one another"—one such winter as this Old Lal had not been seen for three weeks. This fact did not cause any anxiety to his friend the ostler. But one Sunday afternoon, when he had "four o'clocked his horses" and was putting a sack over his shoulders preparatory to going down to his cottage, who should come up to him but one Trojan—a fox-hound and a respected member of Old Lal's team. The fact that Trojan had part of his harness on, set the ostler thinking that he had cut and run, and that perhaps he had left Old Lal in trouble.

This supposition proved correct; but it was never believed that old Trojan was the cause of Old Lal being found dead on the side of the road some distance off his waggon which was found stuck fast between two fir-trees, with one of the hounds still in harness lying dead beside it. No! It was believed by the ostler that the guilt of Old Lal's death lay at the door of another of the dogs—one Rocket, who turned up at the Sugar Loaf shortly after the arrival of Trojan. For this Rocket, according to the ostler, possessed many traits calculated to give rise to suspicion. In the first place, he was "a younger and more ramblier dog;" in the second place, "he never settled nowhere;" and in the third place, the last that the ostler heard of him was that, "being allers wonderful fond of sport," he had joined a pack of Harriers at Luton. "He was kinder master of them, frequently collecting the whole pack and going a hunting with them by hisself." All three which considerations put together induced in the ostler the very probable belief that Rocket was the instigator of the poor old man's death; that he (Rocket) must have caught a view of a fox, or at any rate have crossed a line of scent and bolted off the road and up through the wood, and "after he had throwed the old man out, continued the chase till the waggon got hung fast to a tree and tied them all up." The jury, it may be remarked in conclusion, who sat on Old Lal's remains, did not rise to this very lucid explanation of the cause of their session; for according to the ostler, they contented themselves with observing "That Old Lal was a pauper wagrant, that he had committed accidental death, and the coroner sentenced him to be buried in the

Courtyard of the Saracen's Head, Towcester.

parish in which he was last seen alive." He was buried in a square box accordingly, and the ostler and Trojan the fox-hound were the sole assistants at the rite.

But what of the coachmen on this celebrated coaching road? More celebrated even than the most celebrated of their rivals, it is time that I should make some mention of them here: of their appearance when in the flesh, of their characteristics as artists, of their fate. And, to begin with—speaking of coachmen's fate—few I should surmise have met a more ignobly ironical one from a coachman's point of view than did poor Jack Matthews who drove the Oak and Nettle coaches from Welshpool to Liverpool, which were run in opposition to the Holyhead Mail and were often too fast to be safe. For poor Jack fell no willing victim to his own indiscretion, but was killed—it is with a blush for the departed that I write it—in a railway accident. In a foolish moment he took it into his head to go to Liverpool for a day's outing, in a foolisher moment, if there be such a word, he got on a railway which was only half finished. He got on to this railway at Wrexham, intending to go as far as Chester. This feat the unfinished railway accomplished for him, only however to throw him off a bridge (unfinished too, I suppose) when he got there. Well may his biographer exclaim, "Poor Jack! He would have been safer driving the Nettle Coach, in all probability!" (which "in all probability" gives us a very fair idea of the safety of the Nettle Coach! But this is a digression.) And Jack was as pretty a coachman as ever had four horses in hand. "A good workman in all respects, smart as a new pin."

Another celebrated coachman on this road met as sad, but more consistent a fate, this was Dick Vickers, who drove the Mail between Shrewsbury and Holyhead. He fell a victim to agriculture. That is to say that though in stature he was so little "that he had to get on to sixpennyworth of coppers to look on to the top of a Stilton cheese" yet the deluded man pined to be a farmer. And he was fond of fishing too, a much more profitable pastime. However a farmer Vickers became, in spite of his friends' entreaties, who after a reasonable interval of anxiety found him *sus per coll.* This Vickers, not content with the lack of judgment he displayed while on earth, is said to haunt the scene of his indiscretion still. Though the Mail which he used to drive has long ceased to exist, they do say that at times a rumbling is heard—and so on. Mr. Birch Reynardson, to get to something more tangible about

Vickers, knew him well, as he seems to have known most of the crack coachmen on the Holyhead Road, through Shrewsbury, and has described them as well as he knew them in his *Down the Road.* The ill-fated Vickers, he writes, was a good little fellow, always civil, always sober, always most obliging, and a friend of every one along the road. And Mr. Reynardson had some opportunity of studying his model's characteristics, particularly I should conceive on that one celebrated occasion chronicled, when he sat by him on the box-seat and saw him deal with a team comprised of the engaging attributes of "Three blind 'uns and a bolter", or in the coachman's own words "Four horses, but they've only got two eyes among 'em, and it would be quite a well if that horse had not any so far as I know—for he makes shocking bad use of 'em at all times I can tell you."

Ford's Hospital, Coventry.

A differently organized team was equally successfully coped with by one known to fame as Old John Scott. He drove the Chester and Holyhead Mail, and remarked to Mr. Reynardson, who was using all his art to boil up a trot going up Penmaenmawr (thirty-six miles from Holyhead), "Hit 'em sly—hit 'em sly!" And on being asked the reason for this dark advice alleged that if this particular team heard the whip before they felt it, they would never be got up Penmaenmawr at all. Nor was "hitting 'em sly" with the whip the ingenious Old John Scott's sole method of dealing on heavy ground with this extremely sticky lot. No. He was accustomed, when the crisis came, and the coach threatened to come to a full stop where there was no proper halting place, to play a sort of rat-tat-tat with both feet on the foot-board—and lo! the sticky ones sprang up to their collars at once, as if the author of all evil was behind them. Much exercised by this extraordinary phenomenon,

Mr. Reynardson with a praiseworthy impulse to arrive at the dark truth, remarked, "Well! that's a curious dodge! What do they think is coming?" Upon which Old John Scott, saying, "Wait a pit, I'll soon let you see what they think is coming,"—stooped down and produced from the boot a most respectable and persuasive looking "Short Tommy". This sounds rather like a case for the Society for the Prevention of Cruelty to Animals—did we not have it on the best authority that Old John Scott was a worthy, good little, stout-made fellow, whose B was sounded like P, and who when he said "Shall" pronounced it like Sall.

An artist of a finer mould was Sam Hayward, who drove the Wonder from Shifnal to Shrewsbury (18 miles). Not only was he a fine performer on the Road—but he did a deed in the usual way of business when he got into Shrewsbury which made spectators stare. The Lion yard is just on the top of the hill in Shrewsbury, and is so placed that to coachmen not demigods, to turn into it off a sharpish pitch with a heavy load was to attempt the impossible to an accompaniment of breaking poles and shrieking passengers. All other coaches coming from London went in therefore ignominiously by the backway, though they came out at the usual entrance. Not so Sam Hayward on the Wonder. Secure in the knowledge of accomplished strength he smilingly hugged the kerbstone on the near side, passed the entrance for a few yards—but yards accurately calculated—then described a round and imperial circle, and shot in under the archway a victorious, a classic charioteer. People at first thought him mad—I read, when they saw him thus as it were defying the thunder—but they soon saw that he knew what he was doing, and could do it.

Of quite a different type was one Winterbotham—who drove the Holyhead Mail four stages out of Holyhead and who on one occasion when Mr. Birch Reynardson—the great authority in this part of the world—approached the coach, was described to him by the guard as being "amazing fresh." "Amazing fresh" is not only good in my eyes: it is delicious. And how when Winterbotham presently put in an appearance did he answer to this poetic description? Why, amazingly. "He approached rolling about like a seventy-four in a calm; or as if he were walking with a couple of soda-water bottles tied under his feet." The peculiarity of this gait, which might have been much appreciated on the Metropolitan boards as an eccentric dancer's

The Rows of Chester.

The Falcon and the Bear, Chester.

new departure, did not appeal to the teller of this tale as prophetic of safety from the box-seat of a crack coach. So Winterbotham in all the meridian of his freshness was inclosed, a solitary passenger, in the stuffy inside—and Mr. Birch Reynardson himself assumed the ribbons. At the change near St. Asaph, sixty miles from Holyhead, inquiries were made after Winterbotham's condition. But all his freshness had deserted the cooped-up charioteer! He was however found fairly rational though excessively dejected, and expressed himself thus on an unique experience—"Well I think I'd better get outside now! I aren't used to this. Well! This is travelling

The Bear and Billet, Chester.

The Yacht Inn.

like a gentleman, and inside the Mail to be sure! Well! I never travelled inside a Mail or a coach before; and I dare say I never shall again! I don't think I like the inside of a coach much; and so I'd better get out now! it feels wonderful odd somehow to be inside the Mail; and I really hardly know how I got there."

On the same coach, but further up the road, Dan Herbert did his twenty-four miles between Eccleshall and Lichfield with two changes, and his twenty-four miles back the same day,—an artist perfected in the quiet method, driving bad teams punctually without punishing them, rather by the medium of fine hands and temper coaxing them along. He was upwards of thirty years on the Chester and Holyhead Mail, and in consideration of his faithful and correct attention to business was awarded a scarlet coat on every anniversary of the King's birthday.

And George Clarke was an artist of the same calibre and of like style. He took the Umpire at Newport Pagnell (fifty-one miles from London), and met the down coach at Whetstone returning about nine o'clock. The most valuable of servants, because the first coachman in England for bad horses. Having always weak horses to nurse, the ordeal had worn him down to a pattern of patience. With these and other great weights upon severe ground, he was steady, easy and economical in thong and cord, very light-handed, and sometimes even playful!

An idyllic description of a great coachman's kind qualities this, raising all sorts of pictures to the mind's eye of comfortable journeys performed under a master's direction with no discomfort to the cattle; but we enter into a wilder, a fiercer atmosphere of travel, when we come to consider the great names of John Marchant of the Manchester Telegraph, and Bob Snow of the Defiance. For these men drove opposition coaches, in which speed was the one thing looked to, associated in a mild degree with a more or less reasonable amount of safety. And they drove furiously to beat the record—careful of nothing so long as the coach kept on its wheels, demi-gods whose steel nerves their passengers implicitly trusted, well knowing as they did that if those steel nerves had for an instant failed their owners the whole stock and lot would have gone to the Deuce in an instant.

It was this sort of fiery opposition kept up between the two crack Manchester coaches which called forth some such comment as the following, comments constantly to be culled from contemporary magazines :—

"Whoever takes up a newspaper in these eventful times it is even betting whether an accident by a coach or a suicide first meets his eye.

The End of the Journey.

Now really as the month of November is fast approaching, when from foggy weather and dark nights, both these calamities are likely to increase,

I merely suggest the propriety of any unfortunate gentleman resolved on self-destruction, trying to avoid the disgrace attached to it by first taking a few journeys by some of these Dreadnought, Highflyer, or Tally-ho coaches; as in all probability he may meet with as instant a death as if he had let off one of Joe Manton's pistols in his mouth, or severed his head from his body with one of Mr. Palmer's best razors."

CONCLUSION.

OUR ancestors, on alighting from any of the prolonged journeys I have tried to describe, were used, being fortunate people who lived when life was not all hurry, to sit down quietly over a generous glass and take their ease in their inn. We less fortunate descendants cannot do this now, because time is not permitted us, and we have no inns to take our ease in. We live in an age of hotels, where on touching an electric communicator everything but ease is to be had.

However, though our ancestors' ease after travel may not be ours, we may be permitted some sort of retrospection—such as was often theirs—over the long list of perils past, on many thousand miles of good, bad, or indifferent roads, in vehicles and company agreeably diversified—some final desultory chat on road-bills, coaches, horses, inns, to induce sleep or round the story.

Of road-bills, then, to begin with, here are one or two suggestive specimens—not connected with the roads on which we have been travelling, but none the less illustrative of Coaching Days and Coaching Ways for all that.

"FROM THE SWAN WITH TWO NECKS IN LAD LANE. AUGUST, 1774.

"A post-chaise to Gloucester in sixteen hours, and a Machine in one day—each three days a week. A Machine to Hereford twice a week in a day and a half. A Machine to Salop every Monday, Wednesday, and Friday in two days. A Machine for Wolverhampton every Sunday, Tuesday, and Thursday in one day."

The same bill winds up with the following startling epilogue :—

"The Rumsey Machine, through Winchester, hung on Steel Springs begins Flying on the 3rd of April from London to Poole in one day."

Here is another characteristic announcement from the *Daily Advertiser* of April 9, 1739 :—

"The Old Standing Constant Froom Flying Waggon, in three days, sets out, with goods and Passengers, from Froom for London every Monday by One o'clock in the morning, and will be at the King's Arms at Holborn Bridge the Wednesday following by twelve o'clock noon, from whence it will Set Out on Thursday morning by One o'clock, for Amesbury, Shrewton, Chiltern, Heytesbury, Warminster, Froom: and all other places Adjacent: and will continue, allowing each person 14lbs, and be at Froom on Saturday by twelve at noon. If any passengers have any occasion to go from any of the aforesaid places, they shall be supplied with able horses, and a guide, by Joseph Chavey the Proprietor of the said Flying Waggon. The Waggon calls at the White Bear Piccadilly coming in and going out."

Which reminds me that I have spoken a good deal about Flying Waggons and Machines, but have never described them, so that a brief description of their "more salient features" may here be in place.

I read, then, that they were principally composed of a dull black leather, thickly studded by way of ornament with broad black-headed nails, tracing out the panels, in the upper tier of which were four oval windows, with heavy red wooden frames, or leather curtains. Upon the doors were displayed in large characters the names of the places whence the coach started, and where it was going to—another matter. The shape of the Flying Machine was a matter left much open to choice. You could ride in one shaped like a diving bell; or in one the exact representation of a distiller's vat, hung equally balanced between immense back and front springs; or in one made after the pattern of a violoncello-case—past all comparison the most fashionable shape. If my readers are tempted to cry why this thusness, I can only say because these violoncello-like Flying Machines hung in a more graceful posture—namely, inclining on to the back springs—and gave those who sat within it "the appearance of a stiff Guy Fawkes uneasily seated." But this is a satiric touch, surely. To get on to the roofs, however. These generally rose into a swelling curve, which was sometimes surrounded by a high iron guard, after the manner of our more modern four-wheeled cabs. The coachman and the guard (who always held his carbine ready cocked upon his knee —an attitude which must have made inside passengers wish they had insured their lives) then sat together over a very long and narrow boot which passed under a large spreading hammercloth hanging down on all sides, and furnished with a most luxuriant fringe. Behind the coach was the immense basket, stretching far and wide beyond the body to which it was attached by long iron bars or supports passing beneath it. I am not surprised to learn that these baskets were never very great favourites, though their difference of price caused them to be frequently filled—but another proof of needs must when the devil drives——. And as for the motion of these Flying coaches when well on the road, it was "as a ship rocking or beating against a heavy sea; straining all her timbers, with a low moaning sound as she drives over the contending waves." With which extraordinary simile we may leave Flying Machines behind us—and any description of their successors too. For are not the models of the crack coaches in coaching's primest age to be seen every day in Piccadilly? They are—and some very delightful rides can be had in them too.

Not that travelling in these perfected turn-outs was always like riding on a bed of roses, as I have had occasion frequently to point out, which consideration brings me to the inevitable comparison of the advantages of rail *versus* road. On which great subject much can be said on both sides, as a celebrated Attorney-General for Honolulu once remarked. De Quincey, for instance, may talk of the "fine fluent motion of the Bristol Mail," and call up recollections in our minds of the modern Bristol Mail's motion as anything but fluent; he may glorify "the absolute perfection of all the appointments about the carriage and the harness, their strength, their brilliant cleanliness, their beautiful simplicity, the royal magnificence of the horses;" but here is another side to the picture. I quote from Hone's Table-books, an extract in the style of Jingle, and worthy of him.

"STAGE COACH ADVENTURES.

"INSIDE.—Crammed full of passengers—three fat fusty old men—a young Mother and sick child—a cross old maid—a poll parrot—a bag of red herrings—double-barrelled gun (which you are afraid is loaded)—and a snarling lap dog in addition to yourself. Awake out of a sound nap with the cramp in one leg and the other in a lady's bandbox—pay the damage (four or five shillings) for gallantry's sake—getting out in the dark at the half-way house, in the hurry stepping into the return coach and finding yourself next morning at the very spot you had started from the evening before—not a breath of air—asthmatic old woman and child with the measles—window closed in consequence—unpleasant smell—shoes filled with warm water—look up and find it's the child—obliged to bear it—no appeal—shut your eyes and scold the dog—pretend sleep and pinch the child—mistake—pinch the dog and get bit.—Execrate the child in return—black looks—no gentleman—pay the Coachman and drop a piece of gold in the straw—not to be found—fell through a crevice—Coachman says 'He'll find it.'—Can't—get out yourself—gone—picked up by the Ostler—no time for blowing up—Coach off for next stage—lose your money—get in—lose your seat—stuck in the middle—get laughed at—lose your temper—turn sulky—and turned over in a horse-pond.

"OUTSIDE.—Your eye cut out by the lash of a clumsy Coachman's whip—hat blown off into a pond by a sudden gust of wind—seated between two apprehended murderers and a noted sheep-stealer in irons—who are being conveyed to gaol—a drunken fellow half asleep falls off the Coach—and in attempting to save himself drags you along with him into the mud—musical guard, and driver horn mad—turned over.—One leg under a bale of cotton—the other under the Coach—hands in breeches pockets—head in hamper of wine—lots of broken bottles *versus* broken heads.—Cut and run—send for surgeon—wounds dressed—lotion and lint four dollars—take post-chaise—get home—lay down—and laid up."

So much for coach travelling from a pessimistic point of view. And now a few words on the Coaching Inns.

"There is no private house," said Johnson—it was in the Old Chapel House inn in Oxfordshire, on the Birmingham Road, that he gave vent to the profundity—"there is no place," he said, "at which people can enjoy themselves as well as at a capital tavern like this. Let there be ever so great a plenty of good things, ever so much grandeur, ever so much elegance, ever so much desire that every guest should be easy, in the nature of things it cannot be. There must always be some degree of care and anxiety. The master of the house is anxious to entertain his friends; these in their turn are anxious to be agreeable to him, and no one but a very impudent dog can as freely command what is in another man's house as if it were his own. Whereas at a tavern there is a general freedom from anxiety. You are sure you are welcome, and

A Performance on the Horn.

the more noise you make the more trouble you give, the more good things you call for, the welcomer you are. No servants will attend you with the alacrity which waiters do, who are incited by the prospect of an immediate reward in proportion as they please. No, sir; there is nothing which has yet been contrived by man by which so much happiness is produced as by a good tavern or inn."

Hear, hear! say I; but while on the subject of inns may remark that I have been much disappointed in my ramblings; in truth began some six years too late from this point of view. For in that interval the country has been deprived of many of its finest examples of this hospitable sort of architecture. Of those fine examples—few and far between—which still remain, many are now sinking into a state of irremediable disrepair—witness the great inn at Stilton for one—and will in the near fulness of time doubtless be improved altogether off the face of the earth.

Some of these meanwhile on these direct roads of England which I have up to now treated of, have been preserved by a sympathetic artist's pencil, and the thought is so satisfactory a one that I propose to bestow on three other inns—not on the main roads, but magnificent houses still, the same enviable fate.

At Norton St. Philip, then, in Somersetshire, seven miles south-east of Bath, there still stands in the George Inn, a half-timbered, fifteenth century house, of the finest possible type. Monmouth passed the night of June 26th, 1685, at this George. He watched a skirmish between his outposts and Feversham's from the windows of the inn, was shot at while standing there for his pains, and marched upon Frome next day. At Glastonbury, in the same county, an inn of the same name—the George—with front one splendid mass of panelling, pierced where necessary for windows, the finest piece of domestic work in one of the most entrancing towns in England from an antiquary's point of view, dates from the fourth Edward; while, to go further afield for a fine specimen of a different period, at Scole in Suffolk, the White Hart, erected in 1655 by John Peck, merchant, of Norwich, still retains some fine carving, and had till the end of the last century an enormous sign containing many figures —Diana and Actæon, Charon, Cerberus, and sundry other worthies, carved in wood by Fairchild, at a cost of £1057.

Such splendid monuments of road-travelling as these may fitly round this disjointed story of England's Coaching Days and Ways. In looking back over many miles covered and many incidents missed I find little cause for self-congratulation, save the fact that I have at least kept to my programme. I have traversed an obscure period carefully on well-beaten tracks, and to my pioneers' assistance I hope I have always made due acknowledgment. To give an accurate, a statistical record of the prime age of coaching has been in most cases their object, and they have in most cases attained to it. If a minor measure of success attends my enterprize I shall be content—content, that is to say, if I have caught some flavour of the romance of the Great Roads of England from the time when the Flying Machine of Charles the Second's age lumbered out of the Belle Savage Yard, up to the day when the Holyhead Mail *viâ* Shrewsbury, timed at eleven miles an hour, was our fathers' wonder, and the pride of this perfect road—" Mr. Bicknell's spicy team of greys."

THE END.